Refugee Economies

Refugee Economies

Forced Displacement and Development

Alexander Betts, Louise Bloom, Josiah Kaplan,
and Naohiko Omata

OXFORD
UNIVERSITY PRESS

Great Clarendon Street, Oxford, OX2 6DP,
United Kingdom

Oxford University Press is a department of the University of Oxford.
It furthers the University's objective of excellence in research, scholarship,
and education by publishing worldwide. Oxford is a registered trade mark of
Oxford University Press in the UK and in certain other countries

First Edition published in 2017
Impression: 2

Published in the United States of America by Oxford University Press
198 Madison Avenue, New York, NY 10016, United States of America

British Library Cataloguing in Publication Data
Data available

Library of Congress Control Number: 2016943473

ISBN 978–0–19–879568–1

Printed in Great Britain by
Clays Ltd, St Ives plc

Preface

Most books have a backstory. This one is the culmination of a journey that began nearly two decades ago. Back in 1999, when I was an undergraduate student in economics, I received an opportunity to do voluntary work in a reception centre for asylum seekers and refugees in the Netherlands. While there, I met extraordinary people—from Kosovo, Bosnia, Iran, Iraq, Pakistan, China, Liberia, the Democratic Republic of Congo, and Somalia. A Bosniak lawyer taught me the basics of public international law and an Iranian Olympian taught me table tennis. Despite their talents, the people I met were stuck in limbo while awaiting the outcome of their asylum claims, and denied the right to work until their bureaucratic situation was resolved. This struck me as not only bad for refugees but also for the host society.

When I returned home, I wanted to write my undergraduate dissertation on the topic. But I was an economics student and, back at my university, there was scepticism about whether refugees and economics could really go together. Nevertheless, my supervisor, Frank Bohn, supported my idea to write a dissertation applying ideas from microeconomics to the refugee context. Afterwards, I broadened my research focus towards the politics of refugee protection, believing I would leave economics behind.

But, as I travelled to do research in refugee camps across Africa, the same themes resurfaced. Talented people with the capacity to contribute were left in intractable limbo, sometimes for decades, in refugee camps, where they were denied the right to work. The humanitarian model, based on long-term assistance, was failing. The rare historical examples of host countries giving refugees greater opportunity seemed to rely upon taking a broader development perspective.

Then, in 2010, while spending a year at Stanford, a possibility arose to revisit some of the economic themes that had started my career. Based in the heart of Silicon Valley, I was surrounded by tech, start-ups, and social enterprise. I thought to myself 'This is great—but how is it relevant to me? I work on refugees, and surely that's about what governments and international organizations do?' And then the penny dropped. What if we could rethink the role of markets in relation to refugees? What if we had a better understanding of the economic lives of refugees themselves? Might that offer an opportunity to move beyond dependency and towards more sustainable solutions?

At around the same time, in October 2010, I was invited to Texas for the first time to give a series of lectures. While in Dallas, I was introduced to Stephanie and Hunter Hunt, who had recently created the Hunt Institute for Engineering and Humanity, and become interested in how to create more innovative solutions for refugees. Their visits to camps in Kenya and Thailand had led them to share the frustrations I felt. Why couldn't we find better ways to help refugees to help themselves?

As a result, we co-founded the Humanitarian Innovation Project, based in the Refugee Studies Centre at the University of Oxford. The overall project's basic aim was to understand the role of technology, innovation, and business in relation to refugee assistance, with a focus on the initiative of refugees themselves. Stephanie and I brainstormed ideas for the project's initial focus country, travelling together to Uganda in early 2012, where we had preliminary meetings with UNHCR in Kampala and the Kyangwali refugee settlements.

The decision to focus on Uganda was based on its exceptionalism. Unlike most other refugee-hosting countries around the world, it gives refugees the right to work and freedom of movement, as part of its Self-Reliance Strategy. This offered a unique opportunity to explore what happens when refugees are given basic socio-economic freedoms. It is also a country with a large and diverse refugee population.

We began hiring the Humanitarian Innovation Project team, with Louise and Naohiko joining as Research Officers in 2012 and Josiah following as a Research Consultant in 2013. The aim had been to create an interdisciplinary team. Between us, we had training in anthropology, economics, management, engineering, and political science. Thereafter, Refugee Economies rapidly became the central focus of our research.

Some academic research, notably the pioneering work of Karen Jacobsen, had already taken place on the economic lives of refugees. But much of the existing literature was based on localized qualitative studies. Although extremely important, two things were missing: data and theory. One of our primary research goals became to address these gaps, including through quantitative data collection. To our knowledge, there had been no previous academic studies that had created an original dataset on the economic lives of refugees.

But we also did not want to do what so many economists do: turn up with our clipboards and our pre-designed survey, ask questions, and then simply leave. Instead, we wanted to adopt an approach that would build lasting relationships within the communities, work with refugees as peer researchers, and hopefully leave a positive legacy for refugees and the host society.

To balance these competing imperatives called for methodological innovation. It required us to build trust—including with refugees, the government, and UNHCR—and to be able to work at scale across a number of different research sites, urban and rural. It needed us to use participatory research methods and to invest immense time in building and nurturing research capacity at the national level.

To achieve this, we built a large in-country team, all of who are ultimately the co-creators of the research on which this book is based. The Uganda team comprised three national research coordinators: Clarissa Tumwine, Rashid Mwesigwa, and Hope Zainab Natukunda. It also comprised a large number of researchers who also happened to be refugees: Wardo Omar Abdullahi, Hussein Ahmed Abukar, David Bachy, William Bakunzi, Seinya Bekele, Caesar Bishovu, Osman Faiz, Sada Faiz, Kiflu Hussain, Angelique Kabami, Cosmos Lugala, Abdullahi Mahil, Bernadette Muhongaiyre, Robert Hakiza Ngirwa, Gemus Ngirabakunzi, Ntakamaze Nziyonvira, and Abdirahman Sheik Mahi Yusuf. Without their commitment to the project, this book would simply not exist.

Survey assistance was also provided by our team of enumerators: Emmanuel Baraka, Emmanuel Mbabzi, Clovis Bosco, Jean Claude, Mohamed Hasan, Patricia Kalambayi, Rosemary Kamariza, Alexis Kubana, Hellen Mabonga, Emmanuel Mfitundinda, Abdalla Muhamed, Aisha Muhamood Abdi, Eugenie Mukandayisenga, Damien Ndemezo, Christopher Okidi, Abdifatah Hassan Osman, Bosco Pagama, Christian Salumu, Richard Tombe, Richard Veve, Jimmy Wamimbi, Joseph Yuggu, and our survey site supervisors, Joan Aliobe and Henry Mugisha.

That team received training in research methods, led by Naohiko and Josiah, and it has been gratifying to see so many of our researchers go on to achieve so much. Robert Hakiza was awarded the Ockenden Prize for his work in developing a skills training programme for refugees at his community-based organization, YARID. Kiflu Hussain was resettled to the United States where he continued to work as a researcher at the Hunt Institute for Engineering and Humanity. Ntakimaze Nziyonvira and Angelique Kabami both received Mastercard scholarships to go and study abroad.

We have also benefited immensely from the research support of our Oxford team. Eli Grant was our main statistician and did most of our data analysis. Andrea Abell van Es also provided assistance on data analysis at an early stage. Other research assistants have included Georgia Cole, Evan Easton-Calabria, Romy Faulkner, Ben Kenneally, and Cherie Saulter. Anneli Chambliss-Howse provided language editing on an early draft of this manuscript. Finally, from within Oxford, our work was only possible because of the role of our research coordinators, Mafalda Picarra and then Nina Weaver.

Institutionally, we are incredibly grateful to both the Office of the Prime Minister (OPM) of the Government of Uganda and the Office of the United Nations High Commissioner for Refugees (UNHCR) for supporting our work, especially in the field. Among the many colleagues who assisted, we are grateful to Charles Bafaki, Douglas Asiimwe, Betsy Lippman, Theresa Beltramo, Line Pedersen, Gaela Roudy-Fraser, Steve Corliss, Sakura Atsumi, Olivier Delarue, and Chris Earney.

The work benefited immensely from a series of presentations and lectures, through which we received incredibly helpful feedback. These included presentations at DFID, GIZ, the World Bank, UNHCR, the Danish Red Cross, Harvard University, Stanford University, and the World Humanitarian Summit's Global Consultations, as well as a seminar series on 'Refugee Economies' held at the Refugee Studies Centre.

We also published an early policy brief with some of our descriptive statistics and human stories as 'Refugee Economies: Rethinking Popular Assumptions', which we launched in July 2014 at our own Humanitarian Innovation Conference. This enabled us to receive further feedback on the work, as well as increasing interest in our Uganda study. We were also able to hold subsequent launch events in both Kampala and Nairobi, generously hosted by UNHCR, as well as one in the Nakivale settlement.

However, it was the so-called European refugee crisis, beginning in April 2015, which created unprecedented interest in our work on Refugee Economies, and especially our Uganda study. The work has received coverage on the BBC, CNN, Al Jazeera, Central China Television, and National Public Radio. It has also been highlighted in *The Guardian*, *The Independent*, *The Economist*, *New Scientist*, *World Finance*, and *Fast Company*, among others. It has also been a focus of talks I have given at TED, the Skoll World Forum, and the Global Philanthropy Forum.

Above all, we are incredibly grateful to Stephanie and Hunter Hunt, not only for funding this research but also for being terrific friends, collaborators, and advocates for our work.

We are thankful for the support of our other colleagues at the Refugee Studies Centre, especially Tamsin Kelk for dedicating so much time to communications relating to the project, and her predecessor, Ian McClelland.

Within and beyond Oxford, we have also benefited from the advice, guidance, and support of many friends, colleagues, and students. These include Jean-François Durieux, Alex Aleinikoff, Paul Collier, Kathleen Newland, Michael Doyle, Christiane Amanpour, Gregory Maniatis, Emily Paddon, Erik Abild, Emily Arnold-Fernandez, Sasha Chanoff, Kate Weaver, Faith Nibbs, Meredith Byrne, Pamela Hartigan, Thomas Gammeltoft-Hansen, Joanna Macrae, Eva Csaky, Mikey Tomkins, Jim Hollifield, Jim Hathaway, Jane

McAdam, Thomas Thomsen, Tanya Meurer, James Milner, Ran Abramitzky, Thomas Ginn, Tino Cuellar, Erica Harper, Vlad Gozman, and Jane Wales.

We are immensely grateful to Adam Swallow at Oxford University Press for showing such enthusiasm for this project and ferrying the book through to publication.

Finally, the authors all have people in our lives that have enabled all of us to commit thousands of hours to the research behind this book—Emily, Alex, Helena, and Akiko.

Alexander Betts

April 2016

Contents

List of Figures and Maps

Figures

Maps

List of Tables

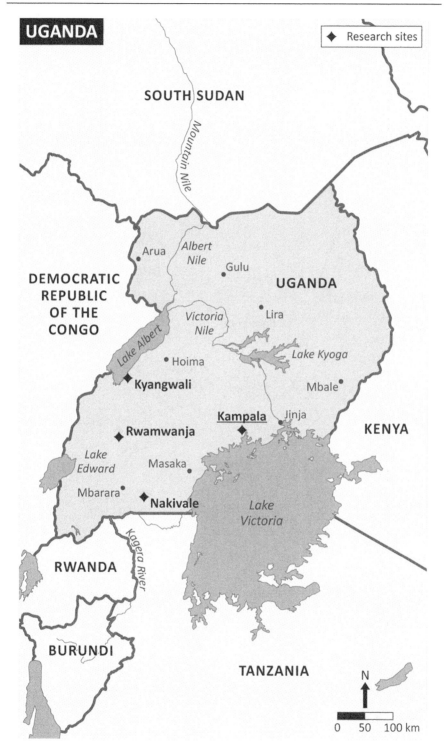

Map 1. Uganda

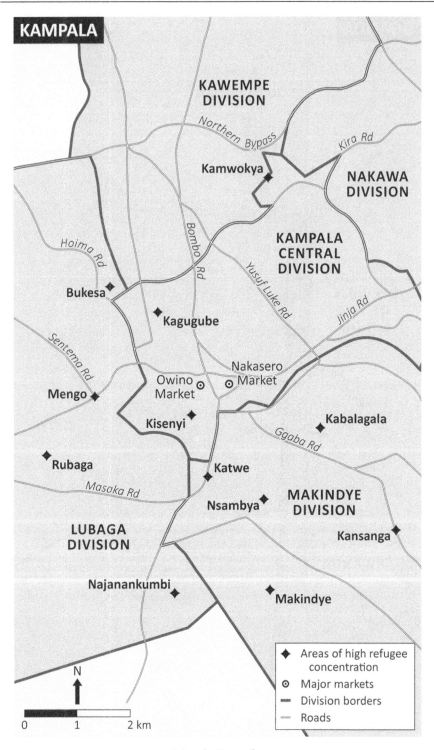

Map 2. Kampala

NAKIVALE

Villages
Major markets
Zone borders
Roads

Rubondo
Trading
Centre

**RUBONDO
ZONE**

Kampala
270 km

Kityaza
Market

**BASE CAMP
ZONE**

Kigali
UNHCR
New Congo Base Camp
Somali Isangano
Village Market

Juru
Market

Lake Nakivale

**JURU
ZONE**

Kahirimbi
Market

Kabingo Mbarara 40 km

N

0   2   4 km

Map 3. Nakivale refugee settlement

Map 4. Kyangwali refugee settlement

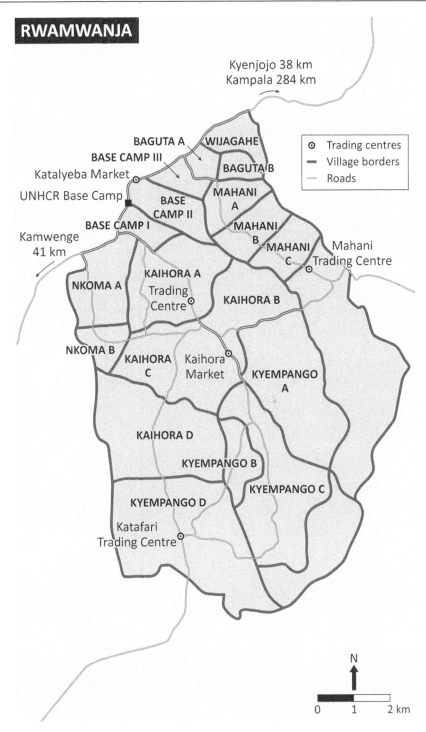

Map 5. Rwamwanja refugee settlement

1

Introduction

There is a global displacement crisis. Around the world, over sixty-five million people—more than at any time since the Second World War—are displaced from their homes by conflict and human rights violations.[1] Nearly a third of them are refugees who have been forced to cross an international border in search of protection. Meanwhile, the causes of displacement are diversifying, with environmental change, state fragility, and water insecurity predicted to become significant contributing factors. Yet, alongside this trend of rising numbers, governments' political willingness to provide access to protection and assistance is in decline. From European countries' attempts to prevent boats from crossing the Mediterranean, to policies adopted in Australia, Kenya, and the Middle East, a growing number of countries are closing their borders to refugees.

In the face of these challenges, the existing global refugee regime is no longer fit for purpose. Created in the aftermath of the Second World War, the existing United Nations architecture continues to view refugees and displacement as a predominantly humanitarian issue. When people have to leave their homes or cross borders, the conventional international response is to meet their immediate needs in terms of food, shelter, clothing, water, and sanitation. For nearly 90 per cent of the world's refugees, this takes place in countries that neighbour the country of origin, and frequently within refugee camps in remote border locations.[2] This approach is broadly effective for providing emergency relief during the onset of a crisis. However, in the long run, it can—and frequently does—lead to dependency.

Over half of the world's refugees find themselves in so-called protracted refugee situations, having been in exile for at least five years.[3] For these people,

---

[1] Up to date at the time of writing (UNHCR 2016).

[2] Data on the global distribution of refugees can be found in UNHCR's annual Global Trends report (UNHCR 2015a).

[3] 6.7 million of UNHCR's refugee 'population of concern' of 16.1 million are in protracted refugee situations (41 per cent). If one includes Palestinian refugees, the number is 11.9 million out of a total population of 21.3 million (56 per cent) (UNHCR 2016: 20).

the average length in exile is now more than twenty-five years.[4] From Kenya to Thailand, many refugees are hosted in camps in which they do not have the right to work or freedom of movement. Effectively, they are 'warehoused' pending an opportunity to return home, with significant implications for human rights and international security.

This conventional approach to refugee assistance is unsustainable. Faced with new mass displacement situations around the world such as those from Syria or Somalia, host countries are less willing to accommodate large numbers of people indefinitely. Several states have closed their borders entirely to refugees. International donors are also increasingly unwilling to support large numbers of refugees within camps indefinitely with their finite humanitarian budgets. Furthermore, without adequate protection and assistance within their region of origin, increasing numbers of refugees are forced to move to urban areas—sometimes illegally—or to embark on dangerous journeys to other parts of the world in search of basic measures of dignity.

However, there are alternative ways to think about refugees. Existing approaches too often ignore the skills, talents, and aspirations of refugees themselves. Yet refugees have capacities as well as vulnerabilities. They need not inevitably be a 'burden' on host states; they have the potential to contribute economically as well as socioculturally. All around the world, even under the most constrained of circumstances—and sometimes under the radar of local authorities—refugees in camps and urban areas engage in significant economic activity. In doing so, they often create new opportunities for themselves and others.

The simple observation that refugees almost everywhere engage in significant levels of market activity offers a window for conceiving of more sustainable approaches. It opens up the possibility that refugees can be thought of not only as a humanitarian issue but reconsidered as a development issue. Rather than assuming that refugees are inevitably dependent, we might help refugees to help themselves, and in so doing simultaneously benefit host states.

Such ideas are not new. There has been a long-standing debate on the transition from 'relief-to-development' in refugee work. However, such approaches have historically suffered from a range of weaknesses. They have generally been state-centric, relying upon the presumption that donor governments might provide additional development assistance to induce host states to commit to long-term local integration for refugees. They have also

---

[4] The average length of stay for refugees in protracted refugee situations within UNHCR's 'population of concern' (i.e. excluding the Palestinians) is twenty-six years (UNHCR 2016: 20). The overall average length of exile for all refugees is more elusive but one of the most commonly cited figures is seventeen years, originating from UNHCR (2006: 109). For discussion of this figure, see White (2015).

assumed that there is a 'magic moment' at which displacement shifts from being a humanitarian issue to becoming a development issue.

What has been lacking in these approaches is a focus on the market-based, economic activities of refugees themselves. How can we build upon such activities to create more sustainable opportunities for refugee self-reliance? Here, research has an important role to play. There is a need to understand the economic lives of refugees better. Rarely have economists worked on issues relating to the economic lives of refugees. By better explaining variation in economic outcomes for refugees, we may be able to rethink the policy and practice of refugee assistance. This approach requires both theory and empirical data.

This book aims to address these gaps. It examines the economic lives and market interactions of refugees themselves. Using the concept of 'refugee economies' to describe the resource allocation system that shapes refugees' lives in exile, we outline a theoretical understanding of what it is that makes refugees' economic lives analytically distinctive. Through qualitative and quantitative research carried out in Uganda, we highlight the factors that shape variation in economic outcomes for refugees, and the untapped opportunities that this offers for rethinking refugee assistance.

Protracted Refugee Situations

The need for refugee protection arises because states are sometimes unable or unwilling to ensure the fundamental human rights of their own citizens. In search of a substitute provider of those basic rights, refugees cross borders. The concept of refugee protection ensures that there can be an alternative provider of those rights, whether another government or the international community. This protection is intended to last for a finite period of time until those people can be reintegrated into the international state system, whether back at home or elsewhere.

In theory, there is an assumed 'cycle' for what should happen to a refugee who goes into exile. She should first receive access to emergency assistance in order to meet her immediate needs. Second, she should receive access to protection, a set of rights including the right not to be returned to a country in which she may face persecution, as well as other basic civil and political, economic, and social rights. Third, she should receive access to a so-called durable solution, such as reintegration into the state system through repatriation to the country of origin, local integration in the host country, or resettlement to a third country.

In practice, refugees all too rarely receive access to timely durable solutions. Repatriation depends upon the end to a conflict or political transition in the country of origin. Host states in the developing world are usually reluctant to provide local integration or a pathway to long-term citizenship for refugees. Meanwhile, resettlement countries in the developed world collectively generally offer resettlement to less than 1 per cent of the world's refugees.[5] The absence of durable solutions means that many refugees are trapped in the host countries of asylum, often in refugee camps designed for the emergency phase, for many years and often with few entitlements and opportunities.

The label of 'protracted refugee situations' has been used to highlight this problem (Loescher and Milner 2005; Loescher et al. 2008). These are situations in which refugees have been in exile for at least five years, often in an intractable state of limbo, and sometimes remaining as refugees for decades. Especially problematic is the denial of the right to work and freedom of movement to refugees, sometimes leaving entire generations of people indefinitely confined to refugee camps. Ranging from the Dadaab camps in Kenya to the Nyarugusu camp in Tanzania and the position of many Palestinians throughout the Middle East, such situations have been described as a 'denial of rights and a waste of humanity' (USCRI 2004).

Today, around 56 per cent of refugees are estimated to be in protracted exile.[6] Such situations are caused by the lack of access to durable solutions, often resulting from political impasse. These contexts have implications for human rights, denying people basic freedoms and the opportunity to participate meaningfully in economic, political, and social life. They also have potential consequences for local and international security, excluding entire generations in ways that sometimes create motives and opportunities for negative coping strategies or recruitment by radical organizations or non-state armed actors. Growing numbers of people in protracted situations understandably seek their own solutions, moving to urban areas or undertaking irregular migration to other parts of the world.

To give one example, in 2009, one of the authors travelled to the Ali-Addeh refugee camp in Djibouti, an isolated, hot, and desolate camp. It lies in the desert along the border with Somaliland and was occupied by 8000 refugees from Somaliland, Somalia, and Ethiopia. Refugees here are not allowed to work, and there are virtually no opportunities for leisure or vocational activities for refugees, young or old, in the camp. There, the author in question met Wuli, a 40-year-old refugee with diabetes, who had been in the camp since he became an adult in 1988. Despite the constraints, Wuli ran an informal school, teaching English and maths to secondary-school-aged children in his tent. He had given up hope for himself but instead insisted on supporting the

---

[5] In 2015, 107 100 refugees received resettlement (UNHCR 2016: 26).

[6] This figure includes Palestinian refugees, without which it would be 41 per cent (UNHCR 2016: 20).

next generation: 'Man does not live on food and water alone but on hope; mine is gone but I now live to support the hope of the next generation.'[7]

The tragedy of long-term encampment is now widely acknowledged and condemned. However, protractedness has become the global norm, and the international community has struggled to find solutions. The failure of states and the United Nations collectively to resolve conflicts or overcome state fragility in countries of origin has left most of the world's refugees in limbo. This poses a massive and unanswered policy challenge in terms of how protracted refugee situations can be both prevented and resolved.

The most obvious solutions to this humanitarian tragedy are political solutions. These rely upon the international community collectively 'doing better' to end conflicts, overcome authoritarian regimes, and reduce state fragility. Addressing these 'root causes' would be the 'first best solution' to resolve protracted refugee situations. However, it would also require serious engagement by the UN Security Council in the areas of conflict resolution, peacebuilding, and post-conflict reconstruction, in ways that are politically elusive.

Failing this, the authors' starting point is the belief that self-reliance offers the most viable way to address the negative consequences of protracted refugee situations. Even in the absence of durable solutions, empowering refugees to help themselves by giving access to the right to work, freedom of movement, and creating an enabling environment for independent economic activity can offer a better path to dignified and autonomous living than the status quo. Done well, such approaches have the potential simultaneously to benefit refugees, host communities, host governments, and donor governments.

This idea has existed for a long time, and yet policies that promote refugee self-reliance have been elusive. Only a handful of countries have been prepared to move beyond encampment policies and support self-reliance. Historically, a number of cases stand out. Throughout the 1960s and 1970s, the norm for self-settled rural refugees in Africa was self-reliance. However, with growing concerns about competition for resources, especially following democratization in host states around the world, support for such ideas waned. Today, a very select few countries actually implement policies that allow progressive economic integration, including Uganda, Zambia, South Africa, and Benin, with varying degrees of success.

Humanitarianism to Development

One of the barriers to self-reliance has been the commonly held view that refugee issues are primarily a 'humanitarian' concern. The belief has been held

---

[7] Interview, Ali-Addeh refugee camp, Djibouti, 25 May 2009.

for too long that the UN Refugee Agency (UNHCR) is mainly a relief agency that should deliver emergency assistance during a crisis and then continue to provide indefinite 'care and maintenance' to refugees until they are able to return home or can be permanently integrated elsewhere. The prevalence of protracted refugee situations demonstrates that this is based on a set of false assumptions.

Refugees are not just a humanitarian issue. Although the emergency phase may require a humanitarian response, including the provision of basic security and subsistence, the risk of an enduring view of refugees as an ongoing humanitarian subject is that it unnecessarily leads to long-term dependency while legitimating social exclusion. Of course, food, clothing, shelter, water, and sanitation may be needed during an initial mass influx. Refugee camps may assist the delivery of relief. However, there is a point at which continuing exclusively with the same response over time becomes counterproductive.

Barbara Harrell-Bond recognized this as early as 1986 in her book *Imposing Aid*. Based on fieldwork with Ugandan refugees in Sudan, she highlighted how long-term humanitarian assistance can undermine agency, failing to adequately recognize and nurture the capabilities of refugees. This argument remains as salient now as it was then. Humanitarian assistance may be necessary early on, but without a transition to greater self-reliance, it risks simply administering misery and dependency.

Humanitarian assistance is, of course, an important component of refugee policy, both in the emergency phase and as an ongoing safety net to support the most vulnerable. However, the presumption that refugees only have vulnerabilities—rather than capabilities—is deeply flawed. Refugees are, as people, no different from anyone else; they are ordinary people in exceptional circumstances. Many have skills and qualifications, and a desire to work and contribute. Yet, existing governance frameworks—both national and international—often inhibit this.

Policymakers have long recognized the need for early transition from relief to development. Indeed, historically there have been numerous attempts to draw upon the toolbox of development practitioners in order to support transition away from humanitarian dependency. The argument has generally been made that if development assistance can be applied to support refugee-hosting countries, it can support self-reliance or even more permanent local integration. If the resulting infrastructure and services create opportunities for both refugees and the national host community, the presence of refugees may come to be perceived as mutually beneficial.

The international community has attempted to bridge this relief-to-development gap through a range of institutional initiatives on an almost cyclical basis over the last few decades. These include the International Conferences on Assistance to Refugees in Africa (ICARA I and II) of the early 1980s, the

International Conferences on Refugees in Central America (also known as CIREFCA) at the end of the Cold War, and UNHCR's Convention Plus initiative of the early 2000s (Betts 2009). The common features of such initiatives have been the attempt by UNHCR to work more collaboratively with development agencies such as the United Nations Development Programme (UNDP) and the World Bank; encouragement of 'additional' development assistance from donors; and efforts to persuade host governments to consider self-reliance and local integration for refugees.

These initiatives have had a mixed record, but most have been a failure. Donor states have generally been unwilling to provide additional development assistance to support such approaches, frequently viewing refugees as being under the purview of exclusively humanitarian budget lines. Without significant additional funding, host state governments have had very little incentive—or electoral ability—to support self-reliance, let alone local integration. Furthermore, without donor or host state commitment, development agencies have often had very little reason to view refugees as anything other than 'a UNHCR issue'.

The underlying problem has been that these past initiatives have been almost exclusively state-centric. They have been intergovernmental initiatives premised upon the idea of achieving what is in practice an elusive North–South cooperation between donor and host governments, and they have relied upon successfully persuading two sets of governments that they can all benefit from refugee self-reliance. Only occasionally has this been effective.

Yet, today there are opportunities to look at the problem differently. Rather than taking an exclusively state-centric approach to targeted development assistance, it may be possible to take a broader view of the political economy that shapes possibilities for refugee self-reliance. Outcomes for refugees are shaped not only by states but also by markets. Historically, the international community has looked at the issue in terms of the relationship between states and refugees. However, the real question is for us to consider the relationship between states, markets, and refugees if we want to maximize opportunities not only for protection and assistance, but also for autonomy and human flourishing.

Engagement with the private sector has often been viewed with suspicion by organizations working with refugees. Yet, alongside a role for states, market-based approaches offer a potentially game-changing opportunity for refugee self-reliance. Refugees represent opportunities for business and entrepreneurship. Perhaps more importantly, they themselves can be entrepreneurial and create businesses. Even though their activities may not always be recognized, refugees almost everywhere in the world are engaging with markets. In a globalized world, they have economic networks that are both national and transnational. Far from being exclusively dependent upon international assistance, they often create economic opportunities for themselves and others even in adverse conditions.

Refugee Economies

Pioneering research has already taken place on the economic lives of refugees, drawing attention to and describing key aspects of the economy of refugee camps and urban areas (Jacobsen 2005; Werker 2007). What has been largely missing, however, is a firm grounding in data and a clear theoretical framework. This is in part because although economists have focused on immigration more broadly, they have rarely looked at questions relating to refugees and forced migration (Ruiz and Vargas-Silva 2013).

The existing work on the economics of refugees and forced migrants broadly divides into two areas, which can be categorized crudely as 'livelihoods' and 'impacts'. The former seeks to understand the different income-generating activities developed by refugees and to examine the success or failure of external livelihood projects and programmes. The main weakness of this stream of research has been that it has tended to look at livelihoods and livelihood interventions in abstraction from a broader and more holistic analysis of the economic lives of refugees. The latter area seeks to understand the impact of refugees on host states and societies. Its main weakness is that it is primarily concerned with hosts, rather than refugees themselves.

Away from academia, each of these strands of work has mainly been developed by international organizations for a particular instrumental purpose: either to enhance livelihood interventions, or to justify the inclusion of refugees in national development plans. Neither of these aims is unproductive, but their focus may obscure a broader and more holistic understanding of refugees' own economic lives. Going beyond these two strands of work, we therefore seek to develop a theoretically informed and data-driven approach to understanding the economic lives of refugees.

In this volume, our key theoretical undertaking is to develop the concept of 'refugee economies'. We define 'refugee economies' as the resource allocation systems relating to the lives of refugees. This represents an attempt to look holistically at what shapes the production, consumption, finance, and exchange activities of refugees, and to begin to explain variation in economic outcomes for refugees themselves. Our goal is to examine refugees' own interactions with markets, both for their own sake and as a means to understand how externally driven programmes might build on what already exists rather than be based on abstract—and sometimes arbitrary—interventions.

What makes refugees' economic lives distinctive is the unique institutional context of being a refugee. As we know from a body of economic theory called

New Institutional Economics, markets are shaped by their institutional context (Williamson 2000; North 1990). 'Refugeehood' represents a particular institutional framework that introduces a set of constraints and opportunities into the economic lives of refugees. Building on the insights of New Institutional Economics, we therefore identify the institutional factors that make refugees' economic lives distinctive compared to citizens or other groups of migrants.

We will argue that refugees are in a distinctive economic position because of their positioning between three different sets of institutions. First, they lie between state and international governance. They are partly under the authority of the state and partly under the authority of international organizations. Second, they lie between the formal and informal sectors. They usually have some legitimate access to the formal economy but also frequently face regulatory restrictions compared to citizens. Third, they lie between national and transnational economies. Given their differing networks, their primary sources of exchange and capital may sometimes be trans-boundary.

These three areas are stylized categories, and they apply to different refugee populations to different degrees. But they serve to illustrate the important ways in which 'being a refugee' conceptually places refugees in an institutionally distinctive position. In different ways, they draw attention to the way in which the institutional context of 'refugeehood' leads to both constraints and opportunities.

We also know from economic theory that the market imperfections and distortions that result from particular institutional contexts can have distributive consequences. This may in turn create opportunities for some people to innovate, adapt, and engage in forms of arbitrage across regulatory environments. We suggest that this is also the case for refugees, whose economic outcomes are not only shaped by institutional structures but also by the agency and capacity of particular individuals—'innovators'—to transform constraints into opportunities for themselves and others.

Based on this theoretical starting point, 'refugee economies' seeks to empirically explore variation in economic outcomes for refugees. The literature in the economics of immigration has already explored a range of such questions. It has asked, for example, what explains variation in migrants' incomes, what explains their selection of alternative geographical locations, and what explains differences in the impact of migrants on natives (Abramitzky et al. 2012; Borjas 2014). Such questions have not been systematically explored through either qualitative or quantitative data collection in relation to refugees.

Uganda as a Case Study

In order to explore refugee economies, we focus on one particular country, Uganda. This case study is not in any way intended to be representative. On the contrary, we have chosen it because it represents an outlier. It is a country that has adopted a relatively progressive refugee policy called the Self-Reliance Strategy (Sharpe and Namusobya 2012; Dryden-Peterson and Hovil 2004). Unlike many other refugee-hosting countries around the world, it has given its 420 000 refugees the right to work and a significant degree of freedom of movement.[8]

Although Uganda's treatment of refugees is far from perfect, it has offered an unusually high level of socio-economic freedom to refugees. Uganda therefore enables us to explore what is possible—in terms of what refugees can do and contribute economically—when given basic economic freedoms. While not representative, it can therefore provide important insights and lessons into what might be possible if other host countries were prepared to also adopt similar policies.

Uganda also offers enough internal variation within its refugee hosting practices to provide a useful context for comparative research within a single country. First, it hosts a significant number of urban refugees. Second, it has protracted rural refugee settlements. Third, it also hosts an emergency relief context with recent arrivals from violence in the Democratic Republic of Congo. Uganda also hosts a range of nationalities, including Somalis, Congolese, South Sudanese, Rwandans, and Burundians. This variation is especially useful for our attempts to explain different economic outcomes for refugees.

We have adopted a participatory and mixed-methods approach. We selected four research sites in Uganda: the capital city, Kampala, host to the largest urban refugee population in the country; the Nakivale and Kyangwali refugee settlements in the south-west of the country, the most populated two settlements in the country at the start of the research; and the Rwamwanja settlement, reopened recently to provide an emergency response to the mass influx of Congolese refugees fleeing violence.

Across each of these sites, we have used participatory research methods, employing national research coordinators and refugee researchers, whom we trained as peer researchers and enumerators. This approach played a crucial role in ensuring access, building networks of trust, and improving the quality of our research. We also felt strongly that it provided a way to ensure our research had a positive legacy within the community.

Our data collection was based on both qualitative and quantitative methods. We began with qualitative research, using a range of methods from transect walks to semi-structured interviews, focus groups, and participant and non-participant observation. This enabled us to get an understanding of the communities we were working in and the overall context of our

[8] As at June 2015, UNHCR recorded 428 397 refugees in Uganda (UNHCR 2015a).

work. We then moved on sequentially to quantitative research, using survey methods in order to collect representative data. Drawing upon UNHCR's sample frame in the settlements and using a technique called respondent-driven sampling in the city, we were able to build an unprecedented data set on the economic lives of refugees, based on a total sample size of over 2000 households. The total period of data collection took place over eighteen months, during which we had almost constant in-country presence.

This Book

We have taken an interdisciplinary approach to explore refugee economies in Uganda. Although we will draw upon ideas within economics, the book is not an economics book; it is a self-consciously interdisciplinary study. We will integrate ideas and research methods from economics, anthropology, sociology, and political science, and this range of perspectives is reflective of the academic training and background of the authors.

The book is not intended to be the definitive, final word on either the economic lives of refugees nor the economics of refugees. Rather, it seeks to be a starting point for building a wider research agenda on refugee economies. Its central contribution is to advance the theories and methodologies we have developed for understanding the economic lives of refugees. The single case study represents an opportunity to provide unprecedented depth in terms of qualitative and quantitative data, which might then inform the development of subsequent work in other contexts. In this sense, it is intended to be part of a theory-building exercise and a means to generate greater interest from economists and researchers from other disciplines in the economics of refugees and forced migration.

Our overall argument is that refugees have complex economic lives. Despite the significant constraints of having to adapt to new regulatory environments, new social networks, and new markets, refugees are consumers, producers, buyers, sellers, employers, employees, and entrepreneurs. They engage in market-based activities that are worthy of understanding. This, we argue, opens up exciting new avenues for research and enables us to better understand what is analytically distinctive about the economic lives of refugees.

Furthermore, if we are able to recognize these economic lives and to explain variation in economic outcomes for different groups of refugees, this in turn offers a means to radically rethink refugee assistance. Rather than designing abstract projects and programmes that exist in a vacuum, this understanding might enable international organizations and NGOs to build meaningfully upon and nurture the skills, talents, and aspirations of displaced communities.

This may enable us to move collectively from a logic of dependency towards greater sustainability within our responses to refugees.

In order to make this argument, the book proceeds in a number of stages. First, we begin by outlining the history of refugees and development from 1919 to the present. We show how a 'refugees and development' approach is not new, but that a range of institutional approaches have been tried over a number of years with varying degrees of success. Second, we outline a theoretical framework for thinking about 'refugee economies' that seeks to identify both what is distinctive about the economic lives of refugees and to generate testable propositions about the variation in economic outcomes for refugees. Third, we explain the methodologies we have used in our Uganda research so that they can be understood, replicated, and improved. Fourth, we outline our main empirical findings from the Uganda research, looking in turn at the urban, rural protracted, and rural emergency contexts. Fifth, we highlight two key trends from our research that have historically been neglected in wider work on refugees and development: the role of business and the role of innovation. Finally, we conclude by highlighting the book's implications for research, policy, and practice.

2

The history of refugees and development

Self-reliance has arguably been the holy grail of the global refugee regime. In the absence of opportunities to return home or permanently integrate into another society, ensuring refugees are not indefinitely confined to camps has depended upon persuading host states to allow refugees a minimum set of socio-economic rights. It has depended upon the willingness to provide refugees with freedom of movement, the right to work, and a range of other entitlements such as access to banking facilities.

However, with few exceptions, self-reliance has been extremely difficult to achieve. Most host governments have been reluctant to reallocate scarce resources from citizens to non-citizens and have perceived self-reliance to be synonymous with permanent local integration. Over time, the norm has therefore become encampment, with donor governments paying for the care and maintenance of refugees in remote and geographically confined border areas, pending the end to conflict or political transition in the country of origin.

At various historical junctures, it has been recognized that beyond the emergency phase of displacement, encampment benefits nobody, and alternatives have been sought. The most notable means to overcome protracted refugee situations and enhance refugees' rights and opportunities has been the attempt to close the relief-to-development gap. Rather than seeing refugees as a purely humanitarian issue, successive attempts have been made to recast refugees as a development issue and to use this as a way to promote more sustainable solutions for displaced populations.

These attempts to rethink refugees as a development issue have been almost cyclical in nature. At times of mass influx or protracted displacement, the international community has often revisited the idea of development-based approaches to refugees in the hope of promoting solutions that can simultaneously benefit refugees, host states and societies, and donors. In the simplest of terms, the logic of these approaches has been that if development assistance can be used to support refugees and hosts simultaneously, then this can lead to 'win–win' outcomes, empowering refugees to be a 'benefit' rather than a 'burden' and reducing the long-term drain on finite humanitarian assistance budgets.

It is important to be aware of the lessons of history. Attempts to bridge the humanitarian–development gap in order to promote refugee self-reliance are not new. Appearing as early as the interwar years to address refugee crises in Europe, they were used again to respond to displacement during the partition of India and became the norm for refugee settlement in postcolonial Africa. During the late Cold War period, the so-called 'refugee aid and development' (RAD) approach led to two major institutional attempts to promote refugee self-reliance in Africa and Central America, known as ICARA I and II and CIREFCA. From the early 2000s, self-reliance came to be characterized as a means to overcome protracted displacement situations.

In order to distil lessons from the past, this chapter provides an institutional history of refugees and development. It outlines five periods: the prehistory of refugees and development (1919–79), ICARA I and II (1979–84), CIREFCA (1987–95), Convention Plus (2003–5), and the Solutions Alliance (2014–). In each case, it shows how the relationship between refugees and development was conceived, examines how attempts to promote self-reliance were developed, and explores factors that led to success or failure.

Overall, the chapter argues that the impact of refugee aid and development has been limited by some common factors. In particular, the initiatives from the 1980s to the early 2000s relied upon achieving international cooperation between Northern donors and Southern host states. They depended upon achieving an elusive and interlocking commitment between host governments' willingness to consider moving beyond encampment policies and donor governments' willingness to provide additional development assistance. The chapter concludes by arguing that there are today new opportunities to reconceive approaches to refugees and development in ways that go beyond intergovernmental negotiations on development assistance.

The Prehistory of Refugees and Development (1919–79)

It is often assumed that attempts to conceive of refugees as a development issue began in the 1980s. Contemporary initiatives have often recalled this history in ways that have begun with ICARA I and II.[1] Yet, as Claudena

---

[1] For example, at its inception, the Solutions Alliance produced a document called 'Unlocking displacement solutions—Storyline' outlining the history of refugees and development. The document began with the 1980s: 'UNHCR promoted the concept of Refugee Aid and Development (RAD) during the 1980s which formed the basis of the International Conference on Assistance to Refugees in Africa (ICARA) in 1981 and 1984, and the International Conference on Assistance to Refugees in Central America (CIREFCA) in 1989'.

Skran and others have shown, 'refugees and development' has an important prehistory. In the early refugee regime, prior to the conception of refugees as a 'humanitarian issue' and the invention of the modern refugee camp, development-based approaches were an important part of the solutions toolbox. In interwar Europe between 1919 and 1939, the League of Nations High Commissioner for Refugees created settlement schemes planned by the League, often with a central role for the International Labour Organization (ILO) in facilitating employment and vocational training for refugees in ways that could contribute directly to national development plans in host countries.

One of the earliest and best-documented examples of this relates to the Greek refugee crisis of 1922–4. Following the Lausanne Convention of 1923, it was agreed that there would be a population exchange established in Turkey of Muslims of Greek nationality for Greek Orthodox Christians of Turkish nationality. This led to around 1.2 million Greek refugees entering Greece against the backdrop of a population of just 5.5 million (Skran 1985; Zürcher 2003).

The Greek Refugee Settlement Commission (GRSC) was established after Greece requested support from the League of Nations to manage this influx (Howland 1926; Mears 1929). The GRSC became one of the first documented commissions focusing specifically on refugee rehabilitation, and these 'League initiatives in helping refugees achieve self-sufficiency were a dramatic departure from the past' (Skran 1985: 113). Financed through a loan by the League of Nations (Howland 1926: 8), the GRSC employed mainly Greek refugees in its key posts (Skran 1985: 179). This approach led to the establishment of new settlements and townships in historically underdeveloped areas of Greece (Zürcher 2003: 5). Refugees were explicitly recognized as making a strong economic contribution to the Greek economy:

> The refugees have caused vast changes in rural Greece. Wastelands have been transformed into orchards, vineyards, grain fields, and tobacco plantations... better breeds of livestock are being introduced, and nomadic shepherds are being replaced by stock breeders who raise forage crops on their own land. Fallowing has given place to artificial fertilization, and new tools supplied by the Refugee Settlement Commission are gradually causing the peasants to discard antiquated methods of agriculture. As a consequence, production of almost all kinds of agricultural products has increased enormously since the refugees began to flood the country in 1922–23. (Mears 1929: 279)

The League of Nations High Commissioner built upon this experience to develop similar schemes across Europe in collaboration with the ILO. In Bulgaria, for example, Bulgar, Armenian and Russian refugees were given access to over 132 000 hectares of land for settlement. The scheme led to the construction of roads, drained swamps, cleared land, built villages, and established farmers. By 1933, around 125000 refugees had been integrated within Bulgaria (Skran 1985: 48).

Many of the schemes that were initiated looked significantly like contemporary 'innovative' ideas for refugee integration. Vocational training, agricultural production, and even microfinance were employed as a means to foster refugee self-reliance. Notable, however, was the incorporation of refugees into these projects as benefactors as well as beneficiaries, which led refugees' livelihoods to hold a central role in both relief and development efforts that was not emulated in later eras (Easton-Calabria 2015). Refugees' own skills and financial capability were emphasized due to a lack of prior experience in refugee relief and as a result of the League's 'no-charity' philosophy, itself borne out of a restricted budget. Across Europe and the Middle East, the ILO worked to match refugee skills with employers in third countries, resulting in the resettlement of over 50000 refugees (ILO 1928: 84–5). Refugees also funded loans for refugee entrepreneurs through the so-called Nansen Stamp Fund, a revolving loan created out of fees paid for the Nansen Passport, a refugee travel document (League of Nations 1934: 69). These examples serve as a timely reminder that far from refugee camps being the historical norm, there is a nearly century-old alternative that has helped refugees to help themselves and contribute to their host societies, through access to employment, loans, and training.

The modern refugee regime that followed the Second World War mainly focused on integrating refugees in Europe. However, as refugee challenges began to emerge in Europe, the dominant approaches followed a development-based approach. From the 1960s, increasing numbers of refugees were displaced within Africa as a result of colonial liberation struggles and, increasingly, Cold War proxy conflicts. Yet at that stage there was very little institutionalized humanitarian response to refugees in Africa. Instead, large numbers of spontaneously settled refugees were supported primarily through development-based responses. Consequently, throughout the 1960s and 1970s the predominant response was not for the international community to establish and run refugee camps. Instead, it was to explore ways in which refugees could be integrated into national development plans for the benefit of both refugees and hosts.

The archive of Tristram Betts, held by the Refugee Studies Centre in Oxford, reveals many of these approaches. Betts was Field Director for Oxfam throughout much of the 1960s, and a strong advocate of refugees' potential for self-reliance and the resulting advantages for host countries. In a 1965 report on new refugee settlements for Rwandan refugees in Uganda (which included Nakivale and Kyangwali), for example, Betts discussed the importance of refugee participation as well as regional development benefiting both refugees and locals. He argued that approaches to refugees 'should dove-tail closely with those envisaged under the Development Plan' and that similar pro-grammes should be applied for both refugees and hosts 'because it will not always be possible or advisable to separate refugees from the Ugandan popu-lation'.[2] He further suggested that such an approach could be supported through external financing.

The Betts collection reveals a host of other similarly conceived projects across Africa. Betts' 1966 comparative review of settlement projects for refu-gees highlights a series of projects across East Africa intended to promote refugee self-reliance through development assistance.[3] ILO projects across Burundi, Uganda, and Tanzania were all conceived as integrated development projects. From road building to credit unions to agricultural cooperatives to integrated provision of health and education services for hosts and refugees, a range of integrated rural development projects were viewed to be the answer to refugee assistance. In his analysis, Betts reveals a number of common conditions for success: (1) being well planned; (2) adopting a participatory approach by including refugees in the projects; (3) the focus on supporting cash crops to increase food self-sufficiency.

However, Betts also highlights the pitfalls of self-reliance if it is presumed to be a panacea, or sought without the true involvement of refugees themselves. In the case of Rwandans in Burundi, for example, hubris about the viability of self-reliance led to refugees being 'more or less dumped wherever land was made available with local consent, and without prior planning or reference to soil fertility... the result has been the establishment of rural slums, partially self-subsistent and with the minimum spirit of initiative' (Betts 1966: 15). Such situations demonstrate a top-down institutional approach towards refu-gee self-reliance characteristic of the post-war period, where often ill-planned steps towards self-reliance were promoted without the consent or participa-tion of refugees themselves (Easton-Calabria 2015). Although many of the efforts to foster refugee self-reliance have been the same throughout the history of the international refugee regime, the post-war era held an often authoritarian approach, where livelihoods in settlements were chosen for refugees based on host countries' needs (Trappe 1971: 10). However, Betts also suggests that with careful research and piloting, community development approaches have immense potential 'to inspire among the people a new spirit of initiative' (Betts 1966: 22).

By 1967, the UN Economic Commission for Africa viewed refugee self-reliance as the mainstream approach to protection in Africa, highlighting

---

[2] 'Draft report of the survey mission concerning a possible project for the integration of refugees in Uganda, research undertaken November–December 1965', Betts Collection 55.

[3] 'Refugees in Eastern Africa: A comparative study', T. F. Betts, Field Director, Oxfam, 6 May 1966, 58 pages.

'the need for training programmes, vocational guidance and employment placement services for our refugees'.[4] A conference that year in Addis Ababa made a series of recommendations on how to address 'the refugee problem', including: (1) integrating refugees into national development plans; (2) selecting pilot countries for new development approaches; (3) improved education and vocational training for refugees to meet 'placement and manpower requirements'; (4) using 'zonal planning' to support and utilize refugees in underdeveloped areas.[5] Meanwhile, voluntary agencies working on refugee livelihoods and self-reliance in settlements across Africa—from the Lutheran World Federation to Catholic Relief Services—mainly funded agricultural projects that supported host countries through the exportation of cash crops, further demonstrating the intertwined nature of refugee self-reliance and national development.[6] Indeed, an agricultural development model aiming to foster refugee self-reliance was the dominant model for the assistance of refugees in Africa until the end of the 1970s.

These historical insights show that there is a neglected prehistory to 'refugees and development'. Many of them happened as a result of institutional support from the ILO and development NGOs, but they were relatively localized in nature. It was not until the early 1980s that UNHCR began to lead international initiatives intended to promote self-reliance through large-scale international cooperation.

The International Conferences on Refugees in Africa (1981 and 1984)

By the end of the 1970s, some three to four million refugees were spontaneously settled across Africa. During the 1960s and 1970s, it had been generally assumed that most of these people would go home as soon as independence was achieved. However, by 1979 it was clear that the majority of Africa's refugees were in protracted displacement as a result of intractable Cold War proxy conflicts in states such as Burundi, Chad, Ethiopia, Angola, Uganda, and Zaire. This recognition led a number of host states to argue that their commitment to hosting refugees had become an 'open-ended burden'

---

[4] A Statement by the Executive Secretary of the Economic Commission for Africa (delivered at the ceremonial opening of the conference), Conference on the Legal, Economic, and Social Aspects of African Refugee Problems, Addis Ababa, 9–18 October 1967. Afr/Ref/Conf. 1967/No. L. 4, Betts Collection, Box no. 15, General Work.

[5] 'Recommendations', Conference on the Legal, Economic, and Social Aspects of African Refugee Problems, Addis Ababa, 9–18 October 1967, Betts Collection, Box no. 15, General Work, 59v.

[6] 'Assistance to African Refugees by Voluntary Organizations', Conference on the Legal, Economic, and Social Aspects of African Refugee Problems, Addis Ababa, 9–18 October 1967. Afr/Ref/Conf. 1967/No. 13, 71 pages, Betts Collection, Box no. 15, General Work.

(Stein 1987). Refugees were using the same agricultural land, natural resources, and social services as the host communities, placing a strain on national infrastructure.

Consequently, the Organization of African Unity (OAU) convened the Arusha Conference on the Situation of Refugees in Africa (7–17 May 1979). The conference explored how African states could share responsibility more fairly for hosting refugees amongst themselves and with the wider international community. Among its recommendations, the Arusha Conference sought a new form of burden-sharing involving development projects. These recommendations suggested that targeting both refugees and host communities might contribute to promoting the self-reliance of refugees, pending their eventual repatriation.[7]

This call led UNHCR and the African states to convene the International Conference on Assistance to Refugees in Africa (ICARA I) in 1981 and a second conference in 1984 (ICARA II). The conferences represented two one-off donor events, held in Geneva. At both conferences, the African states submitted a range of development projects and programmes (jointly compiled by UNHCR, UNDP, and host states in the region) to prospective donor states. The main aim of the African states in submitting these proposals was to attract greater development assistance from donors that would support both refugees and host communities simultaneously.

ICARA I, held on 9–10 April 1981, had three stated objectives: (1) to 'focus attention on the plight of refugees in Africa'; (2) to 'mobilize additional resources to assist both refugees and returnees'; (3) to 'aid countries of asylum in bearing the burden imposed upon them by the large number of refugees'.[8] The event's focus was largely on burden-sharing, and it was primarily a pledging conference that set out few ideas, principles, or guidelines. The resulting funding commitments were also relatively short term in focus.

The participant African states were invited by UNHCR to compile project proposals with the technical assistance of UNHCR, which would then be submitted to the conference. The intention of the call for submissions was that these projects should focus on supporting long-term infrastructural development that could simultaneously compensate host communities while improving refugee protection and the prospects for durable solutions. Bearing in mind the neglect of increasingly protracted rural and border settlements, much focus was directed to meeting basic needs such as food provision. For example, the UNHCR's Chief of West and Central African

---

[7] UNHCR, 'Recommendations from the Pan-African Conference on the Situation of Refugees in Africa', 1984. Recommendations 10 (1) and 10 (3c), in particular, set out the notion of development for integration and self-reliance.

[8] UN General Assembly Resolution 35/42 of 25 November 1980.

operations argued that the priority for the funds falling within UNHCR's mandate should focus on 'immediate needs', such as shelter, clothing, and blankets;[9] meanwhile, $175m of the $560m initially pledged at the conference was earmarked for food aid.[10]

The UN Secretary-General, Kurt Waldheim, proclaimed in his concluding statement that the conference had been a success. In relation to the conference objectives, he claimed 'we have made major strides on all three fronts'.[11] In commenting on the $560m in conference pledges, he went on: 'one may conclude, therefore, that the immediate priority requirements will be met, and that a solid base has been laid for the development of the necessary support to accommodate the long-term needs involved'. In the immediate aftermath, numerous state representatives in African capitals wrote to congratulate the High Commissioner on the initiative.[12]

However, it was only later that the extent to which these pledges had been earmarked by states became increasingly apparent. By September 1981, the steering committee in charge of post-ICARA coordination noted that further specifications by donors left only $144m unearmarked, leaving UNHCR with an estimated $40m available for the high-priority projects that did not fall into its regular or specific programmes. Consequently, a ceiling of $2m per country was fixed, and this was focused on humanitarian assistance needs, such as food, water, shelter, and the delivery of medical services.[13] In Loescher's (2001: 227) words, 'almost all of the $560m offered by donor states was earmarked for projects and allocated to most favoured nations. Very few funds went to especially hard hit nations like Ethiopia and other countries in the Horn of Africa.' When the UN General Assembly subsequently reflected on the achievements of ICARA I, it regretted 'that in spite of efforts made, the assistance provided to an increasing number of African refugees is still very inadequate'.[14]

ICARA I therefore ultimately failed to satisfy host states in Africa because the donors' financial contributions did not meet their expectations. In the words

[9] Mr Bwakiri, Acting Chief West and Central Africa Region, to Mr Asomani, Officer-in-Charge of Post-ICARA Coordination, Memorandum SACO/1153, 'Note on selecting priority projects, falling within/outside UNHCR's mandate', 27 July 1981 (Fonds UNHCR 11, 391.62/374).

[10] UN Middle East Information Centre, 'ICARA: Press release' 66/1981, 28 April 1981 (Fonds UNHCR 11, 391.62/306A).

[11] Concluding Statement by the Secretary-General to ICARA, 10 April 1981, Report to the UN on ICARA, 21 April 1981 (Fonds UNHCR 11, 391.62/300A).

[12] The Foreign Minister of Cameroon, for example, proclaimed the $560m pledged 'une premiere manifestation significative de solidarite internationale', Correspondence Foreign Minister of Cameroon to High Commissioner, 11 May 1981 (Fonds UNHCR 11, 391.62/318A).

[13] '3rd Draft of Steering Committee of Post-ICARA Coordination Meeting', held 15 September 1981, New York, HCR/NY/572 (Fonds UNHCR 11, 391.62/460).

[14] UN General Assembly Resolution 36/124 of 14 December 1981, cited in J. Milner, 'Golden Age? What Golden Age? A critical history of African asylum policy', paper presented at the Centre for Refugee Studies, York University, 28 January 2004.

of the Chair of the African Group of states, 'Although ICARA I had succeeded in certain respects, it had not raised the additional resources hoped for.'[15] This brought calls for 'additionality': Egypt, for example, concerned that other development resources destined to states' citizens might be diverted into refugee protection, stressed 'the need to increase the developmental assistance to asylum countries'.[16] Equally, the legacy of ICARA I failed to satisfy Northern donor states, particularly the United States, which after observing that no greater access to durable solutions for refugees resulted from its $285m pledge, remained on the fringes of ICARA II. The concerns of Northern donors were largely that financial commitments had not translated into durable solutions for refugees but had either been squandered on short-term assistance or had been used by African states simply to fund outdated development projects that offered little benefit to refugees.[17] Gorman (1993) diagnoses the failure of ICARA I ultimately to meet its third goal of addressing refugee-related development needs as a consequence of its failure to involve UN development agencies systematically in the conference planning and project proposal preparations.

ICARA I did, however, have an intellectual legacy. While its focus had mainly been on basic needs, much of the rhetoric of the conference and many of the projects submitted by states focused on building infrastructural capacity in order to facilitate the hosting of refugee populations. This represented the starting point for UNHCR's 'refugee aid and development strategy' (RAD). For example, the General Assembly resolution establishing ICARA I identifies the need 'to strengthen the capacity of countries of asylum to provide adequately for the refugees while they remain in their countries, as well as to assist the countries of origin in the rehabilitation of genuine voluntary returnees'.[18] Self-sufficiency through capacity-building was a major theme in the conference speeches. For example, the Secretary-General emphasized the need to 'promote self-sufficiency of refugees through various local integration programmes'.[19] Meanwhile, Siaka Stevens, as Chair of the OAU, claimed:

> The assistance of the world community . . . should aim at helping them [refugees] to help themselves, particularly in cases where repatriation could no longer be envisaged. Refugees should not be assisted in ways which would create

[15] 'Meeting on ICARA II with African missions', 5 October 1983, HCR/ETH/610 (Fonds UNHCR 11, 391.78/373).
[16] Ibid.
[17] Evident from the comments of European states at the informal meetings of ExCom representatives. For example, 'Note for the file: Summary of statements relating to ICARA II', 27 May 1983 (Fonds UNHCR 11, 391.78/215).
[18] UN General Assembly Resolution 35/42 of 25 November 1980, preambular paragraph 8.
[19] Concluding Statement by the Secretary-General to ICARA, 10 April 1981, 'Report of the UN ICARA' (Fonds UNHCR 11, 991.62/300A).

overdependence. Rather, they should be guided and enabled to become self-supporting as quickly as possible.[20]

Reflecting the limitations of ICARA I, ICARA II drew on many of the under-developed ideas that had been implicit in the first conference. ICARA II was seen by donor states as needing to be, in the words of the Austrian Ambassador, more of a 'think tank' than a 'pledging conference'.[21] The second conference (held in Geneva, 9–11 July 1984) benefited from far greater planning time than its predecessor. Soren Jessen-Petersen was appointed the Head of an ICARA Unit, which coordinated the Steering Committee and Technical Teams from 1983. He noted that the need for the second conference was the failure of the first in terms of capacity-building: 'It fell short of meeting the expectations of the African Governments for support towards strengthening their institutional capacity to receive refugees... Hence, resolution 37/197 calling for the convening of ICARA II.'[22] The objectives of the conference were set out as to: (1) 'thoroughly review the results of ICARA I and the state of progress of projects submitted to it'; (2) 'consider the continuing need for assistance with a view to providing, as necessary, additional assistance to refugees/returnees in Africa for the implementation of programmes for their relief, rehabilitation and resettlement'; (3) 'consider the impact imposed on national economies of the African countries concerned and to provide them with required assistance to strengthen their social and economic infrastructure to cope with the burden of dealing with large numbers of refugees and returnees'.[23]

The central theme of ICARA II was 'Time for Solutions', which the High Commissioner explained represented 'a joint responsibility for all participants... I am thinking particularly of the relationship between relief and development aid, and the primacy of durable solutions'.[24] This reflected the 1983 UNHCR Executive Committee (ExCom) resolution on durable solutions, which 'recognised the importance and timeliness of ICARA II in connection with the pursuit of durable solutions to refugee problems in Africa'.[25]

Consequently, where ICARA I had ultimately focused on short-term relief, ICARA II was intended to direct funds towards durable solutions, acknowledging that this would require a greater developmental emphasis. ExCom noted

[20] Statement by Dr Siaka Stevens, President of Sierra Leone (and Chair of OAU), ICARA, 9 April 1981 (Fonds UNHCR 11, 391.62/316).
[21] 'Note for the file: Summary of statements relating to ICARA II made at informal meetings of ExCom representatives', 27 May 1983 (Fonds UNHCR 11, 391.78/215).
[22] Memorandum Mr Jessen-Petersen to Mr Moussalli, 'Talking points on ICARA II', 23 November 1983 (Fonds UNHCR 11, 391.78/399).
[23] UN General Assembly Resolution 37/197, 18 December 1982, Operational Paragraph 5 (a) to (c).
[24] High Commissioner's Opening Remarks at the 3rd Steering Committee Meeting on ICARA II, 14 November 1983, Jessen-Petersen's summary of the debate (Fonds UNHCR 11, 391.78/398A).
[25] See 'Conclusions adopted by the Executive Committee on International Protection of Refugees', Excom Conclusion No. 29 (XXXIX) of 1983, paragraph (l).

that 'Given the economic and social fragility of those African countries receiving refugees, UNHCR's work needs to be complemented by efforts of a more developmental nature.'[26] This acknowledgement led UNHCR to attempt to build partnerships with development agencies. For example, the Steering Committee for ICARA II included UNDP 'because of the development aspect'.[27] This reflected a growing awareness of the need to address the now-famous transition 'gap' between relief and development.[28] UNICEF's report in the aftermath of ICARA I, for example, noted that:

> It was also apparent that during the first emergency phase, donors wished to see their commitments applied for humanitarian purposes only. A number expressed the view that the longer-term aspects of the refugee problem and the strengthening of infrastructure should be considered as part of the international agencies involved with development in co-operation with the Governments concerned.[29]

By mid-1983, consideration of the 'gap' was emerging in UNHCR's thinking. In representing the organization at a Symposium on African Refugees in Tokyo, UNHCR's Dessalegne Chefeke noted that while the 'most ideal solution' for refugees was voluntary repatriation, 'there are, unfortunately, also situations where voluntary repatriation is most unlikely' and these require 'local integration' and 'self-sufficiency'. He argued that 'ICARA II will try to bridge the gap between the humanitarian aid to refugees and development aid to the countries concerned', claiming 'the process leading to refugee integration is not simply a succession of phases, i.e., relief, self-reliance and development. These phases overlap.'[30]

In preparation for the conference, the ICARA Unit invited submissions from African states under the heading of 'Proposals for Development Assistance to Areas with Refugee Concentrations' in which states were to focus on, firstly, government policy in regard to refugees (including efforts to reach durable solutions); secondly, the impact of refugees on the national economy; and thirdly, overall plans designed to deal with refugee problems *particularly through development projects*. In outlining the 'additional resources sought',

---

[26] 'For the information of ExCom: ICARA II', Geneva, 21–3 May 1984 (Fonds UNHCR 11, 391.78/307).

[27] Memorandum Mr Jessen-Petersen to Mr Moussalli, 'Talking points on ICARA II', 23 November 1983 (Fonds UNHCR 11, 391.78/399).

[28] The so-called relief-to-development 'gap' refers to the long-standing separation of humanitarianism and development in global governance. It has been suggested that this gap has negative practical implications because in complex humanitarian emergencies there is often inadequate institutional collaboration to ensure the smooth transition in responsibility from humanitarian agencies to development agencies.

[29] UNICEF document for Executive Board on Cooperation with African Countries, E/ICFF/P/L.2094 (Fonds UNHCR 11, 391.62/319), paragraph 29.

[30] Dessalegne Chefeke, Keynote Address to Symposium on African Refugees, Tokyo, 24 May 1983 (Fonds UNHCR 11, 391.68/234).

they were required to provide a 'statement of refugee-related development projects which are already underway'.[31]

During this process, Tanzania's prior experience of incorporating refugees in national development projects as a means of achieving self-sufficiency and local integration was championed as the pioneering example of success.[32] The Tanzanian model was used particularly as a means of encouraging involvement from UNDP. For example, in a letter from the UNHCR Representative in Dar-es-Salaam to UNDP's Resident Representative, an enclosed background paper set out some key illustrations of the success of local integration through self-sufficiency. It looked at the self-sufficiency achieved by Barundi refugees in Katumba, Ulyankula, and Mishamo and by self-settled Zaireans in Kigoma, showing how 'with the assistance of settlement and project personnel the refugees themselves are responsible for land clearance and for building their own homes, as well as for various community projects designed to foster a community spirit of self-reliance and cooperation.' The paper argued that the government's encouragement of refugee agriculture and the construction of infrastructure such as roads, water systems, education, and health facilities had promoted this integration, and called upon UNDP to contribute through ICARA II to strengthening this process.[33]

After receiving project submissions from states, the UN technical team for ICARA II conducted a series of visits to the fourteen states concerned. The aim of the visits was to compile reports on the states' 'infrastructural burden of dealing with large numbers of refugees' and to assess and prioritize project submissions 'that would enhance the capacity of the country to support refugees'. All the visits lasted between three and ten days, involved meetings between UNHCR, UNDP, donor countries, host states, and NGOs, and reviewed the current situation and policy while describing and prioritizing projects. The projects in the report all focused on infrastructural development initiatives planned and 'owned' by the host governments, with the explicit intention of providing 'development' facilities such as health, education, road access, agricultural training, equipment, and other forms of vocational training that would better provide a social and economic link between the refugee populations and the state's own citizens.[34]

[31] 'ICARA II: Guidelines for country submissions on the impact of refugee problems on national economies and possible development assistance required to alleviate these problems', YZF 306-03, 15 March 1983 (Fonds UNHCR 11, 391.78/91).

[32] For example, paragraphs 12 and 13 of the 'Report of the UN Technical Team for ICARA II on Tanzania' note 'The deep-rooted and internationally well-known humanitarian concern of the Government of the United Republic of Tanzania towards refugees', 29 August 1983 (Fonds UNHCR 11, 391.78/45).

[33] Letter from Abdellah Saied, UNHCR Representative to Dar es Salaam to Mr D. Outtara, Resident Representative of UNDP re. Proposed Development Assistance Projects from ICARA II, 7 June 1983 (Fonds UNHCR 11, 391.78/227A).

[34] All the reports of the UN Technical Team are in UNHCR archives, Fonds UNHCR 11, 391.78.9.

When the conference met in July 1984, it aimed to raise $392m to meet 128 aid schemes in the fourteen African states over a period of three years, and the Chair, Leo Tindemans, proclaimed the event a success.[35] Although only $81m was pledged at the conference, the consensus reached in Geneva was seen as a starting point and not an 'end unto itself'. In particular, there was optimism that the Final Declaration and Program of Action set out generic principles that could be built upon. These included: firstly, the need for ongoing assistance; secondly, acknowledgment of Africa's disproportionate refugee burden; thirdly, the desirability of 'additionality'; fourthly, the need to mainstream the process institutionally within development planning (Gorman 1987).

However, the causes of failure were once again primarily a North–South polarization in expectations and interests and a lack of commitment on the part of both donors and recipient states. Stein suggests that there was a North–South division in the understanding of the purpose of the conference. While the African states wished to focus on burden-sharing, the donor states wished to focus on the durable solutions theme reflected by the conference title, 'A Time for Solutions'. Stein suggests that while donors did not reject the notion of expanded burden-sharing per se, an increased economic commitment needed to be directly linked to expanded access to durable solutions other than voluntary repatriation. In other words, they wanted 'results' rather than 'an open-ended claim on their resources'. Most donors had regarded ICARA I as a major commitment and were highly suspicious of African motives for convening a second conference (Stein 1987: 67). Donors were therefore no longer prepared to commit to providing significant funding unless the projects were clearly linked to durable solutions.

Another reason for ICARA II's failure was the severe drought and consequent famine of 1985, which affected much of sub-Saharan Africa and diverted donor attention and resources away from ICARA towards emergency relief. Once the initial momentum was lost, ICARA was largely displaced by short-term humanitarian concerns. In the absence of additional resources, achieving concrete partnerships with development agencies became increasingly difficult. Despite unprecedented commitment from UNDP in coordinating project planning and implementation, the absence of state commitment created insufficient momentum to move beyond the 'piecemeal' institutional coordination set out by ICARA II.

In summary, the ICARA process resulted in North–South polarization because of a failure to reach meaningful consensus on the concept of 'additionality'. African states wanted additional resources, while Northern states were unwilling to provide significant unearmarked assistance without

---

[35] 'Press clippings on ICARA II', 26 July 1984 (Fonds UNHCR 11, 391.78/1019C).

a guarantee that this would translate into durable solutions. In the absence of a firm commitment to provide new resources, or of a North–South agreement on unambiguous general principles, the prospects for mainstreaming either the concepts or the resulting inter-organizational partnerships collapsed when new humanitarian and political priorities emerged amongst Northern states in the context of the Ethiopian famine.

The International Conference on Refugees in Central America (1987–95)

During the 1970s and 1980s, the civil conflicts in Central America led to the displacement of around two million people, some 150000 of whom were recognized as refugees by UNHCR. Towards the end of the Cold War, the prospect of a regional peace deal opened up possibilities for refugees to receive access to durable solutions, either returning home or being locally integrated. The prospect of peace opened up new possibilities to seek long-term solutions for the region's refugees.

In response, UNHCR conceived the International Conference on Central American Refugees (CIREFCA[36]). The conference was similar to the ICARA conferences inasmuch as it was based on the notion of refugee aid and development, attempting to use development assistance as a means to enhance refugees' access to durable solutions. However, in terms of outcomes, the contrast between ICARA and CIREFCA could hardly have been greater. CIREFCA was highly successful, leading to sustained levels of donor support and an unprecedented regional commitment to refugee self-reliance.

From early in its planning CIREFCA was 'conceived not only as an event, but, perhaps even more significantly, as a process'.[37] Rather than being a one-off conference, CIREFCA's work ran from 1987 until 1994. Beginning with two Consultative Working Group sessions in 1987 and drawing upon the input of experts from the region, CIREFCA was conceived as a follow-up to the 1984 Cartagena Declaration but received new impetus as a result of the peace deal (Esquipulas II) agreed by regional heads of state in August 1987. This allowed UNHCR to draw on the commitment to peace and development of countries in the region as well as on donors, and to channel this into a commitment to finding solutions for the displaced. CIREFCA received much of its legitimacy from Article 8 of Esquipulas II's reference to displacement,

---

[36] CIREFCA represents the acronym for the Spanish title of the conference, La Conferencica Internacional Sobre Los Refugiados Centroamericanos.

[37] 'International Conference on Central American Refugees, Guatemala City, May 1989: Preliminary information', Memo, Mr Deljoo to Mr Asomani, 5 December 1988 (Fonds UNHCR 11, Series 3, 391.86, HCR/NYC/1466).

and the CIREFCA Concerted Plan of Action itself was incorporated as the chapter on displacement of UNDP's wider post-conflict reconstruction initiative, known as the Special Programme of Economic Cooperation for Central America (PEC).

The underlying ethos of CIREFCA was to find durable solutions for displacement through an integrated development approach, closing the gap between relief and development. This meant that collaboration between UNHCR and UNDP was a central feature of CIREFCA. The agencies jointly ran a permanent secretariat for the initiative, the Joint Support Unit (JSU), based in San José, Costa Rica. Both organizations provided seven regional states with technical support in developing their own 'priority projects', both for initial submission to CIREFCA and for submission to the International Follow-Up Conferences. Integrated development was seen as a means simultaneously to address the needs of refugees, returnees, and the internally displaced, while also benefiting local communities.

The conference, taking place in Guatemala City, adopted a Declaration and a Concerted Plan of Action. The Concerted Plan of Action provided an initial portfolio of thirty-six projects that required US$375 million over a three-year period, which was later added to. The initial project submissions were compiled by states with the support of a five-week UNHCR mission to the region in mid-1988. The Concerted Plan of Action also established a set of 'Principles and Criteria for Protection and Assistance' as guidelines for the submissions. Implicitly, the adoption of policies, standards, and legal norms was posited by UNHCR as a condition for states receiving financial support through CIREFCA. However, in practice, the availability of relatively large amounts of unconditional funding from UNDP and the Italian government's simultaneous PRODERE ('The Development Programme for Displaced Persons, Refugees and Returnees in Central America') project, which principally targeted internally displaced persons (IDPs) rather than refugees, undermined the credibility of this implicit conditionality.[38]

Significantly, and in contrast to ICARA, the Guatemala City conference, as the focal point of CIREFCA, was explicitly not conceived as a pledging conference. Instead, its primary aim was to establish a political consensus upon which UNHCR could build a multi-year process. The strategy for how to develop political support and subsequently translate this into the mobilization of resources was clearly elaborated from an early stage in the preparations.[39] A tactical proposal for the promotion of funding was divided into

---

[38] Interview with José Riera, Programme Officer to the JSU during CIREFCA, UNHCR, 24 October 2005.

[39] 'Procedures for the preparatory activities of the Conference itself and the establishment of follow-up mechanisms—Proposal submitted to the Organizing Committee Meeting, Guatemala, 24 January 1989' (Fonds UNHCR 11, Series 3, 391.86.3, HCR/NYC/0102).

four phases, going from the 'lead-up phase' prior to the final preparatory conference until the post-conference follow-up. The initial stages of the strategy explicitly shunned a financial emphasis in favour of fostering political support. It noted of the 'lead-up phase':

> The top priority must be promotion of policy/political/diplomatic support for the Conference as such and for the strategies it represents. In this perspective, fund-raising of any active or specific kind is dangerous. Too much pressure on the fund-raising issue now could even affect the yet-to-be determined level and quality of political/policy support for the Conference.[40]

Rather than encouraging pledging, the pre-conference priorities included support for the process, encouraging a high level of participation at the Conference, and 'mention[ing] discretely that "it is...the hope of UNHCR that policy support would be translated at a later date into a financial contribution/commitment."' CIREFCA itself was seen primarily as a political event, with the Declaration and Concerted Plan of Action being an inter-state consensus rather than a programmatic list intended to attract money.[41] In this sense, its approach contrasted with that of ICARA. The tactical plan for funding envisaged that the financial issue would be raised informally, at least until political will had been mobilized and consolidated. A meeting for ExCom members in Geneva in May was the first point at which the financial issue was raised directly with donors, and this was simply to forewarn delegations that, at the Guatemala Conference, 'UNHCR would like to meet each donor delegation informally outside the plenary session to discuss with them possible contribution levels.'[42]

The project proposals varied from country to country, depending notably on whether the state was primarily a country of origin or asylum and, in the latter case, how tolerant or restrictive that country was towards freedom of movement and the socio-economic integration of refugees. In Guatemala, the projects focused on facilitating reintegration for returnees in Huehuetenango and El Quiche by strengthening health, education, and sanitation services, and by improving basic infrastructure. In Costa Rica, the projects aimed primarily to promote labour market integration to allow refugees and another 250000 'externally displaced' people from El Salvador and Nicaragua to integrate socially and economically through, for example, improved access to the job market and health care. In Mexico, they focused on self-reliance for Guatemalan refugees, notably through agricultural projects in Chiapas and

---

[40] Memo, Kevin Lyonette to Leonardo Franco, 'Tactical proposal for promotion of funding of CIREFCA projects', 19 April 1989 (Fonds UNHCR 11, Series 3, 391.86.3).

[41] Ibid.

[42] Memo, Kevin Lyonette to Leonardo Franco, 'Tactical proposal for promotion of funding of CIREFCA projects', 19 April 1989 (Fonds UNHCR 11, Series 3, 391.86.3).

the rural resettlement projects in Campeche and Quintana Roo. In Nicaragua, the focus was on rehabilitation and reintegration activities for returnees, mainly from Honduras. In Honduras, given the state's restrictions on freedom of movement, attention was paid to strengthening UNHCR assistance in camps, pending refugees' return to Guatemala and Nicaragua. In Belize, the project focused on improving self-reliance and local integration opportunities for refugees, mainly through strengthening the existing integrated rural development project at the Valley of Peace and improving infrastructure in the Northern Orange Walk and Western Cayo districts. In El Salvador, aside from nominal support for Nicaraguan refugees and returnees, PRODERE, in particular, envisaged meeting the basic needs of the country's IDPs.

The CIREFCA process evolved as it went along in order to integrate new approaches and enlarge its portfolio of projects. In particular, the Italian government decided to allocate its US$115m budget surplus to a development project in Central America, expanding the embryonic PRODERE territorial development project already underway in El Salvador under the auspices of UNDP. Meanwhile, late in the process, UNHCR also developed complementary initiatives such as its Quick Impact Projects (QIPs) to support the immediate developmental needs of returnee integration, and Forefem, which created a forum for mainstreaming a gendered approach to protection and solutions. A crucial component of CIREFCA's political momentum was also its follow-up mechanisms, coordinated by the Joint Support Unit (JSU). The National Coordinating Committees facilitated ongoing formulation of projects and solicited financial support for them. Perhaps most significantly, though, the JSU contributed to convening two International Follow-Up Meetings in New York in June 1990 and San Salvador in April 1992. These meetings, unlike the 1989 Conference, were explicitly conceived as pledging conferences and allowed CIREFCA to remain an ongoing donor focus.[43]

In total, CIREFCA is estimated to have channelled US$422.3 million in additional resources to the region, and the process has been widely credited with helping to consolidate peace in Central America. This financial support emerged gradually as the process evolved. US$245m was pledged by the First International Follow-Up Meeting in New York in June 1990 and a further US$81m was pledged at the Second Follow-Up Meeting in El Salvador in April 1992. Of the initial pledges, the Italian government's commitment of US$115m to fund PRODERE was by far the largest. Throughout the process, the most significant group of donors was the European states, both bilaterally and through the European Economic Community (EEC).

---

[43] 'From conflict to peace and development: Note on implementation of the concerted plan of action of CIREFCA', Pablo Mateu (JSU) to K. Asomani (RBLAC), 17 March 1992 (Fonds UNHCR 11, Series 3, 361.86.5).

In its immediate aftermath, CIREFCA was generally seen as a 'success' in terms of enhancing refugees' access to protection and durable solutions (UNHCR 1994). Although there has been little formal monitoring of the projects implemented under CIREFCA, the extent to which the process raised a significant proportion of its required funding clearly distinguishes it from the limited legacy of ICARA I and II. A General Assembly Resolution on CIREFCA passed at the 85th Session in late 1993 expressed 'its conviction that the work carried out through the integrated conference process could serve as a valuable lesson to be applied to other regions of the world'.[44] Furthermore, over time, UNHCR has increasingly highlighted CIREFCA as a 'model' because many of its achievements have been so difficult to replicate.[45] The initiative is seen as an example of successful international cooperation between regional host states and countries of origin, on the one hand, and donor states beyond the region, on the other, in order to improve access to durable solutions, to enhance protection within the region, and to address the root causes of displacement through peace-building. The way in which CIREFCA contributed to each of these outcomes will be highlighted in turn.

In terms of durable solutions, CIREFCA contributed to voluntary repatriation through the protection principles it elaborated in the Plan of Action, through both the resources it allocated to support reintegration and notably through political dialogue in relation to the Tripartite Agreements. This work allowed the repatriation of some 27000 Salvadorans, 62000 Nicaraguans and the return of 45000 Guatemalans from Mexico.[46] These returns were supported by what might be considered to be the precursor of UNHCR's 4Rs framework (UNHCR 2003). Indeed, PRODERE's approach to integrated-development-linked assistance for local communities with that for returnees by developing social services and infrastructure in border regions.[47] Within the framework of CIREFCA, UNHCR and UNDP also developed the notion of Quick Impact Projects (QIPs), supporting basic needs and short-term productive infrastructure for 70000 returnees in Nicaragua.[48]

[44] 'International Conference on Central American Refugees', GA Resolution A/RES/48/117, 85th Plenary Session, New York, 20 December 1993 (Fonds UNHCR 11, Series 3, 391.86.5).
[45] For an account of the difficulties that UNHCR has had in replicating the success of CIREFCA, see for example UNHCR (2006), chapters 5 and 6.
[46] For an evaluation of UNHCR's repatriation reintegration programmes in Guatemala, see UNHCR, 'Lessons learnt from UNHCR's involvement in the Guatemalan refugee repatriation and reintegration programme (1987–1999)', EPAU Evaluation, 1999 <www.unhcr.ch>.
[47] UNHCR, 'Questions and answers about CIREFCA', prepared for Seminar on the Implementation of a Human Development Approach for Areas Affected by Conflict in Central America and Related Strategies for the Post-CIREFCA Process, June 1993 (Fonds UNHCR 11, Series 3, 391.85.5).
[48] For an evaluation, see UNHCR, 'Quick impact project: A review of UNHCR's returnee reintegration programme in Nicaragua', EPAU Evaluation Report (by Jeff Crisp and Lowell Martin), 1992.

The projects were also notable for the extent to which they facilitated self-sufficiency and local integration. The most obvious case study for successful self-sufficiency was in Mexico in Campeche and Quintana Roo in the Yucatàn Peninsula, where consolidation of the local agricultural settlements and the development of integrated service provision benefited not only the 18 800 refugees but also the host communities. In Chiapas, self-sufficiency was also encouraged, but a shortage of land was an obstacle to allowing refugees to become equally engaged in agricultural activities. In Campeche and Quintana Roo, local integration and repatriation were promoted simultaneously from 1996, while in Chiapas local integration *followed* repatriation from 1998 onwards. The self-sufficiency and local integration projects ultimately provided education, health services, access to markets, and sustainable livelihoods. For the Mexican government, the projects were seen as an attractive means to develop the poorest areas of the country, particularly in the Yucatàn Peninsula.[49]

CIREFCA also provided local integration for Salvadoran refugees in Belize, particularly through the Valley of Peace project. Although the project had begun in 1983 and had been widely criticized for relocating refugees to a jungle area with poor roads and poor-quality land, CIREFCA helped to resurrect the Valley of Peace project.[50] By 2003, some 300 families remained and were integrated alongside the Belizeans of predominantly Maya Quechi ethnicity. The refugees were supported initially with food aid, a fund to build housing, tools, and seeds, and many of the Salvadorans now work in the tourism industry or in local employment, receiving social services alongside the Belizean community.[51] There was also a degree of local integration in Costa Rica. This took place on a smaller scale and was mainly for Salvadoran refugees in urban areas, who were few in number and were perceived to be 'hard-working'. This contrasted with the Costa Rican approach to the Nicaraguan refugees, who, although they were given a degree of self-sufficiency in agricultural production, had been largely confined to camps and were not given the same level of opportunities to integrate.[52]

The success of CIREFCA was due to a range of particularly auspicious circumstances. The European Community and its member states were by far the most significant donors to CIREFCA, a commitment that arose as a result of the desire to stabilize Central America; as UNHCR noted, 'the Community has regarded CIREFCA as an integral part of efforts towards peace, development and democracy in Central America'. In financial terms, the EC provided

---

[49] Interview with Ana Low, intern, researching self-sufficiency and local integration in Southern Mexico, UNHCR, 25 October 2005.
[50] Interview with Pablo Mateu, former Programme Officer in the JSU, UNHCR, 18 October 2005.
[51] 'From conflict to the valley of peace', *El Diario de Hoy*, 18 October 2005.
[52] Interview with Pablo Mateu, former Programme Officer in the JSU, UNHCR, 18 October 2005.

US $110m for CIREFCA projects between 1989 and 1993, 45 per cent of the total mobilized during that period.[53] Sweden also openly claimed that 'the support of Sweden for CIREFCA was inextricably linked to its support for the Central American peace process'. The statements of the European Commission and Norway explicitly stated that their motivation for contributing to CIREFCA was its relationship to post-conflict reconstruction and development within the Esquipulas II framework.[54] While CIREFCA has therefore rightly been proclaimed a success, its achievements owed much to a particular juncture of history and may be difficult to replicate elsewhere.

UNHCR's Convention Plus Initiative (2003–5)

By the end of the 1990s, there was renewed recognition of the growing number of protracted refugee situations around the world. In 1999, the 'Brookings Process' was launched, reflecting an emerging consensus on the need to address 'transition issues', including linkages between short-term humanitarian assistance and longer-term sustainable development interventions. Building on the insights of the Brookings Process, UNHCR began to revisit the earlier themes of the refugee aid and development debates. In 2003, it launched the *Framework for Durable Solutions for Refugees and Persons of Concern* with three components: (1) the 4Rs framework (repatriation, reintegration, rehabilitation, reconstruction), (2) Development Assistance for Refugees (DAR), and (3) Development through Local Integration (DLI), with the first focusing on countries of origin and the latter two on self-sufficiency and local integration, respectively, in host countries (UNHCR 2003).

The *Framework* attempts to highlight the causal connections relating to how development assistance can enhance the prospects for durable solutions for refugees. UNHCR (2004, 2006: 136–7), for instance, supported these causal claims empirically, highlighting development 'success stories', such as its Zambia Initiative (ZI) and the Ugandan Self-Reliance Strategy. UNHCR (2005) emphasized the relationship between development assistance and protection through consolidating 'successful' examples of 4Rs, DAR, and DLI in a *Statement of Good Practice for Targeting Development Assistance*.

This new area of work was carried forward as part of an intergovernmental process known as UNHCR's Convention Plus initiative, which ran under High Commissioner Ruud Lubbers between 2003 and 2005. Convention Plus was

---

[53] Jenifer Otsea, CIREFCA JSU, to UNHCR Brussels, 'CIREFCA: A strategy for solutions', 8 February 1993 (Fonds UNHCR 11, Series 3, 391.86.5).

[54] 'Reunion Tecnica Informal Sobre CIREFCA', San José, 15–16 February 1994. On file with the author.

based on the premise that while the 1951 Refugee Convention addressed key areas on a state's obligations to provide asylum, it did little to establish states' normative commitments to engage in burden-sharing. Consequently, it sought to negotiate a set of new 'soft law' agreements between states in three interrelated areas: 'resettlement', 'targeted development assistance', and 'irregular secondary movement', which could then be applied to address regionally specific protracted refugee situations.

The overarching logic of Convention Plus was premised upon the notion of 'protection in the region of origin'. If Northern donor states provided improved burden-sharing for protection in the South, there would be less need for Northern states to provide territorial asylum to spontaneous-arrival asylum seekers in the North. Hence, donor states would be able to manage irregular migration better, and host states would receive more compensation and support through development assistance and resettlement.

The logic of the South 'providing protection on behalf of the North' in exchange for financial compensation by the North was explained by the representative of the African Group in Geneva:

> Let's face it, it is cheaper to take care of a refugee on the continent than it is for them to be taken care of in Europe . . . the Netherlands, for example, was spending about 10000 Euros/yr/capita just on processing and 10000 Euros, if this were transferred to a refugee-hosting country in Africa, would do a lot.[55]

He went on to claim that Ghana could provide refugee protection for just $29 per month for each refugee. This argument almost exactly echoed the same logic put forward by the Netherlands, which claimed:

> UNHCR had a total budget of about USD 1 billion at its disposal in 2002 for refugee protection for 20 million people worldwide. In that same year, the Netherlands spent 1.4 billion on national refugee determination procedures, personnel, reception facilities for about 80000 refugees and asylum seekers in the Netherlands. Other destination countries spend comparable amounts of money on comparable numbers of asylum seekers, many of whom are not recognized as refugees, but are economic migrants. This phenomenon has as a result that a significant amount of the money spent worldwide does not reach genuine refugees.[56]

It was this logic that placed the idea of Targeted Development Assistance (TDA) at the core of Convention Plus. In order to negotiate a formal agreement on TDA, a series of intergovernmental meetings were held. These took place within five Convention Plus Forums convened by the High Commissioner for Refugees, as well as within a smaller Core Group on TDA, co-chaired by

---

[55] Interview with Sylvester Parker-Allotey, Deputy Permanent Representative of Ghana, Geneva, 16 September 2004.
[56] Statement of the Netherlands, First Convention Plus Forum, 27 June 2003.

Denmark and Japan. However, the TDA strand resulted in polarization between North and South. Donor states were reluctant to commit to 'additionality' in development funding, and host states were reluctant to offer a commitment to what they perceived to be local integration.

Many of the African states in particular recalled their historically bad experiences of being pushed by the international community to consider integrating refugees locally. For example, in an interview, the Tanzanian Minister for Home Affairs, Omar Mapuri, pointed to Tanzania's experience since the late 1970s of using local integration:

> We have had a bitter experience in this ... It provided income-generating activities and open markets to them. But immediately once we introduced that, then the international community washed its hands. So they left the whole burden with us. We fully provided education, health services, water, and all other social services to these settlements. And when we invite the international community to come in, they say 'we are preoccupied with the asylum-seekers'. True, we understand that and we have not been complaining about it. But, of late, Zambia and Uganda came with a similar arrangement and it is being treated as something new [laughter]. For the first time in the world the international community is experiencing self-reliance to help refugees.[57]

The African Group of states commented that 'it is our view that the current debate on this strand is taking place largely without any information on past similar practices and precedents (e.g., lessons learnt of the two International Conferences on Assistance to Refugees in Africa [ICARA I and II])'.[58] This suspicion meant that many Southern states approached the language of the North in cynical terms. In the words of one member of UNHCR staff: 'Ideas such as self-sufficiency were seen as synonymous with local integration; "burden-sharing" was understood as "burden-shifting"; and secondary movements were about readmission.'[59]

This dynamic of mistrust was exacerbated by the nature of the process. For example, host states were initially excluded from inter-state dialogue on TDA, which was 'donor only' until September 2005. In response, the African Group[60] showed its objection:

> We are disappointed that discussions relating to this strand seem to be about assistance to major refugee-hosting countries or countries of origin and not discussion with such countries ... we wish to caution that the work in this strand

---

[57] Interview with the Hon. Omar Mapuri, MP, Minister for Home Affairs, Tanzania, Geneva, 7 October 2004.

[58] Letter from DRC, as African Group Coordinator on Refugee Matters, to Jean-François Durieux, Head of Convention Plus Unit, UNHCR, 8 March 2005.

[59] Interview with José Riera, UNHCR, 17 November 2005.

[60] The African Group is a regional coalition of states that speaks on behalf of African states in UN debates in Geneva.

should be transparent and also include the participation of refugee-hosting countries.[61]

The African Group further argued that 'separate discussions of groups of states unfortunately do not add to a transparent and open process',[62] complaining that there was no Core Group on TDA as initially envisaged and that there was no consultation on the writing of the 'Statement of Good Practice'.[63] The first TDA meeting to be convened with both donors and host states together took place on 16 September 2005; yet by this point, African states were so disillusioned by the lack of transparency of the North that they rejected further discussions, stating: 'I have to inform that the African Group has come to a conclusion that the need for setting up a [Core] Group [on Targeting Development Assistance] is not timely' partly because 'several African delegations have been informed that it is not "realistic" to expect financial or other commitment or assistance in this regard'.[64] Indeed, the head of the Convention Plus secretariat acknowledged that throughout Convention Plus there has been a failure to adequately consult the host countries in the South:

> The most critical point remains . . . who is going to approach the authorities of Kenya (and also Tanzania etc.), and when, with a view to bringing these authorities on board even though, in fairness, they have not been the initiators of these projects? I can see a rather bad scenario developing unless UNHCR . . . approaches the 'target countries' before the projects are a complete 'fait accompli'.[65]

Furthermore, the credibility of suggestions by UNHCR that host state self-reliance would result in additional resources was undermined by the difficulties in developing meaningful partnerships with development agencies. UNHCR built a range of new partnerships, joining the United Nations Development Group (UNDG) and working with the World Bank and UNDP to explore the extent to which displacement issues are systematically incorporated within national development plans. However, the difficulty for UNHCR was that development agencies were only willing to incorporate the displaced insofar as this was based on the principle of 'recipient country ownership' and backed by donor support.

As a UNDP staff member argued at the donor meeting on TDA on 22 September 2004, the key to making DAR and DLI viable was first 'to

---

[61] 'Statement on behalf of the African Group at the Third Meeting of the Forum', read by Sylvester Parker Allotey (Ghana), 1 October 2004.

[62] Chairman's Summary, Inaugural Meeting of the Forum, 27 June 2003.

[63] African Group Statement to Fourth Forum, read by Sebastien Mutomb Mujing (DRC), 20 May 2005.

[64] 'Statement by Nigeria on behalf of the African Group on the occasion of an Informal Meeting on Targeted Development Assistance', 16 September 2005.

[65] E-mail, Jean-François Durieux to Ebrima Camara et al., 'Project proposal on Somali refugees', 17 October 2003.

convince governments and provide more convincing studies to show to governments that refugees are not just burdens but a potential asset'.[66]

The Solutions Alliance (2014–)

In 2011, UNHCR and UNDP, in collaboration with national governments and other partners, launched the Transitional Solutions Initiative (TSI) to more effectively integrate displacement issues on the development agenda, with initial pilots planned for East Sudan and Colombia. This was complemented by the UN Secretary-General's Policy Committee Decision on Durable Solutions in the same year, 2011, to help guide and inform the way the UN system approaches solutions in the immediate aftermath of conflict. Similar to TSI, the SG's Decision aimed to mainstream displacement issues into recovery and development strategies as a step towards peacebuilding, and it developed initial pilots in Afghanistan, Kyrgyzstan, and Ivory Coast.[67] For a brief period, the two initiatives were grouped together within an initiative known as 'Transitional Solutions Initiative Plus' (TSI+).

Against this backdrop, UNHCR and UNDP, with support from the Netherlands Ministry of Foreign Affairs, organized a 'Transitions and Solutions Roundtable' in Amsterdam on 18 and 19 April 2013 to take stock of the developments of the last years and chart ways forward. The meeting reflected upon past attempts to engage in development-based approaches to displacement, and attempted to build a more coherent intergovernmental and inter-agency strategy around the issue. The roundtable's key recognition was that 'today there are new opportunities that enable us to do better'. These included a 'greater willingness to learn from the past and apply lessons learned', 'greater donor interest in finding ways to finance transitional activities', and 'the greater potential to engage the private sector and to leverage non-state sources of funding'.

The Chairman's summary of the meeting highlights the steps forward that were agreed. The initiative's core objective was 'to create the enabling environment for self-reliance and resilience, moving us beyond a culture of dependency in close collaboration with communities'. The mechanisms envisaged to achieve this would include new potential funding mechanisms, a Strategy and Engagement Group to engage in dialogue with affected countries, and the aspiration to select future TSI+ countries to be 'champions' for

---

[66] Betsy Lippman, UNDP, comments at the Informal Meeting on Issues Involved in Targeting Development Assistance, Palais des Nations, Room VIII, Geneva, 22 September 2004.
[67] Transitions and Solutions Roundtable Amsterdam, 18–19 April 2013, Background Note.

the initiative. For virtually the first time, the private sector as well as displaced populations themselves were recognized as potential key actors.[68]

In the immediate aftermath of the TSI+ meeting, however, discussions between UNHCR and UNDP broke down as a result of a difference in vision for the initiative. UNDP felt that UNHCR's emphasis was too much on refugees, while their interest lay primarily in supporting post-conflict recovery and hence in IDPs. As a result, agreement was reached to rethink and rebrand the next steps of the initiative.

After a year's interregnum, a new meeting was convened in Copenhagen on 2–3 April 2014. The background papers to this Roundtable on Solutions described the mission statement for a new approach, referred to only as 'the Initiative', which it explained would build out of TSI+:

> Building on the valuable experience of pilot activities in Colombia and Eastern Sudan under the Transitional Solutions Initiative+, and furthering the Secretary General's Policy Committee Decision on Durable Solutions for Displaced People and the IASC Framework for Durable Solutions for internally displaced people, the Initiative seeks to address the challenge of helping prevent protracted situations and to unlock those that have become protracted. While TSI+ continues in the existing pilot countries, the new Initiative will work separately but in coordination with TSI+, and on the basis of a shared commitment across a more inclusive range of actors representing affected states, local level authorities, and UN agencies.[69]

As Thomas Thomsen, Head of Humanitarian Policy at the Danish Ministry of Foreign Affairs, explained in Copenhagen, the meeting built directly upon the discussions in Amsterdam a year earlier. Following subsequent meetings at the Dutch and Japanese embassies in Geneva, however, it had been decided to take forward a more ambitious initiative distinct from the earlier TSI+ roots, with 'the overall objective to promote and enable the transition for displaced persons away from dependency towards increased resilience, sustainable self-reliance and development'. He outlined that the initiative would involve new types of partnerships and funding mechanisms, look beyond seeing displaced populations as a burden, and involve affected states 'from day one'. For UN Deputy High Commissioner for Refugees, Alex Aleinikoff, the key was fundamentally to reconceive the relationship between displacement and development beyond 'relief to development', and to identify opportunities for 'progressive solutions' between the extremes of encampment and durable solutions:[70]

> The growing number of people in protracted displacement represents a collective failure of the international community and requires new thinking . . . Humanitarian

---

[68] Amsterdam Roundtable on Transitions and Solutions, (TSI + SG Decision on Durable Solutions—TSI+), Chairs' Summary, on file with the authors.

[69] Transitions and Solutions Roundtable, Amsterdam, 18–19 April 2013, Background Note.

[70] Copenhagen Roundtable Report, on file with the authors.

approaches are not focused on solutions, and development is not focused on displacement. Development and humanitarian actors need to come together with holistic approaches focused on solutions and based on co-ownership and co-responsibility. To achieve this, coordination is not enough; it will require conceptual and structural change, based on formal and predictable engagement...While solutions are the end goal, in the absence of immediate solutions, it is important to promote self-reliance and improve the quality of asylum for displaced people.

By the end of the meeting, 'the Initiative' had been renamed 'the Solutions Alliance'. It was to be a multi-stakeholder initiative, and its initial co-chairs were announced as UNHCR, International Rescue Committee (IRC), and the Colombian and Danish governments, with the Danish Refugee Council providing initial secretariat support. The meeting endorsed a proposed Mission Statement and Governance Structure for the Solutions Alliance. At the heart of the Solutions Alliance was the goal of 'reframing displacement crises as development opportunities':

> Displacement is pre-eminently a humanitarian and human rights challenge, but development-led approaches to displacement can challenge the notion of the refugee burden and recognise that in the long run and in aggregate terms, refugees can become self-reliant economic actors. Substantial economic opportunities exist in displacement, and many of the negative impacts of refugees can be compensated by market-led adjustments in the local economy.

The Solutions Alliance initially began its work with a series of working groups. Three of these were thematic, focusing on the private sector, the rule of law, and on research, data, and performance management. Two were national: one focusing on Somali refugees and the other on Zambia.[71] Following the meeting in Copenhagen, the Solutions Alliance acquired a small Geneva-based secretariat, and this became the most recent institutional vehicle through which the international community is attempting to take forwards the development and displacement agenda (Betts 2016).

Conclusion

The institutional history of refugees and development is a long one. It provides significant and important lessons. For a large part of that history, however, the attempts to use development assistance to enhance refugees' access to self-reliance were mainly conceived in state-centric terms. They were premised upon the idea of development assistance being a relationship between

---

[71] Tanzania and Uganda were subsequently added as national working groups following the Solutions Alliance Roundtable held in Brussels on 9–10 February 2016.

donor states and host states. Consequently, their success or failure relied upon achieving intergovernmental cooperation.

Historically, refugees and development initiatives succeeded when a series of conditions were met. First, donor states needed to provide 'additionality' in development assistance. Second, hosts states needed to be willing to recognize that with additional development assistance they would consider opening opportunities for refugee self-reliance. Third, UNHCR and development agencies needed to work together effectively to implement projects that could credibly benefit hosts, donors, and the displaced.

Understandably, these conditions have rarely been met. CIREFCA provides a historical example of success. On the other hand, ICARA I and II and the Convention Plus Initiative illustrate the elusiveness of achieving North–South cooperation to promote refugee self-reliance. Yet, more recent thinking is beginning to recognize that 'refugees and development' does not need to be conceived in purely state-centric terms, and it is about more than achieving donor–host state cooperation.

Today, there may be 'game changing' opportunities to think more broadly about how development relates to refugees. 'Development' does not need to be understood to be synonymous with development assistance. Instead, it can be conceived more broadly in market-based terms. The private sector, innovation, and recognition of the skills, talents, and aspirations of displaced populations themselves may instead hold the key to opening up opportunities to enhance self-reliance. Yet, realizing these opportunities in turn relies upon developing a new way of understanding the economic lives and impact of displaced populations.

3

Refugee economies

Understanding the economic lives of refugees matters because it creates an opportunity to rethink refugee assistance based on a model of sustainability rather than dependency. A growing literature has recognized this (Jacobsen 2005; Werker 2007). However, it is an area that lacks theory. In her recent book *Displacement Economies in Africa*, Amanda Hammar (2014: 3) emphasizes that to date there are no conceptual frameworks with which to make sense of the economic lives of displaced people. In particular, there is, as yet, no satisfactory answer to a simple theoretical question: what difference does it make, in economic terms, to be a refugee? This question could be asked empirically by comparing refugee populations with neighbouring host populations, but it can also be asked theoretically.

We suggest that what distinguishes refugees economically is that they occupy a particular institutional position vis-à-vis the state and the international system. Refugees have been forced to flee from their country of origin. Having been excluded from the state protection, refugees fall outside the 'normal' state–citizen relationship. As a result, refugees occupy a particular legal status and position, which in turn places the economic lives of refugees in a distinctive institutional context. Indeed, the central aim of this chapter is to outline an analytical framework that can make sense of what is institutionally distinctive about 'refugeehood' and what this means for the economic lives of refugees.

Neoclassical economics recognizes that in practice, all markets are subject to market imperfections and distortions. The nature of these distortions is shaped by regulatory environments and by institutions. Indeed, we know from New Institutional Economics that institutions shape how markets work (North 1990; Williamson 2000). They create particular sets of opportunities and constraints for the actors engaged in those markets. The regulatory environment, as well as the broader structure of formal and informal institutions, shapes how a particular economy works, and what opportunities and constraints are available to individuals and groups.

We argue that there are three broad ways in which the institutional context of refugeehood is distinctive. Collectively, these differences lead to different market environments from non-refugee populations, including host communities or other migrants. Refugees lie at three different institutional intersections: (1) state/international; (2) formal/informal; (3) national/transnational. In each case, refugees' blurred position across different institutional boundaries shapes what is economically distinctive about being a refugee. These institutional differences create opportunities and constraints for arbitrage. This different regulatory framework justifies 'refugee economies' as a distinct area of inquiry, which overlaps with but is analytically distinct from the wider national economy.

Yet all of these elements also make understanding 'refugee economies' an especially hard economics problem, which—because of the institutional context—belies many of the simplified assumptions of neoclassical economic analysis. By definition, understanding 'refugee economies' requires an interdisciplinary toolbox. It requires that we go beyond the existing, predominantly policy-driven literature and develop a new way of thinking about the economic lives of refugees.

Refugees and Economics

With a few notable exceptions, there have been few economic studies on refugees or displaced populations (Czaika 2009; Ruiz and Vargas 2013), and there has been limited interdisciplinary enquiry into the economic lives of refugees (Jacobsen 2005; Werker 2007). Although there is a literature on the economics of voluntary migration (Borjas 2014), which explores questions such as the assimilation, selection, and impact of migrants, there is comparatively little research on the economics of forced migration. This is in part because refugee protection and assistance have historically been seen as a humanitarian issue rather than a development issue, as much by theoreticians as by policymakers. Refugees and displaced populations have therefore too rarely been conceived as economic actors engaging in resource allocation decisions that affect their own trajectories and those of the communities with which they interact.

Over time, there have been periods when the economic potential of refugees has been recognized. During the 1980s and 1990s, a number of authors argued for the need to reconceive of refugees as a development issue. They highlighted that if development assistance were applied to support the self-reliance and local integration of refugees in host states and societies, this could lead to outcomes that would be beneficial to refugees and host communities, simultaneously reducing the long-term costs of humanitarian assistance

(Gorman 1987; Stein 1987). Some of these ideas were implemented by international organizations such as UNHCR and UNDP in regions such as Africa and Central America (Betts 2009).

Nevertheless, the general trajectory of Refugee and Forced Migration Studies has neglected the economic lives of refugees, and many of the core ideas of development economics and international development have not been explored in relation to refugees and displaced populations to explain, for example, variation in economic outcomes for refugees. Why do some refugees have higher incomes than others? Why do some refugees choose to live in urban areas rather than rural camps and settlements? Under what conditions do refugees make a positive economic contribution to the host economy?

Despite this general neglect of refugees as economic actors, an embryonic literature has begun to emerge, which seeks to rectify some of these gaps. A small number of pioneering academics, together with policy-focused research by UNHCR and the World Bank, have started to tackle these questions. However, this research has until now taken a particular approach. It has explored two broad areas, which can be described as the 'refugee livelihoods' and 'refugee impacts' literatures. Both literatures offer significant building blocks towards understanding the economic lives of refugees. However, both approaches, we argue, have limitations and have stemmed mainly from particular policy-driven agendas. Here, we outline those two literatures and their limitations, and suggest that there is an alternative way to think about what we call 'refugee economies'.

First, the 'refugee livelihoods' literature emerges from a concern to understand refugees' income-generating activities. It draws upon a wider literature that defines livelihoods as an individual's or household's 'capabilities, assets and activities required for a means of living' (Chambers and Conway 1992: 7), recognizing poor peoples' agency in developing income-generating own capacities despite living in adverse circumstances (de Haan and Zoomers 2005; Kaag et al. 2003). The wider 'livelihoods' literature has been recognized as relevant to policy because of its capacity to highlight populations' capacities rather than their vulnerabilities, and to build upon them as the basis of policy interventions (Farrington et al. 2002: 2). The most enduring policy framework for understanding livelihoods has been DFID's Sustainable Livelihoods Framework (SLF) (DFID 1999).

A number of scholars have applied this approach to examine refugee livelihoods, particularly in protracted refugee situations. Karen Jacobsen's (2005) work in particular has drawn the livelihoods approach into Refugee Studies, using it as a basis on which to describe refugees' income-generating activities. The approach has recognized that refugees have the skills and capacities that, if recognized, can support their own self-reliance (De Vriese 2006: 6; Jacobsen 2005: 73). Initially focused on camps, this work has extended to include urban refugees from Johannesburg to Nairobi (Dryden-Peterson 2006; Crisp et al. 2012; Pavanello et al. 2010; Campbell 2006). The burgeoning literature on refugee livelihoods has extended to include recognition of the role of microfinance (Conway 2004; Jacobsen 2005; Jacobsen et al. 2006), remittances (Lindley 2007a,b, 2008a,b, 2010; Horst 2004, 2006; Al-Sharmani 2004), and social networks (Stigter and Monsutti 2005; Andrews 2003; De Montclos and Kagwanja 2000; Kaiser et al. 2005), for instance.

A significant part of the literature drawn upon the Sustainable Livelihoods Framework (SLF) is descriptive and mainly qualitative (De Vriese 2006; Women's Refugee Commission 2011; Korf 2004; Jacobsen 2006; Horst 2006). For instance, in their research on Darfur, Young et al. (2007) use the SLF to help distinguish how conflict has had an impact on components of livelihoods such as assets and strategies, as well as how some livelihood strategies have in turn fuelled conflict. UNHCR has been increasingly influenced by—and interacted with—academics in this area, adopting the SLF in its *Livelihood Operational Guidelines* (UNHCR 2012: 19), and rolling these *Guidelines* out as its main framework to understand and support the livelihoods of displaced populations.

One of the biggest weaknesses of the livelihoods literature has been its abstraction from wider market conditions. Much of the academic literature has been based on description of specific income-generating activities rather than a more holistic analysis of the underlying market context within which that economic activity takes place. This has carried over into livelihood-based interventions by UNHCR and other actors, which have frequently identified and supported activities that have been abstracted from a deeper understanding of underlying demand and supply conditions. For example, around the world, UNHCR has too often ended up supporting arbitrarily selected income-generating activities, from beekeeping to tailoring, that may not be based on a data-driven understanding of the economies into which they are superimposed.

Second, the 'impacts of refugees' has become an increasingly important strand of the debate. Building on a long-standing question of whether refugees represent a 'burden' or 'benefit' for host states, a growing number of studies have explored how to quantify these effects. Scholars have sought to challenge the assumption that governments and communities are inevitably burdened by the refugees they are hosting (Campbell 2005; Kuhlman 1990; Whitaker 2002). This has been predicated on a recognition that, as Jacobsen (2002: 577) writes, 'while refugees impose a variety of security, economic and environmental burdens on host countries, they also embody a significant flow of resources in the form of international humanitarian assistance, economic assets and human capital.' Much of this work builds upon cost–benefit analyses of immigration, developed in research on voluntary migration (for instance, see Borjas 2008, 2014; Metcalf 2012).

Only recently have a number of studies begun to conceptualize and quantify some of these impacts on host communities. In particular, Zetter et al. (2012) develop a framework within which they examine the macro- and microeconomic impact of refugees on host populations and the host state. At a macroeconomic level, refugees can have significant effects on economic growth through their impact on consumption and production. At a microeconomic level, they show that refugees can have a redistributive effect creating 'winners and losers', notably through impacts on labour markets and prices. However, the existing empirical evidence suggests these impacts are ambiguous and contingent on context.

Assessing the macroeconomic effects of refugees has been methodologically challenging. While there has been significant demand in government and advocacy circles to determine specific macroeconomic impacts of refugee-hosting, such as effects on GDP growth, making such assessments at an aggregate level is often impossible. What is possible, however, is to estimate localized impacts. A Danish-funded impact evaluation in 2010 of the Dadaab refugee camps estimated direct and indirect benefits for the surrounding hosting areas at US $82 million for 2009 (Enghoff et al. 2010). A World Bank assessment for Lebanon predicted that the impact of the Syria crisis will decrease the national GDP by 2.85 per cent annually in 2014, double the unemployment rate, and increase the national deficit, costing US $7.5 billion from 2012–14 (World Bank 2013). Others, however, claim that refugees can stimulate the national economy by increasing demand, consumption, and economic growth, as well as through monetary 'injections' of international aid spending and the development of infrastructure (Zetter and Ruaudel 2014). For example, in the Kurdistan region of Iraq (KRI), some analysts attribute some of the projected 8 per cent GDP growth for KRI in 2014 to Syrian refugees (Sood and Seferis 2014).

In terms of wage effects, refugee influxes may reduce wage levels depending on whether an increased labour supply outweighs any increases in demand for labour, although refugee influxes also tend to result in increased demand for goods and services. Some case studies have demonstrated that following a major refugee influx, a large increase in labour supply results in lowered wages for the local or regional population (Maystadt and Verwimp 2009; Alix-Garcia and Saah 2010; Zetter et al. 2014). Whitaker (2002: 348) notes, for instance, that in western Tanzania following the refugee influx, casual labourer wages 'dropped by 50 per cent in many areas'. However, depending on the nature of the refugee influx, research has also shown that local skilled labourers may in fact benefit from a refugee influx through higher wages and a higher availability of jobs, since increasing consumption and the presence of aid agencies often increases demand for skilled labour through local employment (Whitaker 2002; Alix-Garcia and Saah 2010).

In terms of price effects, increases in demand may raise price levels in ways that have redistributive consequences (Alix-Garcia and Saah 2010; Callamard 1994; Maystadt and Verwimp 2009; Whitaker 2002; Zetter et al. 2012; Zetter et al. 2014). While there is some evidence that higher numbers of displaced people correlate with increased food prices (Alix-Garcia and Saah 2010; Maystadt and Verwimp 2009; Ruiz and Vargas-Silva 2013), this has been contested in other studies (Landau 2004; Enghoff et al. 2010). A 2010 study on the impact of the Dadaab refugee camps, for example, found that the price of basic commodities within refugee camp towns was approximately 20 per cent lower than in similar areas without a refugee presence (Enghoff et al. 2010). Additionally, a 2003 study by Landau found no significant impact on basic commodity prices in the Kasulu district of Tanzania following a refugee influx in the 1990s, despite widespread belief to the contrary (Landau 2003: 26–7).

As this brief review highlights, existing findings relating to refugees' impacts are ambiguous and highly dependent on context. This is in part due to methodological challenges in measuring impacts, and in part due to the number of confounding variables that make causal attribution of impacts to refugees often problematic. It is especially difficult to establish a counterfactual that enables comparison, and identification of the economic impact of the refugee presence on host populations is extremely challenging (Ruiz and Vargas-Silva 2013: 778). Furthermore, as Jacobsen (2014) notes, existing work suffers from the absence of reliable and rigorous quantitative data. In particular, the absence of comparative or longitudinal data has hindered the ability to make more general conclusions about impact (Ruiz and Vargas-Silva 2013).

The Need for Theory

Both the 'livelihoods' and 'impacts' literatures frame the questions they ask in focused but narrow ways. This is in part because a significant proportion of the work has been driven by immediate policy needs. Much of the livelihood work has been driven by UNHCR's concern to programme livelihood interventions, while much of the impact literature was initiated by the World Bank's need to demonstrate discernible negative or positive impacts of refugees on national development.

A more holistic exploration of the underlying market structures that characterize the economic lives of refugees has been missing. The livelihoods literature has tended to look at income-generating activities in isolation. Meanwhile, the primary concern of most of the literature on economic impacts has focused on effects for the national host economy, rather than the economic lives of refugees per se. In other words, neither literature has looked more holistically at ways to understand the wider structures that shape refugees' economic lives.

A significant exception is the work of Karen Jacobsen. In *The Economic Lives of Refugees* (2005), she provides a broader structural account of the income-generating activities of refugees that includes recognition of their production, consumption, and finance-related activities, as well as accounting for refugees' interactions with host communities and wider transnational networks. The book is written largely from an economic sociology perspective and draws in a wide range of qualitative examples from field research and secondary literature to illustrate its observations.

Jacobsen (2014) also argues for the necessity of a theory of 'displaced livelihoods'. Theory is important in order to navigate complexity. It can enable extrapolation beyond context and help to guide questions. In turn, having a theoretical framework can help to generate hypotheses about what explains variation in economic outcomes for refugees. For example, what difference does it make to live in a camp versus an urban area? What difference does it make to live in a particular part of a camp? What difference does it make to be a 'refugee' versus a host community? Without theory, it becomes challenging to organize data, whether qualitative or quantitative.

We therefore seek to begin a conversation about how we can build theory relating to the economic lives of refugees. We wish to develop a set of concepts that can enable us to recognize what is distinct and interesting about the economic lives of refugees, and build propositions about what explains variation in a range of economic outcomes for refugees. In doing so, we are fortunate to have a range of tools to draw upon from economics, political economy, economic sociology, and economic anthropology, for example.

Our core concept is 'refugee economies'. An 'economy' is generally understood as a system of resource allocation, referring to how societies make choices and use limited resources to produce goods and services (Samuelson and Nordhaus 2010; Stiglitz and Walsh 2006). Following this broad definition, 'refugee economies' can be broadly defined as 'the resource allocation system relating to refugee populations'.

Our argument is that refugees can be understood to be part of a distinct sub-economy because they occupy a distinctive institutional context. 'Refugee-hood' brings with it a particular institutional context, which in turn shapes the nature of refugees' interactions with markets. To be a refugee is to occupy a particular legal status and position vis-à-vis the state. This institutional context, we argue, creates the set of market imperfections and distortions that enable and constrain refugees differently from other populations. It is this that theoretically justifies refugee economies being looked at as a distinct sub-economy.

The concept of 'refugee economies' outlined here is important in order to understand the entire market structure relating to refugees, rather than reverting simply to instrumental questions relating to 'livelihoods' and 'impacts'. Understanding refugee economies has academic value because it allows us to understand and explain a variety of economic outcomes for refugees. It also has value for policymakers by highlighting the levers through which policy can enable, build upon, and create a positive environment for markets to support refugees more sustainably.

Why Institutions Matter

The central conceptual pillar of refugee economies is the recognition that markets are structured by their institutional context. Markets do not function simply in a vacuum. They are inevitably characterized by some degree of market failure. The degree and type of market distortion is a function of the institutional context. For example, the regulatory environment and property rights structure relating to markets are central to their functioning. Institutional contexts thereby create an enabling and constraining environment for market actors.

Our starting point is the most basic neoclassical understanding of economics. Within microeconomics, markets represent ways in which buyers and sellers meet and trade for a given good or service at a particular price and quantity. In theory, markets lead to an efficient allocation of resources. However, in practice, microeconomics recognizes that markets have imperfections. Imperfect information, transactions costs, and market concentration, for example, are basic examples of long-recognized market imperfections.

For us, these distortions are a central part of the story. As economics has also long recognized, market failure is a function of its wider institutional context, notably its regulatory environment. Laws and norms on issues such as property rights and the enforcement of contracts shape the functioning of markets. Crucially, market distortions created by the institutional context of a market can create both winners and losers. This is because they lead to both opportunities and constraints for market actors.

The recognition that institutions matter for the functioning of markets and for explaining market behaviour is central to New Institutional Economics (Williamson 2000; North 1995). New Institutional Economics is an attempt to incorporate a theory of institutions into neoclassical economic theories (North 1995: 17). It is a theory that speaks to the conceptual relationship between states and markets. It represents a corrective to neoclassical economic assumptions that individuals have perfect information and unbounded rationality (Wilk and Cliggett 2007: 69; Ménard and Shirley 2005). These

47

authors start from the reality that information is rarely complete, and that individuals have different ideas or mental models of the way in which they make choices (Harris et al. 1995: 3). Instead, markets are subject to asymmetric information, property rights, challenges of contract enforcement, bounded rationality, social, cultural, and religious norms, monopoly and oligopoly, and social capital and networks.

Consequently, the institutions that shape and make corrections for these distortions shape how markets work in practice. As North's (1995) work recognizes, the historical centrality of regulation and property rights demonstrates that neo-liberalism fails unless it is based on sound underlying institutions. New Institutional Economics defines institutions as the rules of the game of a society, or human-devised constraints that structure human interactions and behaviour (North 1995: 23). They are composed of formal rules (laws and regulations), informal constraints (conventions and codes of conduct), and enforcement mechanisms (Williamson 1975, 2000). Institutional economists assume that a mixture of legal, political, social, cultural, and economic institutions have crucial impacts on economic decisions and performance (Joskow 2008: 5).

For our purposes, New Institutional Economics offers a useful starting point for theorizing the question of 'what is different about refugees?'. It enables us to recognize that a given population may be faced with different market structures than another population. Rather than refugees being inherently different from the host community as human beings or economic actors, their different institutional context may mean they face different opportunities and constraints in terms of their participation in markets.

Indeed, a wide range of existing literature shows how refugees are subject to a distinctive regulatory environment, shaped by the different international and national legal frameworks that shape their position vis-à-vis the state. Refugee communities are also subject to a range of informal institutions that shape their economic lives. As Kibreab notes (2004: 25), during exile, previous norms are sometimes replaced by new practices, rules, and institutions that emerge as a result of the refugee experience. For example, Horst (2006) highlights how Somali refugees in the Dadaab refugee camps in Kenya have developed norms of mutual support within the refugee camps. These formal and informal institutional differences distinguish refugees' position from that of citizens or other migrants.

These formal and informal institutions create different sets of market distortions and hence also different economic opportunities and constraints for both refugees and others. Werker's (2007) work on refugee camp economies is one of the few systematic studies by economists on refugees. Drawing from research in Uganda, his article highlights how some of these formal and informal barriers result in different types of market distortions in a refugee camp economy, as follows. First, in terms of *policy distortions*, he highlights how restrictions on refugees' mobility hinder them from participating in markets outside the camp. This, in turn, means that refugees may not be able to sell their products or services at the most profitable price or will incur transaction costs in waiting time or uncertainty when applying for travel permits (Werker 2007: 471). Second, in terms of *isolation distortions*, he highlights how the remoteness of refugee camps from commercial centres makes transporting goods or people between the two places extremely costly, while increasing the cost of gathering market information (Werker 2007: 467). Third, in terms of *distortions related to refugee status and identity*, he argues that insecurity and discrimination by host societies gravely circumscribe refugees' access to external markets (Werker 2007: 470).

Although Werker's examples relate exclusively to camps, they provide clear support for the idea that refugees frequently face a different set of market distortions created by their distinct institutional environment. What is crucial to recognize is that these distortions are not just a source of constraint but also of opportunity. In particular, they lead to opportunities for arbitrage for both refugees and host communities, taking advantage of artificial scarcity and abundance, asymmetric or incomplete market information, and elevated transaction costs.

To provide an example, in the Nakivale settlement in Uganda, many Somali shops sell tins of tuna fish. The tuna is from Thailand, and is imported via Saudi Arabia, Mombasa, and Kampala. It sells in large quantities and at elevated prices because of the significant Somali demand for tinned tuna, and yet it is almost completely absent from the Ugandan market. In the same settlement, a Rwandan refugee runs a maize-milling business. During the height of a mass influx of Congolese refugees into Uganda in 2012, UNHCR commissioned that Rwandan entrepreneur to mill maize to meet emergency food assistance needs. Further afield in the Za'atari refugee camp in Jordan, Syrian refugees make bricks using cement smuggled into the camp beyond the entry controls imposed by the government. The bricks are manufactured in semi-clandestine workshops, and within a camp in which housing is predominantly based on prefabricated housing containers, this brick-based construction achieves artificially elevated returns.

The Institutions of 'Refugeehood'

This presents a challenge to identify the specific institutions that make 'refugee economies' qualitatively distinct. We have argued that refugees are not inherently different from anyone else, and what makes their economic lives distinct is the institutional context of 'refugeehood'. The tendency within the existing literature, though, has been to describe the general characteristics and conditions of displacement, rather than to theorize what institutional structures are inherent to refugeehood. Werker (2007), for example, offers important observations about the kinds of market distortions present in refugee camps in Uganda, but what is unclear is which of these distortions are inherent to refugeehood and which are specific to the context he observes.

In order to begin to theorize 'refugee economies', we posit that there are three key characteristics of refugeehood that collectively suggest 'refugee economies' can be thought of as having specific institutional aspects. These are: (1) the intersection of state and international regulation; (2) the intersection of the formal and informal economy; (3) the intersection of national and transnational economies. Any of these characteristics may individually apply to other groups, such as migrants more generally. However, we suggest that refugees are relatively uniquely affected by these three ambiguous institutional positions when taken collectively. We argue that these institutional characteristics shape the relationship between refugees, states, and markets.

Intersection of State and International Institutions

The governance of refugees frequently lies between host states and international organizations. By the definition of being a refugee, the assumed citizen–state–territory relationship with the country of origin has been severed (Haddad 2008). Consequently, responsibility for protection transfers primarily to a host state of asylum, insofar as that state is a signatory of relevant international treaties. However, in practice—to a greater or lesser extent—refugees are governed by both the host state and international institutions. This is particularly the case for refugees who are hosted by states with limited protection capacity, which often delegate significant governance functions to UNHCR and its partners. Having been placed at the intersection of different governing bodies, refugees suffer from a simultaneous absence and surfeit of statehood; as refugees, they lack territorial citizenship, but they are also subject to the exercise of sovereign authority by the host government and aid organizations (McConnachie 2014: 12).

The paradox of a 'double chain of administration' (Colson 2004: 108) is particularly visible in refugee camps. For instance, whereas the 1951 convention stipulates refugees' freedom of movement, most refugee-hosting countries in the global South have a policy of keeping refugees in segregated camps with limited freedom of movement (Kibreab 2003: 60). Some countries, such as Kenya and Thailand, have official encampment policies towards refugees, placing restrictions on mobility and the right to work. This hinders refugees' ability to participate in markets on the same terms as nationals. In addition to central government regulations, local or provincial authorities sometimes place additional restrictions on refugees' socio-economic activities (Bakewell 2014; Rogge and Akol 1989; Bascom 1993).

Especially in refugee camps in developing countries, UNHCR and its partner agencies take on a key role in camp management and the provision of basic services for refugees. Milner (2009), for example, describes how Kenya adopted an 'abdication' policy to render refugees 'an international community issue'. Similarly, others have described how in refugee camps around the world, UNHCR often assumes the role of a 'surrogate state'. Kagan (2011) and Grabska (2008) highlight how refugees have claimed that 'we live in a country of UNHCR', seeing the international community rather than the host government as the sovereign authority in refugee camps.

Kagan (2011) shows how in many host states in the Middle East, a gradual 'responsibility shift' has taken place, in which key protection functions of the state, from refugee status determination to protection and assistance provision have moved over time from the host state to organizations such as UNHCR and UNRWA. While these functions vary and the degree of responsibility transfer exists on a spectrum, these observations highlight that a significant feature of the institutional context of refugeehood is that governance is shaped not just by states but also by international organizations, and by the nature of the interaction between the two.

Critics of refugee camps—such as Verdirame and Harrell-Bond (2005)—have identified this relationship as a major source of constraint on refugees' agency, removing opportunities for self-reliance and full engagement with the rights and entitlements provided to citizens within host states. While this may be partly true, the implications are arguably more complex. Being partly subject to international governance often leads to both economic constraints and opportunities. For example, international assistance provided to refugees can lead to a variety of opportunities for exchange, arbitrage, and entrepreneurship that would be absent in a purely state-governed institutional environment. Indeed, the pluralist governance regimes that shape refugeehood construct parallel opportunity structures to those available to citizens (McConnachie 2014).

Intersection of the Formal and Informal

Refugees' economic lives almost inevitably straddle the formal and informal sectors. The 1951 Convention sets out a series of rights for refugees, but they are not the same rights as those of citizens. This applies particularly to socio-economic rights, which are usually interpreted as relative to the wider socio-economic situations of the country. The right to work is in practice rarely provided to refugees, particularly in host countries of first asylum in the South. Only a minority of host states explicitly provide such a right within national legislation (Asylum Access 2014).

However, even in states such as Uganda and Zambia that formally provide the right to work, refugees face other institutional barriers to full participation within the formal economy. A range of restrictions, including prohibitive and expensive work permits or the non-recognition of foreign qualifications, often make it hard for refugees to work in the formal sector. Refugees in Ghana have been required to secure special work permits from the host government to work in the formal sector, but this is a cumbersome process which takes several months or even longer, discouraging local employers from hiring refugees (Omata 2013). In countries such as Jordan, for example, the formal right to work for refugees is in practice limited to a tiny minority able to afford such permits (Zetter et al. 2014). Moreover, refugees, like other types of migrants, often find their previous credentials and degrees obtained in the country of origin unrecognized by the host government (see Dick 2002: 18; Porter et al. 2008: 238). As a result of these restrictions, refugees often pursue pre-existing careers within the informal sector.

Beyond the right to work, other barriers exist to full market participation by refugees. Where states are concerned that refugees only remain temporarily, refugees often face restrictions on their ability to own property or to access capital through formal banking systems. Host countries often establish a range of bureaucratic barriers to non-citizens to prevent them from accessing formal economic structures. Even in the absence of official prohibitions, legal processes and fees frequently raise the transaction costs and reduce the viability of participation.

On the other hand, assistance by international organizations is often limited, leaving refugees with little option other than to pursue independent sources of income generation. The result is that refugees end up precariously placed between the formal and informal sectors of the economy. Despite facing barriers to entry into the formal economy, they engage significantly with the informal sector in both rural and urban areas. Even in the most remote refugee camp settings and in countries with explicit restrictions on refugees' right to work, informal markets are often visible, exchange thrives, and a whole series of consumption, production, and finance takes place outside the formal economy. In Kenya, for instance, despite significant legal restrictions on refugees' economic activities, vibrant informal-sector markets exist within both the remote Dadaab camps (Enghoff et al. 2010) and urban areas such as Nairobi's Eastleigh district (Carrier 2015; Carrier and Lochery 2013; Lindley 2010).

An almost universal institutional feature of the economic life of refugees is therefore the virtually constant navigation between the formal and informal economy. This position shapes the economic opportunities available to refugees. To take an example from our research, many refugees in Kyangwali settlement grow sorghum on their allocated plots of land. However, movement restrictions mean that they generally rely upon Ugandan traders travelling to the settlement to buy their produce. A consequence of this dynamic is the asymmetric bargaining power that enables Ugandans to purchase produce at low prices. However, recognition of this has encouraged a group of refugee farmers to create a cooperative called Kyangwali Progressive Farmers Limited, which in turn negotiated a deal directly with a Ugandan brewing company, Nile Breweries, in order to sell sorghum at a collectively negotiated price. This example highlights how refugees' position between the formal and informal economy creates constraints as well as opportunities.

Intersection of the National and Transnational

With major advances in transportation systems and communication technology, trans-boundary connections are a feature of the contemporary world. It is now widely recognized that most people's lives are shaped by transnational economic and social ties. This is especially true for refugees. Refugees are at the intersection of national and transnational connections to a greater extent than most. They are citizens of another state, yet they are also unable or unwilling to be resident on the territory of that state. This places them in a liminal position between two distinct sets of socio-spatial connections: national and transnational. They are not fully integrated into either but are partly alienated from both. Yet, this liminal institutional space in turn creates both economic opportunities and constraints.

Refugees retain—and often develop—significant social and economic transnational networks. These are based on ties with both the homeland and frequently with fellow nationals who have dispersed to other countries as refugees and migrants. Such connections include, but are not reducible to, remittances (Horst 2006; Porter et al. 2008; Monsutti 2005). In the context of limited state protection, refugees rely on informal networks as their fall-back and make use of intricate connections in response to their limited legal, political, and economic rights (Buscher 2013; Al-Shamani 2004; Palmgren 2013; Grabska 2005). For example, mutual assistance between different households constitutes one of the principal livelihood strategies in refugee camps (De Vriese 2006; Hamid 1992; Gale 2006; Golooba-Mutebi 2004; Omata 2013).

Experiences of displacement sometimes result in the construction or expansion of new trans-boundary connections. Some groups of Sudanese refugees in Kenya have a history of frequent displacement and consequently developed new trading and business networks in neighbouring countries which can be traced back to the camps in which they reside (De Montclos and Kagwanja 2000: 213). Somali refugees further illustrate the importance of transnational networks in institutionally structuring refugees' economic activities (Lindley 2006, 2007a,b, 2010; Horst 2006; Campbell 2005).

There is a substantial literature on informal economic activities taking place in border areas. Especially in the global South where the national borders are less strictly controlled by the states, market economies in *de facto* free-trade zones flourish (Chalfin 2001: 219). Since refugee camps are often close to porous borders, important linkages are established between refugee camps and external economies. According to Sohn and Lara-Valencia (2013: 9), borders are an important economic asset because of the ways in which they facilitate arbitrage. In the tri-border area between Ghana, Burkina Faso, and Togo, for instance, traders from each country capitalize on their distinctive strengths and bring in specific items to meet the demand of other sides (Chalfin 2001: 209).

As most trans-border economies in developing countries are informal (or sometimes illicit), participants need to control risks without relying on state protection (Taneja et al. 2003: 3094; Kloosterman et al. 1998: 249). Thus, traders largely depend on their personal contacts with relatives, friends, and co-ethnic groups to mitigate the risk in economic transactions (Konings 2005; Taneja and Pohit 2001: 2263). In a border zone between Cameroon and Nigeria, Nigerian traders make full use of their clan and ethnic bonds on both sides of the border to facilitate their economic transactions (Konings 2005: 285). Therefore, an almost universal institutional characteristic of refugeehood is being liminally situated among national and transnational economic spaces.

Opportunities, Constraints, and Individuals

The theoretical purpose of these three 'institutions of refugeehood' is to highlight the ways in which refugees' different institutional contexts shape their economic opportunity structures. Rather than being inherently different from 'citizens' or 'migrants', what makes them distinct is a set of institutional features that shape their economic lives and interaction with markets.

These three features serve as starting point for theorizing what makes 'refugee economies' distinct. They delineate a key part of what makes it inherently different to be a refugee, beyond a bureaucratic label. They are intended to be taken cumulatively, and of course they are a matter of degree. Some categories such as 'migrant' may have some of these features, but they are unlikely to experience all of them in the way that most refugees will to at least some degree.

Central to this conceptual framework, however, is the recognition that these sources of market distortion create both opportunities and constraints. While sources of market imperfection may include entry and exit controls, scarcity, abundance, illegality, and informal institutions that shape risk and uncertainty, they create opportunities for arbitrage, entrepreneurship, and innovation by both refugees and non-refugees.

While the institutions described in the previous section represent the structural context within which refugee economies take place, it is important to recognize the role of individual or communal agency. Crucially, refugees and other actors have the capacity to transform these institutional constraints into opportunities. Indeed, for neoclassical economics, markets are the structure while rational actors have agency, albeit that markets are conceived simply to maximize utility, subject to a budget constraint. Building on this, economic sociology has suggested that these market actors can instead be conceptualized as inherently social actors. For Weber (2013), for instance, actors are constituted by their context, and deeply embedded cultures influence the capacity of both communities and individuals to shape structural constraints and opportunities.

Therefore, not only can refugees and others exercise agency to recognize and transform market distortions into opportunities, but culture and social networks too can represent a structural resource in this regard. For example, as we highlight in this book, Somalis in particular have strong transnational networks which provide a source of what Bourdieu has called social capital (the capacity of individuals to command resources by virtue of their membership in networks). Somalis' clan networks and culturally embedded economic structure offer a source of community-based agency with which to transcend the institutional constraints of refugeehood. This is exemplified by Somalis' elevated levels of remittance sending, their greater levels of entrepreneurship, and their range of alternative financial mechanisms. Yet, importantly, nearly all different refugee communities have particular forms of social capital and networks which offer alternative ways to transcend economic challenges (Buscher 2011; Al-Shamani 2004; Palmgren 2013; Grabska 2005).

Perhaps less recognized in the existing refugee literature is the role of individuals. While community and culture can indeed offer sources of agency, so too can individual talent and ambition. Yet, the figure of the 'refugee entrepreneur' has generally been neglected from work on the economic lives of refugees. Outliers play a crucial role in any economy, and refugee economies are no exception. While not every refugee can be or will be a successful entrepreneur, the few exceptions who establish businesses play an important and transformative role for themselves and their communities.

We know from innovation theory that individual 'innovators' can be sources of dynamic economic change, including for communities (Schumpeter 1942). Similarly, within refugee communities, while outliers may be in a minority, the 'innovators' can be conceptualized as those who engage in creative adaptation in ways that transform market distortions into opportunities for themselves and the wider community. Whether tapping mains electricity with 'spaghetti wires', reselling food assistance, selling music downloaded onto USB keys, running computer games cafés using recycled games consoles, establishing informal financing mechanisms, or simply hawking scarce commodities, signs of this kind of innovation abound among refugees.

Economy or Economies?

There are multiple and intersecting 'refugee economies'. The institutional sources of refugeehood will play out differently, leading to different sets of constraints and opportunities in different contexts. In particular, refugees may face different sets of market distortions depending on whether they are in emergency, protracted, or urban contexts. In this book, we empirically explore what difference each of these environments makes for structuring the institutional context of refugee economies.

Refugee Economies in an Urban Context

For the first time in history, more than half of the world's population is living in urban areas. Correspondingly, about 50 per cent of the global refugee population now lives in cities (Crisp et al. 2012). Urban refugees find their way to towns and cities for various reasons (Marfleet 2008). It is widely assumed that most of these refugees are from urban backgrounds and opt to come to towns or cities to seek better socio-economic opportunities (Kibreab 2008). However, there are additional factors, including that camp lives in the global South are often marked by complete absence of access to higher education and a good quality of health care. Refugees who previously worked in the modern economic sector may therefore see few prospects for themselves or their children in such places (Fábos and Kibreab 2007).

Some cities are seeing a noticeable increase in the presence of self-settled refugees. In Nairobi, for example, the district of Eastleigh is popularly referred to as 'Little Mogadishu' due to a dominant Somali presence. This population includes a significant number of Somali refugees who have chosen to live in the capital—despite strict regulations imposed by the Kenyan government—because of the comparative socio-economic opportunities available to them in a metropolitan environment (Lindley 2010).

Compared to the wealth of studies on camp-based refugees, the literature on urban refugees remains limited (Fábos and Kibreab 2007). Given the magnitude and scale of recent urbanization in forced migration, however, the question of how to understand the economic lives of urban refugees has begun to draw growing research interest in recent years. Against this backdrop, burgeoning scholarship has highlighted general features of their livelihoods, which we discuss later in this section.

First, whilst urban refugees face similar economic problems as poor urban citizens, research shows that refugees also confront additional, distinct challenges such as discrimination and xenophobia, restrictions on the right to work, and limited access to public assistance (Landau and Duponchel 2011: 13; Grabska 2005; Landau 2004; Jacobsen 2005). Similar to host state perceptions of economic migrants, refugees living in cities are often perceived as 'competitors' with local host people for employment and resources. In Pakistan, for instance, local people believe that the Afghan refugees take their jobs and increase unemployment in the host population because the refugees work for less money (USCR in Jacobsen 2005: 46). Because of this prevailing view, whether true or not, most host governments deny urban refugees the right to work and certain forms of support that are available to local populations.

Second, the majority of urban refugees in the global South are making a living with little access to humanitarian aid. One of the major advantages for camp-based refugees in pursuit of economic success is access to assistance from aid organizations. In non-camp contexts, refugee relief agencies often do not provide meaningful material support. Supplying aid for self-settled refugees is regarded as a 'luxury' (Campbell et al. 2011: 10) by international organizations and is 'not the kind of work the global refugee system is comfortable with' (Rosenberg 2011). In the absence of humanitarian support, urban refugees need to make ends meet with their own, independent income-generating means. In short, they are 'doing it for themselves' (Crisp et al. 2012).

Third, given their limited access to support by humanitarian agencies, social networks play a principal role in refugees' economic lives in urban environments. According to research on urban refugees conducted by the Women's Refugee Commission, robust social capital has proven to be the single most valuable asset for refugees' welfare and livelihood formulation (Buscher 2013: 23). Mutual aid through inter-household networks is widely recognized as a vital livelihood resource for self-settled refugees who have to fend for themselves (Golooba-Mutebi 2004; Grabska 2005). Other studies on self-settled refugees show that contacts with co-nationals help refugees find employment, shelter, and sources of credit (Amisi 2006; Grabska 2005; Jacobsen 2005: 43). A considerable volume of scholarship also highlights the significance of transnational connections in refugees' economic activities. Trans-border ties often enable refugees to access remittances and provide economic opportunities in their host country (see Lindley 2006, 2007a,b, 2010; Porter et al. 2008; Monsutti 2005; Horst 2006).

Whereas the growing volume of literature has revealed some important aspects of urban refugee economies, there also remain critical empirical and analytical lacunas in the scholarship. For one, while there is a general recognition that refugees in urban environments make ends meet on their own, the detailed nature of their economies remains poorly understood. Previous studies on urban refugees generally indicate that the livelihood means employed by refugees largely take place in informal trade sectors (for instance, see InterAid 2009; Women's Refugee Commission 2011; JIPS 2013; Enghoff et al. 2010). Yet very little is known about the diversity and character of those commercial activities, or the myriad ways in which factors related to a refugee's background—such as nationality, ethnicity, or wealth status—shape and define said activities.

Of equal importance, few studies have investigated refugees' economic activities in relation to wider market and economic institutional spaces in their host country. Within the context of a city, a refugee's income generation is likely to be more dependent on local markets and business sectors than in rural areas. The existing literature, however, fails to reveal such patterns of engagement between urban refugees and market actors in the local host communities. Also, whereas the significance of social connections is well documented, surprisingly little research has systematically explored the role of different types of social relations in refugee economies. Besides the advantage of having diaspora networks available for accessing remittances, it is necessary to investigate what other types of networks emerge for refugees, and how these connections enable them to shape their livelihoods in exile.

Protracted Refugee Camps

Refugee camp economies in protracted situations have particular institutional features. Currently, nearly ten million out of 19.5 million refugees worldwide are trapped in protracted exile in poor developing regions where host states and communities often have scarce resources (UNHCR 2015a). When examining refugee economies, one important variable in determining the nature of day-to-day economic life and behaviour is the dynamics of the temporal contexts affecting their capacities to formulate their economic strategies. By their very nature, people's livelihoods change over time in response to the political, economic, and social contexts in which they are situated (Seddon and Hussein 2002: 8; Narbeth and McLean 2003: 3; Kaag et al. 2003: 5). Similarly, in the context of protracted displacement, refugees' economic activities and access to livelihood assets are required to adapt in response to evolving circumstances in their living environment (Horst 2006: 7). The current scholarship draws attention to several defining features which shape camp-based refugee livelihoods in prolonged cases, as follows.

First, compared to those of self-settled refugees, refugees' economic activities inside camps take place under the more direct—and often restrictive—influence of state regulations and UNHCR policy (Kibreab 2003; De Vriese 2006; Whitaker 2002; Horst 2006). Restrictions on camp-based refugees' rights to move freely are particularly prohibitive: host governments across the global South often shackle refugees' mobility outside of camps to prevent them from melting into the host economy. Whilst such policies are typically intended to reduce economic competition over employment opportunities and resources with locals, they also produce critical and wide-ranging distortions in refugee economies (Werker 2007: 471). These constraints on mobility, in particular, hinder refugees from participating in markets or employment opportunities outside the camp. In addition to the formal regulations, informal institutions stemming from relationships with local host populations—such as access to land and other types of natural resources—are a further important factor that affects refugees' economic lives (see Bakewell 2014; Rogge and Akol 1989; Bascom 1993).

Second, access to humanitarian assistance is widely recognized as an important factor in shaping camp-based refugees' economic activities. One of the major advantages for refugees in pursuit of economic success is access to assistance from aid organizations (Jacobsen 2005). While camp-based refugees generally enjoy access to some form of humanitarian assistance, relief aid, especially in protracted refugee camps, is commonly provided on a smaller scale compared to their early phase of arrival. As UNHCR and international donors focus on high-profile refugee crises in which people are either fleeing or repatriating in large numbers, assistance programmes for long-term refugee situations have been deprived of adequate funding (Crisp 2003: 9). With dwindling institutional support over a prolonged exile, camp-based refugees are increasingly forced to help themselves in meeting their basic and other needs with their entrepreneurial and innovative strategies.

Third, the distinct physical environment of rural refugee camps shapes camp-based refugee livelihoods. Most camps are located in isolated and underdeveloped areas. However, these provincial environments may sometimes give refugees access to natural resources such as arable land, river, and forest. This often creates farming opportunities for camps with access to arable land (Bakewell 2014). This does not mean, however, that all refugees living in camps are subsistence farmers. For instance, in Buduburam refugee settlement in Ghana, there are a variety of non-farming economic activities, including retail trading, communication businesses, and transportation (Dick 2002; Porter et al. 2008; Omata 2013).

Fourth, notwithstanding the remoteness of certain camps, no refugee camps, regardless of their locations, are totally closed to traffic in terms of goods, capital, and people from outside (Werker 2002: 462; Ranalli 2014: 428). Especially in protracted situations, some of which have existed in the same area for decades, refugees who live there have become deeply embedded in the host economy. Some move into the surrounding villages to pursue trade and seek employment, while locals in turn enter the camp in search of labour and business opportunities (Phillips 2003: 14). In Kenya, for example, commercial links between the refugee camps and Nairobi have been harnessed by Somali entrepreneurs (Pavanello et al. 2010: 2).

Fifth, refugees' mobility is often recognized in the literature as a crucial livelihood asset in camp settings, one which can be constrained or enabled as a result of freedom of movement proscribed by the regulatory environment. At Utange camp in Kenya, for example, Somali female refugees leave the camp in the morning, 'commute to' Mombasa to purchase vegetables wholesale, sell them at a retail price in the city markets, and then return to the camp again (Hyndman 2000: 159). Certain groups of refugees also take advantage of trans-border movement in their commercial activities, extending trade routes far beyond the borders of both camp and host country itself. In the Afghan refugee population in Iran, pre-war mobility continued during displacement as a livelihood strategy, and there is a clear pattern of multidirectional and cross-border movements in their income-generating enterprises (Stigter and Monsutti 2005: 270).

Finally, social networks have been shown to play a vital role in the economic survival of refugees living in camps, as they do for self-settled refugees living in urban contexts. In particular, contacts with local host communities works as a catalyst to enable refugees to access wider economic opportunities. In the Sembakounya camp in Guinea, for instance, multiple joint businesses have stemmed from networking connections built between refugees and local Guineans (Andrews 2003: 6). Mirroring the wide-ranging mobility of camp-based refugees, their social networks also often extend beyond national borders. Owing to a history of frequent displacement, some groups of Sudanese refugees in Kenya have developed new trading and business networks between the camps in which they reside and the neighbouring countries (De Montclos and Kagwanja 2000: 213).

Emergency Contexts

In refugee contexts, emergency situations occur when people are forced to flee from their country of origin in large numbers due to persecution, conflict, or violence. The UN refugee agency and other humanitarian agencies respond to a refugee movement by launching an emergency relief programme in the country to which the displaced people have fled. The emergency phase typically lasts for one year or a few years at maximum until most of the relief agencies depart, followed by a so-called 'care and maintenance' phase. These forcibly displaced people are pushed out of their familiar moorings and typically seek refuge and succour in a refugee camp in a host country. The existing literature draws attention to several defining features that shape refugee livelihoods in emergency camp settings, as follows.

First, and unsurprisingly, most refugees in the emergency phases are likely to be at a very early stage of rehabilitation from forfeiture of their economic base. As Jacobsen (2014) explains, forced displacement almost always entails some forms of loss of key economic assets such as livelihood instruments or business contacts as a result of flight. In his 'Impoverishment Risks and Reconstruction' model, Cernea and McDowell (2000) identifies various types of losses that increase the risk of impoverishment when people are displaced: loss of land, wage employment, and common property assets. Bereft of their livelihood assets, most refugees need to re-establish their economic foothold under very different institutional circumstances than those in their homeland. In such an emergency context, refugees are often only at the beginning of this economic recovery process.

Second, support from humanitarian agencies plays a key role in refugee economies in emergency situations. During and immediately following the mass inflow of refugees into a host country, camp-based refugees usually have much better access to free goods in the form of relief aid in comparison to self-settled refugees or those in long-term camps. As Crisp writes (2003: 9), UNHCR and donor communities tend to focus on high-profile refugee crises in which people are fleeing in large numbers. There is, therefore, normally an influx of humanitarian support in the form of food aid, shelter, and services like health care and sanitation provided by international organizations or NGOs (De Vriese 2006: 27).

Third, despite deprivation of economic resources, refugees still exercise agency to find ways of survival. Refugees who are caught up with emergency contexts rely on more than just the delivery of external aid, devising or improvising a range of parallel coping strategies. For instance, refugees often develop localized informal networks of survival in the face of acute crises (Calhoun 2010; Stigter and Monsutti 2005; Andrews 2003; Gale 2006; Grabska 2005; Hamid 1992). As one example, in the uprooted populations from the Southern Lebanon in Israel, particularly between women's groups, informal mutual support networks have budded and have provided important livelihood assistance for them whilst their familial relationships in their homeland have been eroded (Doron 2005: 189).

Fourth, in considering refugee-receiving host states, it is important to understand that sudden influxes of refugees can impact host communities and countries in distinct ways. These effects are particularly pronounced at an emergency stage where displaced people are fleeing *en masse* into a host community or country. From the earlier literature (Chambers 1986) to very recent reports (Zetter et al. 2014) it has been suggested that the sudden inflow of large numbers of refugees negatively impacts on host populations. But as several scholars documented, alternatively, major refugee influxes often correlate with a local or regional increase in trade and market activity, particularly in rural or more remote areas (Jacobsen 2005; Kibreab et al. 1990; Kok 1989; Maystadt and Verwimp 2009).

During the process of writing this book, the outflow of Syrian refugees is undoubtedly the largest-scale emergency refugee crisis worldwide. According to various reports, while the influxes of refugees have caused numerous problems for receiving countries, their presence also presents new economic opportunities for local host communities. For instance, Za'atari refugee camp—the home of more than 100000 Syrian refugees in Jordan—hosts hundreds of well-stocked shops owned by both Syrian refugees and Jordanian locals, and this camp is evolving into an important economic hub in the hosting area (Kimmelman 2014).

The literature on prison economies can provide some implications and analogies for refugee economies in a very early phase of exile, particularly with regards to the process of emergence of an economy inside the prison. Research has shown that prisoners in a brand-new prison will quickly form economic linkages within and outside the prison. An internal 'market' economy between prisoners is spontaneously spawned by bartering their free rations (Radford 1945). This intra-prisoner economy later grows in scale by forming trade relationships with external economic actors. This observation applies to emergency refugee contexts. In Kobe refugee camps in Dolo Ado, Ethiopia, for example, newly arrived Somali refugees immediately started selling part of the UNHCR/WFP (World Food Programme) food ration to local traders. Refugees spent the obtained cash on popular staple foods like spaghetti and rice and other necessities such as milk, meat stock, and clothes distributed by Ethiopian traders from surrounding villages or towns (Desert Rose 2012).

Another implication from the literature on prison economies is that even in a relatively small-scale economy inside the prison, specialization gradually occurs. Interestingly, although living in a very similar environment, some entrepreneurial prisoners embarked on providing specialized services, which diversified the camp economy (Price 1973; Goldsmith 1997; Gleason 1978). Similarly, when refugees first arrive in a country of asylum, on the surface, they seem to be more or less in similar situations in terms of material and living conditions. For those who live in refugee camps in rural areas, subsistence farming often becomes their central livelihood option at the outset of their exile. Yet as time passes, not all refugees remain as farmers, and some may embark on specialized non-farming activities.

Conclusion

In this book, we examine the economic lives of refugees from an interdisciplinary perspective. Nevertheless, we suggest that economic theory offers us a useful starting point for conceptualizing that economic context. We know from the most basic microeconomic theory that markets are subject to market failures resulting from, for example, imperfect information, imperfect competition, or transaction costs. Furthermore, New Institutional Economics has long recognized that the variety and impact of these market distortions is shaped by the institutional and regulatory context within which those markets operate.

Building upon the insights of New Institutional Economics, we have argued that what makes refugee economies an analytically distinct area is not any inherent difference in the people per se but that refugees occupy a different institutional structure compared to citizens or other migrants. Refugeehood creates a distinct institutional context, which we suggest can be distinguished by three core institutional features. This in turn introduces a particular set of market distortions, which lead to a distinct set of opportunities and constraints for market-based activity by refugees and non-refugees. Some refugees have the agency to be able to turn this structural environment into opportunities for themselves and their communities, whether as entrepreneurs or 'refugee innovators'.

This conceptual framework thereby offers a theoretical argument for why and how we might view refugees as operating within analytically distinct sub-economies. Yet this is not to say that they reside in a single isolated sub-economy. Rather, there are a number of refugee economies—across urban, protracted, and emergency contexts—that have different economic institutional frameworks but which overlap and interconnect with one another, as well as the wider national and regional economies. Indeed, it is the distinct but overlapping nature of these economies that creates many of the arbitrage opportunities—from brokerage to hawking—that we argue are characteristic of refugee economies. In the next chapters we show how the variation and interconnection plays out by looking at urban, protracted, and emergency contexts in Uganda.

4

Research methodology

Research on refugees and forced displacement has developed considerably over the last two decades. For the most part, though, it is dominated by small-scale, qualitative studies. Qualitative research methods, especially those rooted in an ethnographic approach, are an essential means to draw substantial observations from the complex, informal, and everyday nature of refugee interactions and processes. However, as Jacobsen and Landau (2003) note, research is often carried out over short time periods, relies on small, unsystematic, and unrepresentative sampling, and is therefore limited in the insights it can provide.

In exploring refugee economies in Uganda, we have attempted to balance the strengths of qualitative ethnographic approaches with the pressing need for more rigorous, quantitative scholarship. To achieve this, we pursued a mixed-methods approach in our data collection. We sequenced qualitative research and quantitative research based on large-scale and representative data collection. This approach enabled us to build a deep understanding of context, and to develop the trust and networks required to acquire research access, before embarking on survey design.

First, we drew from a wide range of qualitative ethnographic methods, including unstructured and semi-structured interviews, livelihood mapping, wealth breakdown instruments utilized in focus group contexts, and market-mapping techniques. This enabled us to attain an in-depth understanding of the economic lives of refugees as well as the wider local, national, and trans-national networks within which they are situated.

Second, we paired this qualitative approach with the added rigour of a large-scale survey based on randomized sampling. This allowed us to generate substantial quantitative data. Our survey was carried out in each of our four main research sites. In the three settlements (Nakivale, Kyangwali, and Rwamwanja), we were able to base our sampling on UNHCR's existing sample frame. In Kampala, in the absence of a sample frame, we used an experimental approach to urban refugee profiling—respondent-driven sampling (RDS)—which allowed us to access hidden populations that pose a major challenge to traditional sampling approaches. With a sample size of 2213 refugee households, the survey represents one of the largest quantitative studies of the economic lives of refugees yet undertaken.

Throughout our fieldwork, we were committed to a participatory approach. We hired and trained a core team of seventeen refugee peer researchers and twenty-two refugee survey enumerators. This enabled us to improve the quality of our research but also allowed us to contribute meaningfully to the development of local capacity during our fieldwork. While not without its challenges, this participatory research afforded an important space for refugee ownership in the production of knowledge dealing with their own economic lives.

In this chapter, we offer in-depth discussion of these methodological approaches, supported by personal reflections drawn from our fieldwork experiences. First, we provide an overview of our research design, including our case selection criteria, guiding research questions, and rationale for the sequencing of our fieldwork. Second, we introduce our mixed-methods approach to data collection, including a review of the qualitative, participatory methods we employed and of our survey and sampling strategy. Third, we conclude by assessing the implication of our methodology for future research.

Research Design

Our analytical framework, introduced in the preceding chapter, is informed by premises found in both microeconomic and New Institutional Economic theory. These are that state–market distortions—inherent in economy—are shaped by the institutional and regulatory contexts within which those markets operate. Applying this to the forced migration context, we began by considering how the unique institutional contexts created by 'refugeehood' might introduce their own distinct set of market distortions, and in turn, lead to opportunities and constraints for market-based activity by refugees and non-refugees alike.

In order to explore and refine these initial premises, we selected a single country for in-depth study. Our goal was to build our understanding of refugee economies through iterative observation and analysis, grounded in the same communities and markets across a country where refugees were actively pursuing their livelihoods. To determine where our study should be based, we considered a sample of countries that host large refugee populations in both emergency and protracted contexts, and which could also provide a space to develop some of our experimental methodological approaches for potential future comparative work. Our selection of Uganda was informed by three key case selection criteria.

First, within the international community of refugee-hosting states, Uganda represents a relatively permissive regulatory environment for allowing refugees' economic agency, and it therefore offered a unique opportunity for research on refugee economies. Since the early 1960s, the government of Uganda has maintained an open policy of hosting refugees and is signatory to the central international legal instruments for refugee protection, including the 1951 Refugee Convention, the 1976 Protocol, and the 1969 OAU Convention. Uganda has also adopted two newer pieces of legislation, the 2006 Refugees Act and the 2010 Refugee Regulations, which reflect the government's commitment to current international standards of refugee protection.

Critically, Ugandan policies enacted through the Refugee Department of the Office of the Prime Minister (OPM) have made the goal of self-reliance central to the country's refugee regime. As part of this strategy, refugees in Uganda enjoy the right to work, freedom of movement within the country, access to basic services, and the right to live in local communities as well as in defined settlements (Sharpe and Namusobya 2012). Within the country's refugee settlements, small plots of land are also allocated to each refugee household to facilitate a development-based approach to refugees' self-reliance. This is in direct contrast with neighbouring countries, such as Kenya, whose refugee policies impose far stricter impediments to refugees' economic freedoms and represent formidable barriers to market access. While aspects of these policies are problematic and have attracted well-founded criticism (Dryden-Peterson and Hovil 2004; Hovil 2007; Kaiser 2006), we felt that the policies had on the whole helped to create an environment distinctly well suited for exploring the 'limits of the possible' for refugee economic agency compared to other potential research sites.

Second, Uganda hosts a diverse range of refugee nationalities from which to draw comparative observations and inferences regarding economic systems and behaviours (Table 4.1). With 244 776 refugees and asylum seekers as of

Table 4.1 Refugees in Uganda by country of origin, 2013

Country of Origin	Refugees/Asylum Seekers
Dem. Rep. of the Congo	163 916
South Sudan	25 265
Somalia	18 534
Rwanda	14 613
Burundi	11 364
Eritrea	6 275
Sudan	1 629
Kenya	1 534
Ethiopia	1 450
Others	196
Total	**244 776**

Source: UNHCR Population Statistics 2013

2013, the country hosts a significant number of different refugee populations from across East Africa (UNHCR 2013a). Given our project's time and resource constraints, we were able to engage in depth with only the largest of these groups during our research: Congolese, Rwandan, Burundian, Somali, Ethiopian, Eritrean, and South Sudanese. This diversity nonetheless facilitated a multitude of important comparative dimensions, which have enriched our subsequent analysis.

Third, refugees in Uganda are housed in settlements throughout the country as well as within urban contexts of the capital. This distribution complemented our criteria for exploring refugee economies comparatively across multiple contexts—urban, rural protracted, and emergency—within a single country.

We selected four field sites that fulfilled these two comparative criteria: Nakivale refugee settlement (population 68 406), the capital city of Kampala (58 167), Kyangwali settlement (21 989), and Rwamwanja settlement (50 024).[1] The inclusion of Kampala permitted comparisons between an urban refugee setting and the protracted rural settlements of Nakivale, Kyangwali, and Rwamwanja. Moreover, Rwamwanja—reopened in 2012 in response to an emergency influx of Congolese refugees—provided us with a site for exploring early, emergency stages of livelihood adaptation in Uganda.

In order to examine key features of the host communities within which Uganda's refugees live, we also explored several local centres of trade in close proximity to our research sites. We focused on understanding spaces of commercial engagement between refugees and Ugandans in the towns of Mbarara (near Nakivale settlement), Hoima (near Kyangwali settlement), and Kyenjojo (near Rwamwanja settlement).

Guiding Research Questions and Sequencing of our Fieldwork

With our fieldwork sites selected, we designed a sequenced project plan, informed by several central guiding research questions. These included:

1. What types of refugee economic activities and behaviours can be observed in each research site?
2. What kinds of variation in economic outcomes can be observed across refugee households?
3. What factors explain variation in refugees' economic behaviours and outcomes?

---

[1] Data received from UNHCR internal statistics March 2013, not published. Rwamwanja internal statistics from UNHCR data collection in December 2013.

4. What roles do innovation and entrepreneurship play in refugees' lives, and to what extent do they enable some refugees to transform structural challenges into opportunities for themselves and their communities?

5. How do these preceding factors play out across urban, protracted, and emergency contexts to constitute a distinct but overlapping plurality of refugee economies?

We sought to explore and refine these initial questions via sequential phases of iterative data collection, moving from qualitative to quantitative research.

Qualitative Methodology

In each of our research sites and across several local trade sites, we drew upon a wide range of qualitative research techniques to develop a deep base of contextual knowledge. Our central qualitative methods included unstructured and semi-structured interviews, focus group discussions, participant observation, transect walks, and participatory mapping.

We redesigned our semi-structured interviews at progressive steps throughout the field research to capture emerging themes of interest in line with our overall research design. We also carried out context-specific livelihood mapping and wealth breakdown exercises, to understand general and specific features of refugees' economic activities with reference to their socioeconomic status.

In our qualitative research, we focused primarily on interviews with Congolese, Rwandan, Somali, Burundian, South Sudanese, Ethiopian, and Eritrean refugees. We also interviewed a comprehensive cross-section of non-refugee stakeholders working in both Kampala and the settlements, including Ugandan nationals, Ugandan government representatives, staff members of the United Nations Office of the High Commissioner for Refugees (UNHCR) in Uganda, and UNHCR's implementing partners (IPs) and operating partners (OPs). Lastly, we conducted interviews and focus groups with key groups of Ugandan nationals who regularly interact with refugees. In particular, we consulted a wide range of Ugandan business people—from petty traders and small-to-medium enterprises to large national corporations and multinational corporate franchises with commercial interests in the settlements and Kampala. For confidentiality and security, interviewees are anonymized in this book.

Our qualitative data collection strategy was strongly ethnographic throughout. To develop a more granular knowledge of the day-to-day livelihood experiences of the refugee populations under investigation, our field research team spent significant time conducting participant observation. We also relied on a 'hanging-out' strategy, involving long periods of loosely structured participant observation in the community with key informants, their friends, family, neighbours, and business colleagues (Geertz 1998: 69; Rodgers 2004).

These sessions became invaluable for orienting us to the rich, intercontextual details of daily economic life for refugees in each field site. We developed strong personal relationships with key informants, allowing us to penetrate closed refugee communities and subcommunities based around particular livelihoods. This also served to advertise our presence and research agenda to these closed communities, allowing us to build trust and transparency.

Often, our most interesting cases and observations emerged from casual conversations with refugees held during these relaxed periods of 'hanging out'. For example, we frequently spent time in Kabingo, a small town close to Nakivale settlement's primary entrance. The research team had heard passing comments by Congolese refugees in Nakivale, describing the trend of Congolese teenagers leaving the settlement to work for Ugandans in neighbouring villages as day labourers. However, no one could help us set up a face-to-face meeting with any of members of this particular livelihood group, who chose to 'hide' amongst their Ugandan neighbours, were guarded, and would—we were assured—avoid contact with outside researchers.

Spending time in Kabingo, however, we became familiar with several small-scale industrial sites around its main street, including one small maize-milling plant. This plant, we sensed, would be a natural first stop for Congolese refugee labourers seeking informal daily work. On this hunch, we entered the plant and asked if any Congolese refugees worked there—one did. We invited this young Congolese man for a drink at Kabingo's local bar after work, a place we occasionally used to conduct interviews in an informal, relaxed setting. Our first interview with the respondent was deliberately unstructured, intended primarily to build rapport. The next evening, our respondent was eager to continue the conversation, and brought along three other Congolese refugee teenagers with whom he boarded. Over the next two hours of animated and wide-ranging discussion, we learned a good deal about the strategies, challenges, and motivations behind this small, hidden community: access we would not have gained had we not 'hung out'.

Participatory Research with Locals and Refugees

Central to our approach was a commitment to conduct research both *for* and *with* members of the refugee communities. We therefore incorporated an ambitious agenda of participatory research elements in the design and direction of our qualitative methods throughout all three phases of research design and implementation.

At the most pragmatic level, participatory research methods can improve access and triangulation of data collection. They are often uniquely well suited to enabling the professional researcher, as an 'outsider', to navigate and grasp the deeper complexities of their research subject's complex, unfamiliar, and often contested reality or realities. This is particularly true in the study of refugees and displaced peoples, where the communities researched are often vulnerable, closed, and fearful of outside examination. Access into such communities is often difficult or impossible without willing local participation to facilitate research processes.

Importantly, participatory research also enables social scientists to play a direct role in confronting and solving challenges within communities they are researching—in essence, 'giving back' to the communities under study. By inviting refugees into the formal research process to share their own subjective realities and propose solutions to their own challenges, participatory research can contribute to positive social change while deepening academic understanding of a social phenomenon.

Although not always easy in practice (Voutira and Dona 2007), facilitating and encouraging the growth of a local refugee partner's skills and self-confidence is one of the most important contributions that participatory research can make, and the link between participatory research and local empowerment for policy and broader social change has been clearly recognized (Gustavsen 2003). In our case, we implemented a research agenda in line with Chamber's call for 'eclectic pluralism' in our participatory methods (Chambers 1996), drawing from a number of established participatory techniques in our qualitative data collection. We discuss several in the following subsections.

Participatory Ranking and Scoring Exercises

We relied, firstly, upon participatory ranking and scoring exercises in our focus group discussions with refugee communities across all research sites. This approach provided valuable new insights into the subjective categories, divisions, and hierarchies with which refugees structure meaning in their economic lives. They also supported our contextualization and analysis of quantitative survey data. As such, we implemented both wealth ranking and livelihood mapping exercises with our focus groups, who were asked to qualitatively evaluate the general socio-economic status of households in their local villages, including their own. The purpose was to build qualitative understanding of refugee livelihoods in the four sites, and of socio-economic differentiation between households, through their own words. The exercises followed research templates and guidance documents prepared for each site. Similarly, we asked participants to list the most common livelihood strategies in their communities and then ranked and scored them by a number of subvariables. This allowed us to begin mapping the diversity of livelihood strategies pursued by refugees in each site, as well as to identify the most important income-generating activities to prioritize for greater case study exploration.

Participatory Mapping

Our research team also carried out transect mapping walks through villages, neighbourhoods, markets, and trading centres, led by local refugee guides. The walks were interspersed with informal one-on-one discussions with UNHCR staff, with refugees who were engaging in their livelihoods, and with refugee stakeholders. Topics included livelihood dynamics and challenges, settlement topography, soil quality, common property resources, and major social and economic challenges.

The transect walk process was as much about watching and listening as it was about asking questions and constructing maps. The participants who guided us through their communities sketched out the contours of their daily economic lives. They showed us where they shopped, the infrastructural challenges they faced, and described their perceptions of commercial boundaries between nationalities and neighbourhoods, critical information missing from available UNHCR maps. We were often joined by curious children and by other community members eager to share their perspectives on livelihoods and daily economy. Transect walks also provided another opportunity to raise our exposure within closed communities.

One particularly valuable methodological innovation which we developed over the course of our fieldwork was our adaptation of participatory market mapping to visualize the value chains and linkages surrounding and contextualizing key refugee livelihood activities. We adapted our market maps from the Emergency Market Mapping and Analysis (EMMA) toolkit, an established technique used by relief agencies to quickly generate knowledge of market systems in disaster zones.[2]

Our market mapping exercises began with the identification of key livelihood activities by our peer research team, who then worked alongside and independently of international staff to gather the data needed to fill in a full market map for their particular livelihood of interest. Once this map was constructed, it was used as a template for both written case study analysis and GIS mapping of the market chain.

---

[2] For the full EMMA toolkit package, see <http://emma-toolkit.org/>.

Participatory Visual Methods

We employed a further number of participatory visual methods for our qualitative data collection. For instance, we worked with refugees to draw out participatory maps of their local communities, highlighting key areas of economic activity, innovative businesses, markets, and trading centres, and other features that were identified by refugees themselves as distinct landmarks of their daily livelihood activities. These maps served the essential functions of not only highlighting the topography of livelihood activities and networks across all three sites, but also of providing a degree of fidelity higher than the limited official mapping data from UNHCR/OPM which we had available.

We also worked closely throughout the project with a young Congolese refugee filmmaker and members of our peer research team in Nakivale to produce several participatory documentary films. This footage not only informed our understanding of livelihoods in the settlement, but provided technical skills training to the filmmaker. Perhaps most importantly, the film provided him an opportunity to document, in his own thematic and aesthetic direction, subtle dynamics of livelihood activity within Nakivale.

Participatory Peer Research

Lastly, our research agenda relied strongly on peer research through the development of a core team of refugee peer researchers who were also study participants.

We based a major facet of our data collection strategy around the contributions of more than forty peer researchers, enumerators, and assistants. Building upon an initial pool of key informants organized during the pre-project scoping phase in 2012, we organized our qualitative research around a core of seventeen peer researchers from the Congolese, Somali, Rwandan, Ethiopian, Burundian, and South Sudanese communities. This core refugee research team was later joined by an additional twenty-two enumerators from the same communities as we conducted our survey in Nakivale, Kyangwali, and Kampala.

Through a rigorous hiring process, we hired peer researchers who were bright, motivated, and professional, who enjoyed positions of trust in their communities, and who had developed wide personal networks upon which they could draw in their work within and across research sites.

We attempted to avoid a common pitfall of participatory research, namely that hastily considered participatory research in unfamiliar communities risks contributing to pre-established power differences, privileging the participation and voices of those who already benefit as a result of their gender, age, nationality, ethnicity, or wealth (Ashby and Sperling 1995). To avoid this, constant discussion, thought, and sensitivity were required during the hiring process as we endeavoured to create a team that balanced its ability to provide us deep penetrative access to closed refugee networks with representativeness. We paid particularly close attention to diversity of the team's members regarding nationality, gender, and age.[3]

Our core team of peer researchers proved invaluable in introducing us, as external researchers, to individuals and networks of economic activity which would have been extremely difficult to locate otherwise. These team members were also strongly encouraged to contribute directly to, and challenge, our own observations with their grounded expertise.

Our peer researchers were also given the responsibility and independence to lead their own self-directed research into key economic activities. We began this peer research engagement with general exercises aimed at generating an inventory of the most common livelihoods in each team member's particular national community. This allowed us quickly to populate a list of economic activity priority areas from which to draw our first round of qualitative case studies. In parallel with intensive periods of instruction on qualitative social research methodology, we tasked our team members with conducting their own research into some of the key livelihoods that they themselves had identified. They arranged and conducted interviews, consulted primary and secondary data, and wrote reports on their findings. These self-directed research projects ultimately contributed to some of our project's most important livelihood case studies, discussed further in the following chapters.

Reflections on the Participatory Research Experience

Adopting a peer research approach allowed us, as external professional researchers, to transfer real and sustainable skills to members of the communities we studied. One of the most rewarding aspects of working with these team members was that as their own research skills developed and they uncovered deeper information about the economic systems which

---

[3] For instance, we attempted wherever possible to avoid an over-reliance on refugee elites, which can potentially reinforce socio-economic disparities in researched communities (Ashby and Sperling 1995). This was particularly true in the settlements where leaders of the local refugee political structures, the Refugee Welfare Councils (RWCs), were recommended by UNHCR as our first point of engagement. Although we did ultimately work with several RWC leaders as core team members, they took part in our research alongside an intentionally diverse range of non-RWC peer researchers and enumerators. We also ensured a diversity of ethnic subgroups among each nationality represented, and a gender balance to ensure both male and female perspectives. The HIP refugee peer research team was also characterized by a wide diversity of professions: youth community leaders, farmers, real-estate brokers, small business owners, religious leaders, former lawyers, community health workers, and students, among many others.

surrounded their own day-to-day lives, they gained new insights into their own communities and their own economic agency as refugees. As a project team, we are proud to have left behind participants now better equipped to articulate their own realities and advocate with their own voice in future. We hope that these relationships will continue, providing an ongoing link to the research communities we intend to maintain even though the project's main fieldwork phase is complete.

Our investment in participatory research also generated opportunities for broader critical reflection on our own subjectivities as researchers, and the strengths, weaknesses, and challenges of implementing participatory peer research in 'messy' real-world research settings. Indeed, many of the struggles which emerged from working alongside our refugee colleagues resonated closely with some of the valid critiques levelled against participatory peer research in the social research methodology literature (Cooke and Kothari 2001).

First and foremost, maintaining such a large peer research team demanded significant investment in resources, energy, costs, and time. Our peer researchers, largely from deprived or marginalized communities, were typically lacking in basic academic skills of writing, interviewing, and analysis. While some of our most successful team members possessed an enthusiasm and local knowledge which went far in compensating for their lack of formal education, the investment in training time to develop their basic research skills proved an unavoidable, recurrent struggle throughout our fieldwork.

Given the serious logistical challenges of covering large distances between each settlement and Kampala, it was also often necessary for refugee research staff to pursue their research tasks with a high degree of autonomy. This arrangement called for, on the one hand, extensive training to ensure proper research methods were followed at all times even without direct supervision of international staff; and on the other, placing a high degree of trust in the delegation of important tasks to these same team members.

We were also forced to routinely confront highly sensitive ethical issues from a team formed of refugees from the same communities under study, particularly those refugee communities with high rates of psychosocial trauma. We thus adopted a cautious approach and tried to avoid prying too deeply into our staff members' 'refugee stories' of displacement into Uganda, even as our professional and personal relationships deepened.

Further ethical challenges involved a duty of care for the personal safety and well-being of our staff operating in an often-fluid security environment. These ranged from temporary work absences due to malaria and road accidents to the death and kidnapping of close family members, and—for several staff who were political exiles—fears of physical harm from foreign intelligence services from their country of origin. Equally, it was our ethical responsibility to ensure we did not make demands of our peer researchers which might place them at risk, such as asking them to brave Uganda's notoriously dangerous traffic, or hike treacherous rural settlement roads that became inaccessible during rainfall.

Other challenges arose from the constant blurring and renegotiation of traditional power relations between the 'researcher' and 'researched' inherent in the peer research model. We were routinely struck by the complex and nuanced ways in which roles and positions of power evolved alongside trust throughout the project.

For instance, we had early on identified several important livelihoods for urban Somalis in Kampala involving 'grey market' activities, including selling illegal digital television subscriptions to friends and neighbours. In an unfortunate coincidence, a businessman whom we had interviewed was arrested shortly thereafter, and upon his release accused the research project of being responsible for the police raid.

Kampala's Somali population was already suspicious of outside intrusion as a result of constant government surveillance following the 2011 Al Shabaab bombings. We were thus extremely concerned that loose rumours of the project's complicity with the Ugandan police, although utterly unfounded, could quickly spread through this tightly knit community, causing undue anxiety for its members, and permanently damaging the hard-won trust our team had diligently cultivated.

Fortunately, the matter was resolved through the intervention of one of our Somali team members, a well-respected youth leader who arranged a meeting to clarify the matter with a senior Somali community elder. By deftly advocating on our behalf through his own social networks, he may have well saved our entire relationship with a community critical to our research. Over the course of one very tense week, we found ourselves dependent on this peer researcher's efforts and reliant on the trust we had built together. This emphasized just how dramatically and quickly classical power relations between the professional researcher and the 'researched' can be inverted in participatory field research, and the critical role of trust in this process.

In another incident which highlighted the importance of trust in participatory research, we met with interpersonal difficulties with a key team member in whom we had placed a significant amount of trust. When he demanded a personal loan unrelated to his project salary, we decided we could not reconcile his request with good research ethics. In response, he became aggressive, resigned his position, actively agitated against our presence in his community, and even threatened another team member.

Our true challenge came when we discovered that this same individual, who was already known by the Ugandan Office of the Prime Minister for Refugees (OPM) and UNHCR as a 'difficult' refugee youth leader, was already at risk of deportation or arrest. Although his disgruntled attitude to the project threatened to erode our hard-won community trust, we realized a public rebuttal from our position of external privilege and influence might place him at risk with the authorities, and thus violate our own ethical principle of 'do no harm'. Fortunately, this individual eventually moved on to other priorities, resolving the incident. However, it remained a sobering lesson in the importance of trust, and the occasional, unavoidable volatility of interpersonal relations, during participatory research.

Ultimately, however, we found that our commitment to fostering a peer research role for refugees was worthwhile. Our refugee team members improved their capacities as researchers, which has left them with skills to explore and describe the realities, challenges, and opportunities of their own communities. In exchange, they have provided us with data of exceptional quality and novelty, which would not have been obtainable without such a participatory approach.

Quantitative Methodology

In addition to qualitative methods, our mixed-methods approach centred on the collection of a rigorous body of quantitative data to compliment and triangulate our qualitative observations. To this end, we conducted a large-scale random survey into the economic livelihoods of 2213 refugee households across all four research sites. To our knowledge, this data set represents one of the largest quantitative data contributions on the economic lives of refugees in the literature to date.

Survey Design

We began our survey by choosing the household as our primary unit of analysis. We chose this as households are the smallest economic units at which resources are shared and managed (Holzmann et al. 2008: 132). Households, particularly in developing countries, also typically function as a single decision-making unit for establishing livelihood strategies and for organizing the economic activities of household members. The economic behaviour of an individual can therefore be best explained in terms of the interests and objectives of the household to which he/she belongs (Kuhlman 1991).

However, *defining* the household, especially in developing regions, is a common challenge for researchers due to the sheer diversity of household formation (Landau 2004; Kandiyoti 1999: 502). A household becomes fluid in mobile populations such as refugee camps, where people are sometimes attached to several households simultaneously and are accustomed to sharing resources with non-family members (Clark 2006: 3). We thus defined 'household' as a loose grouping of people, usually but not always related, who share most aspects of consumption and draw upon a common pool of resources for their livelihood strategies.

Due to limited time and resources, we were unable to include every nationality of refugee present in Uganda in our population of interest. As a compromise, respondent populations were drawn from the largest nationalities in each of our four sites. These included the Congolese, Somali, and Rwandan populations in Nakivale; Congolese and South Sudanese in Kyangwali; Congolese in Rwamwanja; and Congolese, Somali, and Rwandan in Kampala.

We based our initial sampling frame on the most current UNHCR statistics available through UNHCR Uganda at the start of fieldwork. For Nakivale, Kyangwali, and Rwamwanja, data on registered refugees was available at village and household levels. In Kampala, only estimates of the cities' total refugee population were available.

Working from this sampling frame, we calculated minimum sample sizes in each survey site to determine the representative number of households for each nationality of interest to be sampled per site. Working with our statistical consultant, we adjusted our final sample size to compensate for an anticipated response rate of 85 per cent. This approach generated sample sizes of 577 respondent households in Kampala, 732 in Nakivale, 284 in Kyangwali, and 620 in Rwamwanja (see Table 4.2).

We approached our survey questionnaire design only after completing our preliminary phase of qualitative research. This ensured consistency between our emerging understanding of the research context and the structure and

Table 4.2 Surveyed refugee populations by nationalities in each site

Location		Population	Sample size (Households)
Kampala Total		58 167	577
Origin	Congo DRC	26 365	193
	Somalia	14 079	181
	Rwanda	3 967	203
Nakivale Total		68 406	732
Origin	Congo DRC	33 865	252
	Somalia	12 973	237
	Rwanda	9 665	243
Kyangwali Total		21 989	284
Origin	Congo DRC	18 863	142
	South Sudan	2 825	142
Rwamwanja Total*		50 024	620
Origin	Congo DRC*	50 000	620
Total		**198 586**	**2 213**

Source: Data received from UNHCR internal statistics March 2013, not published; *Rwamwanja internal statistics from UNHCR December 2013

content of the survey questions. We divided our overall questionnaire into two key thematic sections:

Survey Section A was designed to capture the general economic behaviours of refugee households in each site and across all surveyed nationalities. The section contained a series of questions capturing data on general household demographics, economic activities undertaken by the entire household, and household members' reliance on, and perceptions of, external aid.

In Survey Section B, we presented questions designed to elicit detailed information on specific livelihood strategies. Most households would employ multiple income-generating means. Our goal was to generate a grounded understanding of the complex dynamics that shape not only refugees' income-generating strategies, but also the networks of economic exchange and interaction between refugees and other actors. As such, we decided that an appropriate compromise was to ask each respondent to select their household's single most lucrative livelihood for detailed analysis.

We term each household's single most important income-generating activity the 'Primary Livelihood Activity' (PLA), and the person who conducts it the 'Primary Livelihood Person' (PLP). By restricting our focus to a single income-generating strategy and a single individual responsible for conducting the PLA, we were able to dedicate the entirety of the questionnaire's second section to eliciting insights into the nuanced market dynamics of buying, selling, employment, and challenges which define a range of key PLAs, as well as detailed behaviour data on the PLPs.

Once we decided on the questionnaire content, a significant investment was made to carefully translate and back-translate this instrument into Somali, Kinyarwanda, and idiomatically appropriate Congolese Swahili. In the case of South Sudanese respondents in Kyangwali, the decision was made to employ Acholi instead of Arabic, as this proved the most universal language spoken within their community. The translation process was developed in consultation with two independent teams of professional translators, refined through multiple rounds of testing with our refugee peer researchers and piloted with respective national communities in Kyangwali, Nakivale, Rwamwanja, and Kampala before implementation.

Sampling Strategy and Data Collection in the Settlements

Due to the significant differences between the urban and rural refugee contexts in Uganda, we employed different sampling strategies for the rural settlements and the urban context of Kampala. These approaches were piloted in each site prior to full survey implementation. In Nakivale, Kyangwalia, and Rwamwanja, we pursued multi-stage stratified interval sampling with proportional allocation.

This process included a randomized selection of villages, and second, random interval sampling of households within each village.

In all three settlements, we began by identifying all villages in the settlement occupied by our target nationalities. This was done using official UNHCR data and maps, but on multiple occasions we came across disputed village boundaries—and occasionally entire villages—which required our research teams to physically verify details in person. Each village was thereafter visited by our enumerators, who checked for the consistency of each village's borders against UNHCR-provided mapping data and demarcated clear boundaries when difficult to determine from existing map data.

Once a total selection of villages was prepared for each settlement, we excluded certain villages from our sampling list: those that posed a serious risk to the safety of our respondents (due to factors such as treacherous roads), those that were physically inaccessible during the period of data collection due to rain, and those which OPM requested we avoid due to sensitive political situations and potential security threats.[4]

In order to disaggregate village populations into the specific refugee nationalities we wished to survey, we next stratified the total refugee settlement population according to their countries of origin across each village, ranking villages in order of the numbers of confirmed refugees from the nationalities of interest. We also eliminated villages which hosted a less than proportionately significant number of households for each national stratum. This allowed us to avoid misallocation of the survey team's time and resources to villages with too small a population of interest. From this reduced list of viable villages, we used a random number generator to sample ten villages per settlement for our enumerators to survey. Lastly, for each nationality, we calculated a target number of households to sample in each of the ten villages per settlement, based on the proportionality of each village's population to the combined total population of all ten randomly selected villages. An example of our sampling methodology for one nationality in Nakivale settlement is given in Table 4.3.

Our enumerator teams began by visiting each village for initial site preparation and mapping. During this process, village contact persons were identified, and appointments were made by refugee enumerators to introduce the aims of the project and obtain cooperation from the village inhabitants. Enumerators were also tasked with preparing and mapping routes through

---

[4] Since some villages had to be excluded for these reasons, we can only draw inferences from survey results about households in excluded villages. We assume that sampled households are representative not only of the population of households in their own villages but also of those in non-selected villages. This assumption is supported by the random allocation of refugees to villages, which prevents households from self-selecting to particular villages. This assumption is consistent with observations made during village on-site assessments and with our qualitative research findings.

Table 4.3 Example of sampling calculations for Congolese refugee sample population in Nakivale villages

Sub-zone	Village	Pv	Targeted collection Sv=[Pv/P(tot)]St	Actual collection
Nyakagando	Nyakagando A	1 978	50	46
Base Camp	Base Camp II	1 822	46	46
Nyarugugu	Nyarugugu B	1 283	32	34
Juru	Kajurungusti	952	24	27
Ngarama	Ngarama B	834	21	23
Lake view zone	Isanja D	642	16	17
Kahirimbi	Kahirimbi B	624	16	15
Lake view zone	Isanja C	502	13	16
Kiretwa	Kiretwa C	498	13	16
Kabahinda	Kityaza B	433	11	12
	P(tot)	9 568	241	252

St = 241. Key: Pv = Village population, Sv = Village sample, St = Target sample, P(tot) = Total population
Source: Data received from UNHCR internal statistics March 2013, not published

each village in order to ensure subsequent interval sampling was limited only to households from their respective target nationality. The enumerator teams were aided in this task by local guides and village chairmen to help facilitate the door-to-door sampling of households.

This preparatory work was often difficult. In addition to physical demands of long days spent comprehensively mapping spread-out villages, the work called for painstakingly detailed discussions with community members and leaders to triangulate regularly conflicting information about village boundaries. We also required in-depth explanations from community members about important nuances in door-to-door sampling that we would otherwise have missed. This was essential, for instance, in explaining how three separate houses belong to the same family and were considered, at the village level, a single home. Our reliance on community members' assistance was a powerful validation of the power of participatory collaboration in survey design.

The actual data collection was carried out via door-to-door interval sampling. Due to the extremely low levels of non-response, the number of sampled households per nationality in each village remained proportionate to the total number of households per nationality in that village. Only those respondents who gave full consent and were over 18 years were interviewed. Again, we faced significant challenges in carrying out data collection which demanded an adaptive approach. Surveying farming communities, for instance, required us to time visits to the hours when farmers were not in the field. Here, again, consultation with village leaders and community members, together with their familiarity from our prior ethnographic qualitative exposure, proved invaluable.

Sampling Strategy and Data Collection in Kampala

In Kampala, we faced the challenge of identifying and reaching refugee households hidden—often by choice—within a much larger city environment. This was particularly true in the case of Rwandan refugees, who did not live in clearly delineated neighbourhoods as a result, in part, of Tutsi–Hutu rivalries within the disapora community, mistrust of Rwandan neighbours tied to fears of undercover Rwandan intelligence activity in Kampala, and the relative ease with which Rwandan refugees could simply claim Banyankole and Bamfumbira ethnicity as Ugandans of Rwandan extraction. Such coping mechanisms had become a popular option in the midst of a formal refugee status cessation process for many Rwandans, which was implemented by government of Uganda during our fieldwork period in 2013.

This 'needle-in-a-haystack' aspect of Kampala's Rwandan refugee community challenged our initial random sampling strategy, which was premised around interval door-to-door sampling of delineated neighbourhoods. A natural solution would have been to engage in 'snowball sampling'; the limitation, however, would have been a loss of rigour in our data, in as we would be forced to give up a randomized sampling strategy in exchange for a purposive, qualitative one.[5]

Searching for a solution to these dilemmas, we turned to respondent-driven sampling (RDS). RDS is a pioneering sampling methodology that has increasingly been used by social science researchers who are trying to penetrate hard-to-reach populations. The method combines the advantages of purposive snowball sampling in penetrating closed communities with a mathematical model that allows for a degree of random rigour in the data collection (Heckathorn 1997).

RDS begins with a core set of respondents from a target population—termed 'seeds'—selected by convenience sampling. These 'seeds' are presented with two or three coupons to give to other contacts from the same population, who are then asked to attend a survey interview in exchange for a small incentive. At the end of their survey, these recruited respondents are themselves presented with their incentive. They are also promised a second incentive for handing out another 'wave' of coupons to another set of respondents from the target population. This process continues through several iterations of 'waves' until the pre-established survey sample size is reached, or until the

---

[5] During this survey period, we also confronted security concerns in the Somali community, in which UNHCR had a 'no-go' area due to reported Al-Shabbab activity. Increased police presence in Kisenyi made many Somalis nervous to speak with outsiders. We had to consider the potential risks to our enumerators' personal security, and the possibility that we might create undue anxiety for the local community through what might be perceived as invasive door-to-door sampling.

distribution of participant characteristics reaches a degree of equilibrium. RDS analysis software then applies a correction for the degree of non-random sampling in the selection of respondents, ideally arriving at a final set of unbiased estimates for the target population.

Meta-analysis of RDS-driven social research projects show that RDS generally represents a promising experimental methodology to maximize randomness in situations where only convenience sampling methods are possible (McCreesh et al. 2012). Debate within the statistics literature does, however, raise several recurrent criticisms of RDS. Statistical inferences drawn from RDS approaches can fail, and confidence intervals are often quite narrow (Malekinejader et al. 2008). Nonetheless, after consultation with statistical experts, we felt that RDS offered a practical solution to reaching hidden Rwandan households within Kampala, while also providing a unique opportunity to test the practicality of a cutting-edge social research method that might benefit our discipline more broadly.

To this end, we followed general RDS procedure in our data collection, albeit with several modifications made necessary by the research context. We first approached our core refugee peer research team to provide several initial 'seeds' from their own personal networks. Each enumerator was assigned the task of generating 'waves' of interviews using these seeds, first contacting the seed to conduct an interview and then asking for two follow-up contacts. Each of these two contacts would then be interviewed and asked to generate two additional contacts, increasing the size of each enumerator's 'wave' of respondents from two to four, four to sixteen, and so on until the total quota for that particular nationality was reached.

To facilitate this process, we made several decisions that deviated from standard RDS practice. First, standard RDS practice calls for coupons to be hand-delivered by one respondent to two or three potential recruits. These coupons should then be carried to the interview in person so researchers can verify the recruits' identities. However, we found this sequence logistically untenable due to difficult traffic conditions in Kampala, the limited money for participants to travel around the city, and an ethical concern regarding the safety of respondents travelling through dangerous traffic conditions in order to participate in our research. Instead, we assigned an individual coupon code to each respondent and collected their phone numbers and family names from referees in advance. The phone numbers and names were then verified against the assigned code at the interview to ensure the participant was in fact the correct individual who had been referred to us.

Second, RDS requires researchers to pay a small incentive to participants to encourage cooperation in referring new respondents. We considered the decision to employ incentives carefully. Beyond the added project costs, using incentives also risks potentially increasing reward expectations within a vulnerable population, with possible knock-on impact for future researchers. After consultation, including discussions with our peer researchers regarding which forms of incentives were the most culturally and contextually appropriate for their particular national communities, we decided to provide small vouchers for mobile phone airtime. In certain circumstances where this was inappropriate, particularly among senior members of the Somali community who might be offended at the perceived 'crudeness' of a direct material reward, we gave our enumerator the option of spending an equivalent amount of petty cash to treat the respondent to lunch.

Enumerator Team Composition and Quality Control

As already discussed, we assembled a team of enumerators from each target nationality to collect data in Kampala and the settlements. This team included core peer researchers, a number of new refugee enumerators, and several Ugandan enumerators with past refugee research experience, with sixteen enumerators in Kampala, eleven in Nakivale, six in Kyangwali, and four in Rwamwanja. Teams underwent a rigorous hiring process and a full month and a half of intensive training. They were guided in each location by a team of three Ugandan research supervisors, while research staff circulated between all four research sites. Enumerators were held to strict expectations regarding daily delivery rates of completed surveys, and were offered bonuses as incentives to achieve survey returns above the expected targets.

We employed several layers of quality control to ensure rigour during all stages of data collection. All enumerators were carefully monitored throughout the workday, and all surveys were thoroughly reviewed at the end of each day—once by our Ugandan research coordinator, and again by our Ugandan research supervisor—before being backed up digitally and uploaded by our data entrant. Data collection procedures and entry quality were also closely monitored on a day-by-day basis by researchers in Oxford to ensure adherence to research protocols. Back in Oxford, researchers also rechecked all hard-copy questionnaires against the full data as a final stage of quality control before any statistical analysis.

Statistical Analysis

Once all questionnaire data had been entered, statistical weighting was applied by a consultant statistician, facilitating inferences across the broader population of each site. We prepared and analysed data using open source R 3.02 statistical software, which generated descriptive and correlative data, as well as a range of multivariate regressions for subsequent analysis (R Core

Development Team 2013). These statistics, alongside qualitative data, inform our analysis in the following chapters. The data was also 'weighted back' to allow us to generalize it across the broader refugee population of each site.

We then conducted both descriptive and inferential analyses. For all survey questions, we calculated population estimates for each of the sampled nationalities in order to describe the general characteristics of economic activities and socio-economic status of each nationality. We also experimented with recursive partitioning, a statistical method for multi-variable analysis that creates classification 'trees' or regression models from an exploratory rather than a hypothesis-driven perspective. We employed this method so as to classify patterns of links between a dependent variable and selected sets of possible independent variables.

Although our research was designed to be exploratory, we also conducted several inferential analyses, focusing on livelihood income and perceptions of dependency on external aid. We analysed the correlation between a household's level of livelihood income and other potential variables, such as use of Internet and mobile phone. These analyses proved a valuable means to test our qualitative observations. We also conducted logistic regression analyses using livelihood income and perceptions of aid dependency as dependent variables. As described later in the book, while controlling village-level clustering, we tested some regression models, for example, against the level of education of the household breadwinner, nationality, age, length of exile, and gender.

Conclusion

The methodological contributions pioneered over the course of this fieldwork include helpful lessons that we feel can inform future forced migration scholarship. Taken together, these represent a range of methods which provide a structured means of exploring the economic lives of refugees. In particular, we hope that our experiences with participatory research might encourage other researchers to adopt a similar commitment to empowering research subjects in the production of knowledge regarding their own realities. We have also raised several important cautions that these same researchers should consider before embarking with too much enthusiasm on a participatory path.

Our experiences in Uganda have also offered insights into ways in which our research methods might be extended in future research. There is great potential for exploring experimental and semi-experimental research designs and we are particularly interested in the use of randomized controlled trials (RCTs). Although the body of forced migration scholarship is relatively small and primarily focused on the evaluation of psychosocial interventions in refugee contexts, preliminary work suggests the potential of RCTs in broader refugee research, as well as some of the challenges in terms of practicalities and ethics (Neuner et al. 2008; Ruf et al. 2010). Quantification of the direct economic impact of refugees on the local and national host economy has also begun to attract attention, but few studies have yet produced results (Enghoff et al. 2010). Lastly, as noted by authors such as McMichael et al. (2014), there remains a notable, generalized gap in longitudinal data on forced migration. There seems to be great potential to combine time series data collection with cross-country data collection to generate panel data relating to the economic lives and impacts of refugees.

5

Urban areas

More than half of the world's refugees now live in urban areas. From Nairobi to Beirut to Bangkok, many refugees choose to move from traditional rural camps or settlements to large global cities. Urban refugees find their way to towns and cities for a variety of reasons, particularly to seek better socio-economic opportunities. Refugee camps generally lack access to higher education and good-quality health care, and refugees who have previously worked in the modern economy often see few prospects for themselves or their children in staying in camps. The trade-off is that in moving to cities, refugees give up almost all access to international assistance.

An increasing amount of scholarship has reflected on the challenges of ensuring refugee protection in urban contexts (Campbell et al. 2011; Crisp et al. 2012; Kibreab 2007; Landau 2014; Grabska 2005). Yet, with few exceptions, existing scholarship has rarely examined the range and diversity of refugees' economic lives within urban areas. Previous studies on urban refugees generally indicate that the livelihood means employed by refugees largely take place in informal trade sectors (see, for example, InterAid 2009; Women's Refugee Commission 2011; JIPS 2013; Enghoff et al. 2010). However, relatively little is known about the diversity and character of those commercial activities, nor about the range of factors that explain variation in refugees' economic activities and outcomes within urban areas.

Uganda's 2006 Refugee Law allows refugees the freedom to choose a place of residence outside the settlements. As of 2013, the city hosts about 58000 refugees, making it the second largest refugee hosting location in Uganda after the Nakivale refugee settlement and home to a quarter of the country's refugee population. Kampala is a melting pot of refugees from more than twenty countries. While Congolese refugees constitute nearly half of Kampala's refugee population, the city accommodates refugees from a variety of countries from across the region, including Somali, Eritrean, and Rwandan refugees.

The economic lives of refugees in Kampala are diverse. Different refugee populations have different settlement patterns, and there is variation in economic strategies across the different nationality groups. For example, most Somalis live in the geographically contiguous Kisenyi area and engage in a range of entrepreneurial activities. The majority of Congolese refugees co-reside with Ugandans in the Nsambya and Katwe areas, being associated with a range of economic activities, especially textile and jewellery making. Oromo Ethiopians are dispersed across the city and are commonly involved in the provision of informal financial services, in particular foreign exchange.

We argue that this urban context gives rise to a particular set of opportunities and constraints. Compared to camp refugees, urban refugees face only minimal levels of refugee-specific regulation. Their situation is much closer to that of nationals and other migrants. Nevertheless, we suggest that there are significant differences that make urban 'refugee economies' analytically distinctive.

Kampala for Refugees

With an estimated population of more than 1.5 million people, Kampala is the largest city in Uganda. Kampala's formal business sector has seen an expansion in the service industry in recent years; tourism, telecommunications, financial services, insurance, and construction are frequently mentioned by Ugandan government officials as the most rapidly growing areas. Beyond the formal sector it also has a large and vibrant informal economy. In the midst of this bustling urban centre, refugees live and work side by side with both Ugandan nationals and a cosmopolitan mixture of migrants from across the continent. The city accommodates refugees from a variety of countries, as shown in Table 5.1.

Table 5.1 Refugee populations in Kampala

Nationality	Number	%
Congolese	26 365	45%
Somali	14 079	24%
Eritrean	7 776	13%
Rwandan	3 967	7%
Ethiopian	2 170	4%
South Sudanese	1 439	3%
Burundian	1 325	2%
Sudanese	766	1%
Other nationalities	280	1%
Total	**58 167**	**100%**

Note: These figures represent only those who are formally registered with UNHCR in Kampala. During the fieldwork, we found that some refugee households who are registered as settlement-based refugees have sent some family members to Kampala, mainly for socio-economic reasons. This phenomenon of dispersing family members is particularly relevant for the Somali refugee population in Nakivale.

Source: Data received from UNHCR internal statistics March 2013, not published

In choosing to live in urban areas, refugees renounce access to almost all international assistance. The assistance programmes provided by InterAid, UNHCR's sole implementing partner (IP) operating in the capital, largely concentrate on refugees' education and protection. Some agencies, such as the Jesuit Refugee Service and the International Rescue Committee, operate livelihood programmes with training in areas such as hairdressing, tailoring, and textile design; however, such interventions are small-scale, serving only a limited number of refugees.

Despite giving up formal assistance, urban refugees benefit from access to markets, infrastructure, and economic opportunities unavailable in refugee camps. Kampala's Owino market, for instance, is the largest market in East Africa, sprawling across a grid of narrow passageways and alleys guaranteed to disorient the first-time visitor. A vast array of products and services are sold here by vendors operating from several hundred stalls and storefronts: among these thousands of products, they sell rice, maize, beans, vegetables, fruits, meats, fish, spices, kitchen supplies, second-hand clothing, shoes, barber shop services, and mobile phone chargers. Every day, tens of thousands of people visit the market, and many of its stalls, as well as those along surrounding roads, are run by refugees.

Such opportunities are reflected in the higher average incomes, and greater inequality, for urban refugees relative to those in the camps. Figure 5.1 shows the income distributions for refugees in Kampala relative to our other research sites.

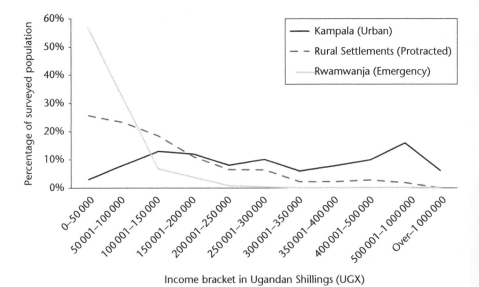

Income bracket in Ugandan Shillings (UGX)

Figure 5.1 Average income distribution by research site (unweighted, in UGX)

Yet urban refugees nevertheless face regulatory challenges. The Ugandan Refugee Act of 2006 formally allows refugees across the country the right to work just like 'aliens in similar circumstances' (Government of Uganda 2006). Interpretation of this, however, is not uniform. Different sectors of government have different views on whether refugees do or do not need to apply for work permits in the country. The Immigration Department interprets this to mean that refugees require work permits, as aliens need work permits to work in the country. On the other hand, the Office of the Prime Minister (OPM) asserts that once a refugee is in the country, she is granted de facto right to work (Women's Refugee Commission 2011: 9).

This inconsistency of interpretation creates varied enforcement of the regulations that guide employment of refugees and often makes employers wary of hiring refugees (Buscher 2011: 25; Macchiavello 2003: 11; Women's Refugee Commission 2011: 9).

The Kampala Capital City Association (KCCA) is the gatekeeper for economic activity in the capital. Refugee entrepreneurs in Kampala, including street vendors, must purchase a licence from the KCCA to set up a business. Registration is, however, expensive. According to the research undertaken by the Women's Refugee Commission in 2011, a licence costs 108 000–280 000 Ugandan Shillings (UGX, about 54–140 USD) depending on the market location, which explains why many refugees keep their businesses unregistered and remain in the informal sector.

A further challenge is access to banking (Women's Refugee Commission 2011: 9). In order to open a bank account, refugees who are formally employed are required to submit a signed letter from their employer with a photocopy of their refugee ID card as a proof of their formal economic status. Self-employed refugees must obtain a recommendation letter from a referee who already possesses a bank account at the same bank.

While opening up a bank account is not impossible for refugees, access to credit is unavailable. According to one Congolese refugee, Ugandan banks do not provide any lending to refugees because refugees are unable to provide property collateral for loans.[1] They are also perceived to be a flight risk. Meanwhile, none of the NGOs provide microcredit programmes.[2] This lack of access to loan programmes, in turn, means that refugees in Kampala need to mobilize their personal or social contacts to draw any finance for building or expanding their income-generating activities.

---

[1] Interview with Robert, a Congolese refugee in Kampala, personal communication, 5 February 2015.
[2] Interview with the senior officer of Jesuit Refugee Services in Kampala, personal communication, 16 August 2012.

Although they are subject to a discrete regulatory framework, refugees' economic lives interact in important ways with the national host economy. Whereas many researchers acknowledge the existence of xenophobia towards refugees in host communities, the levels of discrimination differ in the literature from mild to acute (Sandvik 2011; Macchiavello 2003; Women's Refugee Commission 2011). According to Bernstein and Okello (2007: 48), refugees in Kampala suffer from harsh discrimination in employment sectors and also report concerns relating to their physical security, as well as difficulties in seeking redress when a crime was committed against them.

In contrast, Hovil (2007: 611) writes that in Uganda, the host populations on the whole showed considerable willingness for refugees to engage in economic activity, since refugees were perceived as a net economic benefit to the area. According to an interview with one senior KCCA official who had been interacting directly with refugees since the early 1990s, the tension—while it does exist—generally appears less acute:

> In Kampala, both refugees and locals are in the same markets. So inevitably, there is some competition and tension between them. But I have hardly seen any acute hostility between them such as violence. They seem to be doing OK with each other.[3]

Goods and items bought and sold in the markets often come from across Uganda, as well as from neighbouring countries such as the DRC, Rwanda, Tanzania, and Kenya. Refugees buy and sell in and around these markets. For example, the following is a comment of a Somali refugee who owns a restaurant in Kisenyi:

> I buy rice from Somali traders in Nairobi but I buy all other stuff in Kampala. I receive more than 300 customers per day. So every day, I go to Owino and Kikubo markets to buy meat and ingredients from Ugandan nationals. For vegetables, I sometimes go to Nakasero market. I also purchase soft drinks and water from Ugandan traders.[4]

We asked refugee households to identify the most important category of supplier for their main business activity. As shown in Figure 5.2, regardless of respondents' nationality, refugee households identify Ugandan merchants as the most important supplier of goods and services for their primary income-generating activity. These findings are not surprising, as refugees make up less than 3 per cent of the entire Kampala population. Their access to goods therefore relies heavily on Ugandan suppliers.

---

[3] Interview with the senior KCCA official in Kampala, personal communication, 9 August 2012.
[4] Interview with a Somali refugee in Kampala, personal communication, 25 June 2013. Interview extracts have been transcribed exactly, including disfluencies in English.

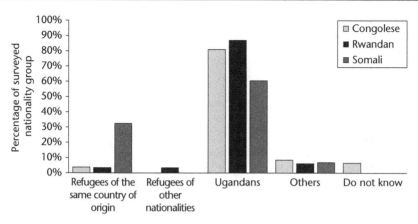

Figure 5.2 Categories of supplier identified as 'the most important' for refugees' primary business

Refugees and locals often provide a source of labour for one another. Some refugees have found employment through Ugandans. For instance, Joanna, a 28-year-old Congolese refugee, had been working as a floor manager at a restaurant owned by a Ugandan in Nsambya:

> I am hired by the Ugandan owner. He doesn't come to the restaurant every day so I am in charge of the daily management. There are three other Congolese refugees and one Ugandan working here as waiters or waitresses.[5]

A considerable number of refugee entrepreneurs rely on Ugandans for staffing and labour in their own businesses. In one of our survey questions, we asked all refugee business owners in Kampala whether they employ anyone from outside their household. Of the 21 per cent who hired from outside of their household, 41 per cent of their employees were Ugandan nationals. In other words, refugees are creating jobs for Ugandan nationals. Such evidence speaks to the contributions that refugees can make to their host economy, a role which many of the refugees we interviewed were notably proud of. For example, over cups of strong Ethiopian coffee, one successful refugee hotel owner explained to us how heavily his business relies on Ugandan staff, including clerks, waiters, cleaners, and cooks:

> I have two lodges in Kampala. In total, there are more than fifty employees. I hire Congolese, Somali, Sudanese, and Ethiopian refugees. But the majority of the employees are Ugandans.[6]

---

[5] Interview with Joanna, a Congolese refugee in Kampala, personal communication, 8 August 2012. The names of some of the refugees have been changed in order to ensure anonymity.

[6] Interview with an Ethiopian refugee in Kampala, personal communication, 12 August 2012.

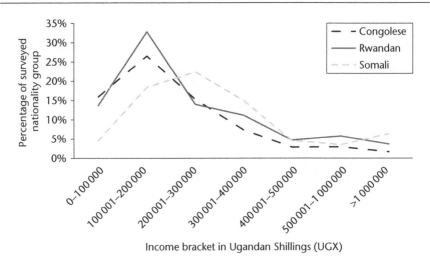

Income bracket in Ugandan Shillings (UGX)

Figure 5.3 Monthly total household income in Kampala

Nationality Matters

Different nationalities fare differently in economic terms in Kampala. This variation in economic outcomes is most clearly exemplified by the differences in average income levels across the groups (Figure 5.3).

Somali Refugees

Most Somali refugees live and work alongside Somali-Ugandans and Somali economic migrants in Kisenyi. The district itself is a maze of roughly two dozen blocks in the heart of central Kampala. Visitors stepping into Kisenyi for the first time are immediately immersed in the sounds, smells, and sights of Somali culture: groups of Somali people chatting in their language on the noisy street, restaurants and shops serving Somali cuisine and rarer delicacies such as camel meat and sour milk, signboards in Somali and Arabic, and calls to prayer at more than ten heavily attended Somali mosques in the area. Meanwhile, other nationalities are more widely dispersed across the city.

Kisenyi has become the seat of a proverbial 'Somali government in exile', the Somali Community Association, which serves as an official representative body of Somali society in Uganda. The Association was founded in 1987 and is formally registered with the Ugandan government. With an overarching aim of 'uniting the Somali to create peace and harmony among the Somalis living in Uganda', it has approximately 13 000 members across the whole country.

The Association collaborates closely with the Ugandan government in the governance of Somali society. For example, during the national census, the Chairperson called upon all Somalis in Uganda to cooperate and participate in the census. It serves as a mediator with police in times of conflict. The Somali community in Kampala also provides some limited public services for the benefit of its members. In Kisenyi, for instance, it runs a number of madrassas—Koranic schools that give Islamic religious instruction to Somali schoolchildren. Normally, the children will go to the Somali religious schools after finishing their normal instruction at their Ugandan schools. As an added benefit, the religious schools generate employment opportunities specifically for Somali refugees, who are employed as teachers, administrators, or service staff.

The community's informal institutional structures shape the economic lives of Somali refugees. Three forms of influence stand out.

First, the Chairperson of the Somali Association urges all Somalis to register their business with the KCCA. The Chairperson explains the rationale for this encouragement:

> We strongly encourage [Somali] refugees to register their business with the government. Even for new arrivals, we ask them to register with the government. In Kampala, the government prohibits non-registered businesses or street vendors. Illegal business is a disgrace to Somali community ... We have been asking clan leaders to financially assist those without money for registration. I think many Somali refugee businesses are now formally registered with KCCA.[7]

Second, they provide a network of support for employment. For example, several large-scale Somali-Ugandan enterprises operate in the oil, petrol, and retail industries and offer employment for a large number of Somali refugees. A senior Somali-Ugandan manager from one of these companies explained to us that while his company has not set a formal policy for helping refugees, hiring Somali employees is nonetheless an uncomplicated decision:

> Somalis have very strong unity. We feel more comfortable working with Somali people because we have a lot in common such as language, religion and cultural habits. Also, there are some levels of mutual trust, so we are comfortable to give more opportunities and responsibilities to Somali refugees in the company.[8]

One Somali-Ugandan-owned oil company alone, City Oil, employs nearly sixty Somali refugees as shopkeepers, cashiers, security guards, and clerks at just one of its more than twenty franchises across the greater Kampala area.

---

[7] Interview with the Chairperson of the Somali Association in Kampala, personal communication, 4 February 2015.

[8] Interview with a senior Somali-Ugandan manager of one of these companies in Kampala, personal communication, 11 August 2012.

Table 5.2 Patterns of employment among refugees in Kampala

Nationality		Self-employed	Employed by others
Congolese	%	95%	5%
	n	110	6
Rwandan	%	78%	22%
	n	151	42
Somali	%	26%	74%
	n	43	123

Note: Figures refer to the number of respondents who belong to each employment category and percentages refer to the ratio of those in the employment category out of the total surveyed households.

Ali, a sales manager at City Oil, arrived in Uganda as a refugee in 2005 after having spent some years in Nairobi. He describes how Somalis leverage their networks to find jobs in the Somali business sector:

> In many cases, Somalis get recruited through their personal or clan contacts. It was not difficult for me to get employed in Kampala. My uncle was already working [at this company] as a chief cashier, and he asked me to come to Uganda and join him. He facilitated my job search.[9]

The result is that nearly 75 per cent of primary income earners from Somali refugee households are employed by other individuals or enterprises outside of their own family, a much higher proportion than our Congolese or Rwandan survey participants (see Table 5.2).

Third, a range of informal social protection mechanisms exist within the community. For example, informal insurance mechanisms known as *ayuto* ('merry-go-rounds') are common practice, particularly among women. Small groups of Somali women come together to contribute a sum of money to the *ayuto* every week or month, depending on the level of their income. These contributions continue for some months until a sufficient pot is collected, at which point the full amount is given to the *ayuto* member deemed to be the most vulnerable in order to help them start a new business. Somali refugees also rely on clan-based and faith-based social protection mechanisms based on forms of Islamic alms-giving, such as *sadaqah* and *zakat*. As one Somali refugee explained:

> As Muslims, every Friday we get an announcement in the Mosque that so and so has a problem. So, contributions in the form of money and in kind are made by the members to help our colleagues to get out of problems.[10]

Our qualitative and quantitative results strongly support the conclusion that Somali refugees conduct their economic lives in a very different institutional

---

[9] Interview with Ali, a Somali refugee in Kampala, personal communication, 25 June 2013.
[10] Interview with a Somali female refugee in Nakivale, personal communication, June 2013.

context from other refugee groups in Kampala. One of our Congolese refugee research assistants, Robert, commented insightfully on the significant difference in internal support mechanisms between Congolese and Somali refugees:

> Somali people are so united! They are religiously and culturally closely tied. Yes, we Congolese refugees help each other but our internal assistance is very small scale. Somali society has a much more systematic support mechanism . . . For example, it is very clear how well new arrivals are received by the Somali community. From the very beginning, their start point is much higher than us.[11]

Refugees from Somalia, therefore, demonstrate a high level of integration into the existing Somali economic systems and into the markets within Kampala, particularly in the formal sector. This network offers a distinctive institutional space within which Somali and Islamic values have been carefully maintained.

Congolese Refugees

Most Congolese refugees in Kampala, for instance, co-reside with Ugandans in the Makindye division, particularly in the Nsambya and Katwe areas. These areas are home to tailoring shops among the dozens of kiosks and stalls lining the unpaved dirt lanes: a speciality associated with Congolese craftsmen, and stalls selling brightly coloured *bitenge*, a traditional Congolese fabric. Congolese churches offer both religious services and initial support, providing temporary shelter for many newly arrived refugees fleeing the DRC. A number of community-based organizations (CBOs), mostly founded by Congolese refugees themselves, offer guidance in Swahili for new arrivals on how to register as asylum seekers and obtain refugee status.

The selling of *bitenge* fabric and jewellery are among the most common income-generating activities of Congolese refugee women. Such small-scale commercial activity is typically referred to as 'petty trade', a useful label in broadly categorizing a wide range of small-scale products sold by informal traders. However, the term obscures the surprisingly complex dynamics that are embedded in such small-scale economic activities.

This street vending is nested in national and global trade chains. *Bitenge*, for instance, is primarily imported to Uganda not only from a wide range of African countries, such as Ghana, Ivory Coast, Nigeria, Tanzania, and the DRC, but also from international producers in China, India, and Holland. Each country produces *bitenge* of varying quality, with Holland supplying the highest-quality fabrics and China the cheapest. Most jewellery sold by the street vendors includes faux-gold imitations that are mass-produced in China

---

[11] Informal conversation with Congolese refugee research assistants in Kampala, December 2013.

and India. Ugandan merchants fly to Beijing, Delhi, and Dubai to purchase these products in bulk. They are even referred to as 'suitcase importers' for their practice of packing as much jewellery into their suitcases as possible before flying back to Uganda.[12] Some authentic Congolese jewellery continues to enter Kampala via the DRC and tends to be of higher quality than the Chinese equivalents. This flow, however, is much smaller and limited to occasional pieces that are hand-carried into Uganda by Congolese merchants.

Congolese refugees gravitate to the sales of *bitenge* and jewellery for two main reasons. First, many members of the Congolese refugee community in the city lack the initial capital to build larger-scale, formal enterprises, and this is particularly true for female refugees.[13] The up-front investment needed to begin selling *bitenge* and jewellery is relatively small (about 20000 UGX, equivalent to roughly 10 USD), which proves attractive to Congolese refugees as a low-entry, informal business.[14] Second, while the low entry barrier is also common to other types of small-scale trading, positive stereotyping of Congolese craftsmanship among Ugandans provides a helpful market opportunity. There is a perception among Ugandans that due to the DRC's vast natural resources, Congolese people themselves, including refugees, may have access to gold and other high-quality minerals. DRC-produced *bitenge* fabrics are viewed in a similar way, as these textiles are traditionally of very high quality.

In their daily rounds, these Congolese refugees find mutually beneficial economic links with Ugandan merchants. They purchase their jewellery stock, for example, almost entirely from Ugandan retailers and wholesalers in a large shopping complex near Owino market. The complex, 'Gazaland', is a vertiginous four-storey building packed with roughly thirty-five crowded shops selling jewellery. The shops are predominantly owned by Ugandan 'suitcase' merchants, who display wholesale jewellery they have purchased from China, India, Dubai, and the DRC in glass cases and small piles of plastic bags.

These Ugandan merchants have come to rely heavily on Congolese refugees, who act as the primary distributors and retailers for their products. As one of the Ugandan jewellery shop owners in Gazaland explained, 'Congolese people are the most important customers for me. I receive about 100 retail buyers per day. Seventy of them are Congolese refugees.'[15] Another Ugandan merchant whom we spoke with was very passionate about Congolese refugees' positive contributions in the jewellery sector in Kampala, explaining, 'we rely

---

[12] Interview with James, a Ugandan jewellery merchant, personal communication, 3 August 2013.
[13] Interview with Helen and Mary, two Congolese *bitenge* sellers, personal communication, 23 July 2013; interview with Ruth, Sarah, and Grace, Congolese jewellery sellers, 23 July 2013.
[14] Interview with Amelia, a Congolese refugee in Kampala, personal communication, 15 December 2013.
[15] Interview with James, a Ugandan jewellery merchant, personal communication, 3 August 2013.

on the Congolese'.[16] Gesturing to the rest of the Gazaland complex, he noted that 'these jewellery shops wouldn't exist without the Congolese vendors'.[17] As a further example of the importance of this relationship for merchants, many of these shop owners also employ one or two Congolese refugee women to help facilitate their daily sales with refugee customers.

As for other vendors in Kampala, the KCCA's prohibition of street trading and non-registered business are major constraints to Congolese *bitenge* and jewellery hawkers. These strict regulations, however, have encouraged refugees to find new ways to avoid government patrols. Female hawkers may choose to escape patrols by venturing into further-away Ugandan towns such as Mbarara, Masaka, Kaseseye, or Hoima, and even over the borders with South Sudan, Kenya, and Tanzania. Leaving the capital city generates important advantages for refugee vendors: demand tends to be higher in these cities and towns where access to imported jewellery and fabrics is limited; there is less competition from other hawkers; and refugees are able to sell on the street without equivalent interference from local authorities. Whereas these 'sales trips' entail lodging and transport costs, the profit margins are often higher, particularly in South Sudanese border towns like Kaya, where demand for these goods is particularly high.[18] As their mobile selling strategies show, Congolese refugee women are working to expand markets throughout Uganda as key distributors.

Refugee street vendors navigate dynamic and competitive markets, and as a result they tend to be extremely conscious of fluid shifts in the demand for their products. Amelia, a Congolese refugee hawker selling *bitenge* and jewellery, has been involved in this business in Kampala since 2008. She described how one recent market trend has shaped the sale of these products in the capital:

> Some Ugandan hawkers have started selling *bitenge* and jewellery in Kampala. The number is small, but it may increase competition in the city... But recently, we found a lucrative market. We now often go to Busia in Kenya [a border town with Uganda on the Kenyan side]. There are many business people there.[19]

Rwandan Refugees

A particular constraint faced by Rwandans has been ongoing persecution by the country of origin. Many Rwandan refugees continue to live in fear of the

---

[16] Interview with John, a Ugandan jewellery merchant, personal communication, 3 August 2013.
[17] Ibid.
[18] Informal conversation with Congolese refugee research assistants in Kampala, December 2013.
[19] Interview with Amelia, a Congolese refugee in Kampala, personal communication, 15 December 2013.

government. In contrast to Congolese and Somali refugees, Rwandan refugees deliberately live in a dispersed pattern throughout Kampala to avoid the attention of both the Ugandan and Rwandan governments. One of our Rwandan refugee research assistants explained this as follows:

> We want to remain invisible. If we are concentrated in a specific area, we will definitely attract attention from others...We know the Ugandan government is very close to the Rwandan regime. The government of Rwanda is searching and monitoring those against the regime even in exile. Rwandan Intelligence Services are all over in Kampala...Other refugee groups live together for security but it doesn't apply to Rwandans...[20]

The concerns of Rwandan refugees are not unfounded; Rwandan intelligence services acting in Uganda and throughout East Africa have targeted Rwandan refugees with documented acts of abuse, kidnapping, and harassment (Betts and Jones 2016). This has a knock-on effect on refugees' economic activities. For instance, a number of Rwandan refugees all echoed that there is no 'Rwandan refugee community' in the capital because Rwandans are suspicious of other Rwandans. Anyone might be an undercover intelligence agent tasked with monitoring them. Mutual support mechanisms among Rwandan refugees are underdeveloped. Many Rwandan vendors are afraid to be found out and arrested by KCCA officials. This seems to reflect a belief among Rwandans that once their identity is revealed to the local municipality, they will be reported to the Rwandan government by the Ugandan government.

Rwandans therefore mainly work in the informal sector as traders, dealing in second-hand clothing and shoes, a choice facilitated by the opportunities provided by their own distinct networks with wholesalers of Rwandan origin in Kampala. Former Rwandan refugees, who fled to Uganda in previous decades, and have gained Ugandan citizenship, offer openings for Rwandan refugees to sell used clothing and shoes in the informal markets across Kampala.

Rwandans from this industry explained that there are three main groups of actors in the used-clothing business.[21] Upstream, there are a handful of major wholesalers that import used clothes directly from their contract partners in Europe, North America, China, and India. There are also a good number of retailers who have their own shops in commercial buildings or have secured selling space. Owino market is particularly known for the sale of used clothing. Retail owners normally buy their stock from wholesalers in large quantities. Downstream, there are the vendors who move in and around Kampala to sell their items, which they purchase mostly from retailers in small volume.

---

[20] Interview with a Rwandan refugee in Kampala, personal communication, 11 December 2013.
[21] Interview with Emelia, a Rwandan refugee in Kampala, personal communication, 15 December 2013.

Almost all of the wholesalers and retail shops are formally registered with KCCA, but the vast majority of street venders remain unregistered, like the Congolese *bitenge* and jewellery hawkers.

Emelia, a second-generation Rwandan refugee, runs one of the largest wholesale shops of used clothes in Kampala. She highlighted for us her long-term involvement in this industry:

> My father first came from Rwanda to Uganda in 1959 as a refugee but now he has Ugandan citizenship...He started selling second-hand clothing in Kampala. He retired some years ago so now I am running this business. There are some other wholesalers owned by Rwandans. I think our shop is one of the largest dealers in Kampala...Many Rwandan refugees buy from us. We receive twenty to thirty customers every day and three to four of them are Rwandans [refugees].[22]

Emelia's office was located on the second floor of a tall commercial building near Owino market, which is fully occupied with numerous shops. She took us on a tour of her office, a big storage space piled floor-to-ceiling with packed bags of used clothing imported from Germany, Canada, the US, the UK, and India. During our conversation, she occasionally pointed to Rwandan refugee retail buyers who were negotiating the price with the sales manager of her shop.

Unlike Emelia, the vast majority of Rwandan refugees involved in the used clothing business are street vendors who purchase small bundles of stock from the retailers and the move on foot around Kampala to sell to customers. Fred, one such Rwandan refugee hawker, explained how he entered this business in Kampala:

> I chose this business because many Rwandans were selling used clothes. I was working for an NGO in Rwanda, so I did not know anything about clothing. I learned how to do this business by looking at others...I go to Owino market and buy cloth from Rwandan dealers there. I don't have my own shop, so I move around busy streets and major markets in Kampala to find customers...Most of my customers are Ugandan nationals. If I have a very good day, I have about fifteen customers per day and make about 30000 UGX profit. But on a bad day, I get a few customers and only make 10000 UGX profit or even less.[23]

Recent KCCA regulations require street vendors to register and purchase trading licences in order to conduct any business in the city. Few Rwandan hawkers can generate adequate financial capital to afford these licence fees. Without a formal licence, they have to elude the eyes of KCCA patrols to avoid confiscation of their products by the government officers. Fred explained how

---

[22] Ibid.
[23] Interview with Fred, a Rwandan refugee in Kampala, personal communication, 14 December 2013.

he and many other street vendors spend their work day constantly on the move to avoid being arrested by KCCA:

> The [KCCA] officers come and try to arrest us. It is hard to predict when they come to which areas. I avoid going to the same selling place again and again. I move around different areas in Kampala. Sometimes I call other hawkers to check [whether KCCA officers are around or not]. But if I see them [KCCA patrols], I grab my stuff and immediately run away.[24]

Ethiopian Refugees

Thousands of Ethiopian refugees live in Kampala, and many of them pursue livelihoods working in restaurants, lodges, beauty salons, and in housekeeping.[25] However, one particular feature is ethnic specialization; FOREX bureaus are run almost exclusively by the Oromo, a specific Ethiopian ethnicity.

The academic literature acknowledges that shared ethnic origins can play the role of 'migrant-supporting institutions' (Massey et al. 2008: 43). These connections can play a significant role in a refugee's choice of income-earning strategy. Ethnic clustering in certain parts of economic sectors or labour markets is already well known. Early immigrants from a particular place of origin may discover job opportunities in a sector and then generate recruitment chains that bring other members from the same ethnicity into the sector (Logan et al. 2003: 345). While such migration theories apply to refugees, the Oromo presented our team with a much more nuanced picture of economic specialization.

At about thirty million, the Oromo constitute the single largest ethnic group in Ethiopia, or more than 30 per cent of the national population. Despite being Ethiopia's largest ethnic group, the Oromo have been dominated and repressed by the minority tribal group, the Amhara, who have monopolized the country's key political and economic posts for many decades. In response to a series of oppressions including forced relocation and military conscriptions, many Oromo have sought refuge in neighbouring countries, including Uganda.

For us, it was much more difficult to research the economic strategies of Oromo people than those of other Ethiopian refugees. Oromo refugees were extremely cautious regarding any communications with non-Oromo Ethiopians; for instance, our Ethiopian refugee assistant, who was not of Oromo origin, was utterly unable to penetrate the Oromo community, perhaps because of continuing tensions from the pre-displacement period in Ethiopia. Only after a well-known Oromo gatekeeper was employed by us were we gradually able to begin to elicit interviews with Oromo refugees in Kampala.

[24] Ibid.
[25] Informal conversation with Ethiopian refugee research assistants in Kampala, 19 February 2013.

Our interviews allowed us to learn that Oromo refugees began to set up FOREX businesses during major displacements in the 1980s. We interviewed several Oromo owners of FOREX companies, and none of them had been involved in any type of financial business before their arrival in Uganda. Ali, owner of three FOREX bureaus and an Oromo himself, traced the origins of this niche industry for us back to his own arrival in Uganda:

> I am one of the very first people who started FOREX bureaus among Oromo people in Uganda. I came to Uganda in the early 1980s. I remember at that point, there were only a few FOREX businesses in Kampala, and many people were changing money in the black market. I thought there would be big demand for money exchange services.[26]

According to Ali, other Oromo refugees began to 'copy' this business format, and FOREX gradually spread among the Oromo community. Ali continued:

> I first hired several Oromo refugees in my FOREX. Later some of them started their own FOREX. There are at least eight owners of FOREX bureaus who used to work at my place. Some of them now have even bigger ones than mine![27]

Idosa, another Ethiopian refugee of Oromo background, used to work at Ali's FOREX in the early 1990s and started up his own bureaus. When we asked him why he chose this line of business, he replied:

> Between 2001 and 2006, I worked at Ali's FOREX. I learned how to run this business from him, so I decided to start my own FOREX . . . I thought this business would be promising. Kampala is a crossroad of East Africa and a common pathway for so many traders. They are always with foreign money.[28]

Whereas the duplication of popular businesses by co-nationals is widely acknowledged in the migration literature, FOREX operate in an economic sector with very high entry criteria. Money exchange requires a special licence, and the business is strictly regulated by the Central Bank of Uganda. All of the Oromo FOREX bureaus that we encountered were formally registered with the government. The cumbersome application process for FOREX licences involves: (1) finding 50 million UGX (about USD 25 000) as a deposit; and (2) providing evidence that the business has an independent and safe office structure. Only after these criteria are fulfilled will the Central Bank assess an application and decide whether it will issue a licence. In this sense, money exchange services are at the opposite end of the spectrum from informal small-scale trading, which requires very little initial capital.

---

[26] Interview with Ali, an Ethiopian Oromo refugee in Kampala, personal communication, 23 June 2013.
[27] Ibid.
[28] Interview with Idosa, an Ethiopian Oromo refugee in Kampala, personal communication, 21 June 2013.

As we learned more about the painstaking procedure of beginning a FOREX business, we were curious to know why Oromo people, specifically, would pursue such a capital-intensive industry which necessitates such stringent assessments by the Ugandan authorities. Ali's and Idosa's comments about the prospective market gap for such businesses only seemed to be part of the answer. With such significant financial capital required to start a FOREX business from scratch, some non-Oromo Ethiopian refugees whom we interviewed in Kampala implied that FOREX bureau owners might be connected with the Oromo Liberation Front (OLF), a political organization initiated by Oromo nationalists to promote self-determination for the Oromo in Ethiopia.

According to these suspicions, many leaders of the OLF are dispersed all over the world, especially in North America and Europe, but remain closely tied to the Oromo in East Africa. Without any direct evidence to draw upon, these non-Oromo Ethiopian refugees told us that they suspected FOREX owners might have received initial capital from OLF members living in the industrialized West. FOREX businesses might therefore be a financial resource for a whole Oromo society. Given the high sensitivity of this topic, with the OLF being labelled as a terrorist organization by the Ethiopian government, we chose not to pursue this line of enquiry further. Nonetheless, this nuanced comment from a senior Oromo FOREX owner gave us reason for pause:

> We Oromo people have to face many handicaps in our life. In Ethiopia, Oromo had many challenges with other ethnic groups and the Ethiopian government. The majority of the country's land belongs to Oromo but we have not been given any political power and voice under oppression by the government. We never had an Oromo president in Ethiopia though we occupy the largest group in the country. This is why we founded the Oromo Liberation Front in 1973 to solve our plight. We need to unite and cooperate in order to survive abroad.[29]

From this and related examples, our team found evidence that the proliferation of FOREX business as a niche Oromo livelihood is likely to have been shaped by cultural or ethnic norms beyond individual pursuit of profit. During our interviews with Oromo owners of FOREX businesses, they continually emphasized the solidarity, bond, and unity among Oromo people: 'No Oromo should suffer.'[30] Often, they described their priorities not in terms of profit maximization, but as contributing to the wider Oromo community's welfare.

This may lend some explanation as to why Oromo FOREX brokers have readily accepted and facilitated other Oromo entering into the same business as competitors. When we asked Idosa whether he felt challenged by competition

---

[29] Interview with a senior Ethiopian Oromo refugee in Kampala, personal communication, 27 June 2013.
[30] Interview with Haider, an Ethiopian Oromo refugee in Kampala, personal communication, 29 June 2013.

with other Oromo running FOREX businesses in this relatively niche market, his response was emphatic:

> Oh no! There is strong solidarity in Oromo society! We don't exclude other Oromo entering this business. We say 'No Oromo can beg others.' We don't want to see any Oromo in misery...Also, the FOREX business needs cooperation for our mutual benefits. For example, if I don't have much USD, I will have to buy it from other FOREX.[31]

The example of Oromo money exchange businesses is not statistically significant for the entire Ethiopian refugee population in Kampala. However, it does provide an illustrative case example that demonstrates how economic activities can be deeply 'ethnicized' and shaped by different institutional resources even within the same nationality.

The Role of Networks

One of the key features of urban refugee economies is the degree to which they are nested within the larger national economy as well as wider transnational networks. Social networks play a crucial role. Access to transnational networks is an especially important factor that seems to differentiate degrees of success between refugees' economic strategies. However, some nationalities have more economically significant social networks than others.

Somali refugees are the most well-networked population within Kampala. Somali entrepreneurs often capitalize on well-established Somali trade networks, which extend far outside Uganda to neighbouring Kenya and as far as Dubai, Pakistan, Saudi Arabia, and India (Campbell 2005).

Mohammed, a Somali refugee, owns a registered retail shop with a wide range of supplies on sale. His well-stocked shelves featured a mixture of typical Ugandan products and hard-to-find, specialist goods popular with Somalis, ranging from dried spaghetti to hair and beauty products. Mohammed explained to us that his business is supplied through both Ugandan merchants and his Somali trade contacts abroad:

> It depends on the items. I buy some food stuff from Ugandan traders in Kampala. But I import basmati rice from Somali agencies in India and Pakistan...I buy tuna cans, pasta, canned milk, cosmetics from Somali traders in Eastleigh, Nairobi.[32]

---

[31] Interview with Idosa, an Ethiopian Oromo refugee in Kampala, personal communication, 21 June 2013.
[32] Interview with Mohammed, a Somali refugee in Kampala, personal communication, 22 June 2013.

The Somali diaspora in particular, play a key role in Somali entrepreneurship (Lindley 2010: 105–6). During our fieldwork, we frequently observed economic connections being established between refugees in Kampala and their diaspora communities in the West. During an interview with Ahmed, a Somali restaurant manager in Kampala, we discovered that the owner of the restaurant is a Somali former refugee who resettled some years ago.

INTERVIEWER: How is your restaurant business?

AHMED: This is not my restaurant. I work here as a general manager.

INTERVIEWER: Who owns this restaurant?

AHMED: The owner is a Somali guy who currently lives in Canada. He got resettled there.

INTERVIEWER: Where did you meet him?

AHMED: I know him from my time in Somalia.[33]

We also found that links with Somalis in wealthier Western countries also equipped refugees with substantial access to remittance support. As noted earlier, refugees in Kampala have very little access to formal loans because they often cannot provide the necessary collateral, legal documentation, and character references. Whereas the majority of refugees in Kampala have struggled to secure initial capital for their enterprise, our interviews and quantitative survey both showed that Somali refugees have utilized their extensive connections with the diaspora to draw financial support. In the main streets of Kisenyi, we observed a number of money transfer businesses congested with (apparently) Somali people. The quantitative survey supports this observation, returning that Somali refugees have a much higher level of access to international remittances than other refugee groups in Kampala. Figures 5.4 and 5.5 show that more than 50 per cent of Somali respondents are the consistent beneficiaries of overseas remittances, with the most frequently remitted amount being between 200001–300000 UGX (about 100–150 USD) per month.

In Kampala, this greater access to remittances and loans from the West often enables Somali refugees to embark on substantial, lucrative businesses. Our interview with Hassan, a 24-year-old Somali refugee owner of a well-stocked supermarket in Kisenyi, illustrates how international money transfers helped him to open up his popular enterprise.

INTERVIEWER: When did you start your business?

HASSAN: I started this shop in 2011.

INTERVIEWER: How did you secure the start-up capital to start such a big shop?

HASSAN: Some of my family members are living in the UK. My brothers remitted me to start this business.

---

[33] Interview with Ahmed, a Somali refugee in Kampala, personal communication, 11 August 2012.

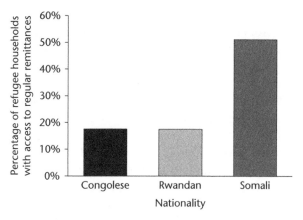

Figure 5.4 Percentage of refugee households with access to regular remittances

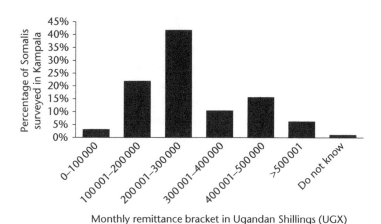

Figure 5.5 The monthly average amount of Somali remittances

INTERVIEWER: How many customers do you receive per day?
HASSAN: 100 to 200 customers per day, I cannot count the exact number because there are too many.[34]

Although Hassan never revealed the exact amount of money he received from his brothers as initial capital, we can easily imagine that the amount was reasonably substantial, given the size and scale of his business.

Better access to transnational networks, coupled with a robust ethnic unity, appear to be key factors that help to explain the better economic status of

---

[34] Interview with Hassan, a Somali refugee in Kampala, personal communication, 11 August 2012.

Somali refugees vis-à-vis other refugee groups in Kampala. Yet other populations also benefit from important national and transnational connections. We found that a number of Rwandan urban refugees have found economic opportunities by taking advantage of their ethnic affinity with co-nationals involved in Uganda's cattle and dairy farms. This employment takes them far outside Kampala to the heart of the country's dairy businesses, particularly Mbarara and Kabale, near the border with Rwanda.

A good proportion of these farms are owned by Ugandan nationals of Rwandan Tutsi origin, who came to Uganda as refugees after the 1960s and subsequently gained Ugandan citizenship. Many Rwandan refugees—largely Tutsi—therefore capitalize on their ethnic and cultural commonalities with farmers, travelling from Kampala in order to seek employment as cattle keepers and farmhands. The work is often seasonal, with Rwandan refugee farm workers splitting their year between the farms in the countryside and other pursuits in Kampala. Others commute back and forth from rural Uganda to the capital. As such, many such Rwandan refugees themselves reject a dichotomous categorization as pursuing wholly 'urban' or 'rural' livelihoods.

Charles is a 20-year-old Rwandan refugee of Tutsi origin. He came to Uganda when he was 11 years old and now works as a cattle keeper on a small farm in Gomba District. His opportunity for employment came about through a combination of good fortune and cultural and linguistic affinity with the farm's Banyankole owner. As Charles explained:

> I grew up around cattle in Rwanda, and I know them very well. In Uganda, I began by walking cows from Gomba farms to the abattoirs in Kampala, then eventually saved enough to buy cattle and bring them to auction or slaughter in Kampala for sale...It was at a cattle auction that I met my current employer. It helped me get the job because he was Banyankole and I was Rwandan, and we both spoke Kinyarwanda. He wanted to hire me.[35]

The milk which Rwandan farm workers like Charles help to collect is distributed to Kampala via a country-wide network of dairy collection points and processing centres. Rwandan refugees also own many shops in Kampala that specialize in dairy products, such as yogurt and cheese.[36] Both ends of this major Ugandan industry can be linked clearly to the urban Rwandan refugee population. Ishmael, a Rwandan refugee owner of a dairy store in Kampala, explained:

> Many Rwandan refugees are working in the dairy industry in Uganda. There are many Rwandans living in Mbarara, Kabale, Kiboga. You will see many dairy farms in

---

[35] Interview with Charles, a Rwandan refugee in Kampala, personal communication, 22 June 2013.
[36] Informal conversation with Rwandan refugee research assistants in Kampala, June 2013.

those areas ... I started this small shop in Kampala a few years ago. I am buying all dairy products from a Rwandan farm owner in Mbarara.[37]

Rwandan-run dairy shops sell the same milk, ice cream, and yogurt products as hundreds of identical, Ugandan-run businesses across the city. However, we encountered one niche product that only Rwandans provide in the Kampala dairy market: a specialty drink known as *kiviguto*, made from sour, unpasteurized ('raw') milk. The drink has gained popularity among Ugandans, and as Ishmael noted in our interview with him: 'more and more, others, Ugandan people, are buying [our product of Rwandan origin] *kiviguto'*.

With farm workers constantly on the move between Kampala and rural areas, our survey with Rwandan refugee households did not always account for the rural activities of those dairy workers. However, a substantial number of interviews conducted with Rwandan refugees in Kampala demonstrated the existence of this substantial institutional space, which takes advantage of ties with Rwandan co-nationals living outside the capital city.

Conclusion

Different groups of refugees have constructed their economic lives differently in response to the particular institutional context of being urban refugees in Kampala. In Uganda's largest urban centre, where nearly two million people live, refugees' economic lives are absorbed into a wider market economy. Their economic lives are largely shaped by similar conditions to the wider non-refugee population. Nevertheless, as we have argued, there are a range of ways in which, even in urban areas, refugees lead distinctive economic lives.

As we have argued in Chapter 3, three defining features shape the institutional contexts of 'refugeehood' in economic terms; namely, refugees' patterns of engagement with formal and informal sectors; with national and transnational spaces; and their relationship to the state and international organizations. In Kampala, similar to non-refugee populations, refugees' economic activities take place both in formal and informal economic spaces. Refugees identify their best survival strategies along a spectrum of formality, adopting particular modes of economic incorporation that enable them to best use their skills and assets.

Refugees' economic lives in Kampala are shaped by wider geographical spaces beyond their immediate urban environment. Various types of networks play an important role in linking refugees with different spaces. Rwandan

---

[37] Interview with Ishmael, a Rwandan refugee in Kampala, personal communication, 14 December 2013.

refugee workers at dairy farms seek their livelihood opportunities outside the capital, although they are formally registered in Kampala. Brokerage businesses are common because they enable refugees to make use of their simultaneous access to markets in their country of origin and in Uganda. In other words, they create opportunities for arbitrage. While all of the communities use transnational networks within their economic strategies, Somali refugees appear the best-positioned, given their close ethnic ties and far-reaching diaspora communities around the world.

It is also evident that a number of institutional actors, beyond the Ugandan state and international organizations are involved in moulding refugees' economic lives in Kampala. Concerning the official regulatory environment, refugee economies in Kampala take place under similar contexts with non-refugee populations. The state authority—namely KCCA—sets out Kampala's regulatory framework to which all economic actors need to conform. On the other hand, KCCA's interpretation and implementation of law varies across populations and it is sometimes applied more restrictively to refugees. For specific groups of refugees like Oromo and Somali refugees, informal governance structures at the community level significantly affect the nature of their economic activities. Furthermore, the government of refugees' countries of origin sometimes seeks to exert extra-territorial influence over refugees' economic lives, as demonstrated with examples of Rwandans in Kampala. Perhaps, this is one of the most distinctive differences that represents 'refugeehood' and reinforces the need for a different interdisciplinary approach for understanding the economic lives of refugees.

What distinguishes Kampala from the rural refugee camp environments in the rest of the book is the wider market-based opportunities to participate. Urban refugees are nested within much broader economic structures. In Kampala, they broadly have the right to work and freedom of movement, making them in many ways less distinguishable from nationals and other migrants. Nevertheless, economic life in urban areas is still subject to distinguishing features that create unique sets of opportunities and constraints for refugees and means they stand apart from the wider population. The way in which refugees transcend these institutional constraints or even transform them into opportunities varies between and within particular nationality groups. It is shaped by communities' own social networks and social capital, as well as the entrepreneurship and human capital of individuals.

6

Protracted refugee camps

Over half of the world's refugees find themselves in so-called 'protracted refugee situations', having been in exile for five years or more (Loescher et al. 2008). Protracted refugee situations can arise in urban or rural areas, but for the most part they are characterized by long-term encampment in rural areas with limited access to services and opportunities.[1] One of the tragedies of many such situations is that refugees are often 'warehoused' without the right to work or freedom of movement. In Uganda, at least, refugees within settlements do have these opportunities. Unlike self-settled urban refugees, however, settlement refugees in Uganda live in a context of tighter regulation by the state and international organizations.

In this chapter, we extend our analysis of refugee economies from the urban context to Uganda's two largest refugee settlements, Nakivale and Kyangwali. The former has existed since 1959 and the latter since 1989. Both settlements are located in the south-west of the country and host an array of different nationality groups. They are formally designated as 'settlements' rather than 'camps' because of their relatively open layout and the economic freedoms afforded to refugees (Svedberg 2014). Upon arrival, refugees in both settlements have historically been given access to a plot of land to cultivate, which can be used for both consumption and commerce.

Over time, both settlements have evolved to take on many of the characteristics of a city, with vibrant economies. They challenge many of our preconceptions about refugee settlements. Life for many refugees remains challenging, but our research findings in this chapter describe an environment of complex economic interactions, interconnected to both national and transnational economic networks. We found that an array of different

[1] In this book, refugee 'camps' and 'settlements' are used interchangeably. There are no standard criteria classifying them. In general, while refugee camps refer to dwelling in a temporary manner, settlements are used to describe long-term permanent settings (Schmidt 2003). But even this difference is not always applicable in the naming of refugee camps or settlements.

businesses and income-generating activities coexist alongside international assistance. While farming activities dominate both settlements, neither one can be understood as a simple agricultural economy. Furthermore, while most refugees spend the majority of their time within the settlements, a whole range of movement in and out of the settlements—of goods, services, and people—is an important characteristic of camp life.

In order to explore the complexity of these settlement economies, the chapter is structured as follows. First, it provides an overview of the economies of Nakivale and Kyangwali settlements. Second, it highlights variation in economic outcomes across communities. Third, we examine how the settlements are embedded in broader economic relationships. Finally, we explore the role of refugee agency in transforming institutional constraint into opportunity. Overall, this chapter argues that even in protracted refugee camps, refugee economies are often nuanced, complex, and deeply connected to wider national and transnational processes.

Refugee 'Cities'

Both Nakivale and Kyangwali settlements have long histories connected to a series of past protracted refugee situations. Nakivale was founded in 1959— one of the oldest refugee camps in Africa—to accommodate the influx of Rwandan refugees who fled the country following the 'Hutu Revolution' of 1957. Since then, Nakivale has opened its gate to large numbers of people uprooted by civil war and persecution. It is now a melting pot of refugees from the Democratic Republic of Congo, Somalia, Rwanda, Burundi, Ethiopia, Eritrea, and other neighbouring countries.

Nakivale is remote. The sprawling settlement lies near the Tanzania border in Isingiro district, Southern Uganda, an hour's drive from the district capital of Mbarara along twisting, bumpy dirt roads. Although different sources give varying figures for the size of the settlement, it is estimated to be well over 100 square kilometres. This enormous area is divided geographically into three administrative zones, Base Camp, Juru, and Rubondo, which contain between them a total of seventy-four individual villages.

Although a much 'younger' settlement than Nakivale, Kyangwali still has more than twenty years of history. It was established in 1989 to receive refugees primarily from Rwanda, followed by Congolese refugees in the late 1990s. It is located in Hoima district in Western Uganda near Lake Albert, the natural boundary between the DRC and Uganda. Like Nakivale, the physical size of the settlement is substantial, occupying over an estimated 90 square kilometres and divided into fourteen villages.

Kyangwali is also remotely located. The journey from the district hub of Hoima to Kyangwali easily takes a few hours along a rugged dirt road. The closer one gets to the settlement, the tougher and more uneven the road becomes. During a rainy season, the main path within a few kilometers of Kyangwali becomes almost impassable, trapping vehicles, minibuses, and motorbikes in a 'muddy sea' impeding entry and exit for residents and visitors.

Both settlements differ very much from the expectations of a first-time visitor who might imagine harshly gated, prison-like refugee camps. For one, a clear physical delineation between the settlement and the surrounding community is surprisingly difficult to identify. In Nakivale an old wooden gate, hand-operated by a local villager, is one of only a few signs indicating the geographical boundary differentiating this long-standing home for refugees from Ugandan villages.

Nakivale and Kyangwali settlements are also deceptively picturesque, even pastoral. Visitors to Nakivale pass by the banks of Lake Nakivale into an immense open plain of tall green grass; they must carefully avoid muddy traps and bunches of grazing Ankole cattle on the way. Near the entrance to Kyangwali settlement, tea gardens shimmer with shiny fresh leaves and offer a refreshing shock of green after hours on the dusty road from Hoima.

While all visitors should in theory obtain a formal permission letter from the Ugandan authorities to enter the camps, we observed that this is not strictly enforced by the OPM. We observed Ugandans from the neighbouring areas entering and leaving the camp areas freely. Indeed, we later discovered that a significant number of Ugandans visit refugee settlements daily from neighbouring villages and cities such as Hoima, Mbarara, and Kampala to sell and purchase products and services. These interactions play a central role in the economic life of many refugees in both settlements.

At the start of our study, we chose Nakivale and Kyangwali as study sites because they were the two largest refugee settlements out of the eight hosted in Uganda. In 2013, more than 68 000 refugees resided in Nakivale, and about 22 000 refugees in Kyangwali.[2] In Kyangwali, 86 per cent of the settlement's population are Congolese, reflecting its proximity to eastern DRC, followed by South Sudanese (12.8 per cent) (see Table 6.1). Nakivale is a more diverse melting pot: refugees from the DRC constitute nearly half of its population, and the rest is made up of Somali, Rwandan, Burundian, Eritrean, and Ethiopian refugee groups, as well as refugees and asylum seekers from other minority nationalities. As in Kampala, we chose to focus our research on the largest national refugee populations in both settlements: Congolese and

---

[2] Data received from UNHCR internal statistics March 2013, not published.

Table 6.1 Refugee population by countries of origin in Kyangwali and Nakivale settlements

Kyangwali		
Nationality	**Number**	**%**
Congolese	18 863	86%
South Sudan	2 825	13%
Rwandan	242	1%
Other	59	0%
Kyangwali Total	**21 989**	**100%**
Nakivale		
Nationality	**Number**	**%**
Congolese	33 865	50%
Somali	12 973	19%
Burundi	10 200	15%
Rwandan	9 665	14%
Eritrean	1 212	2%
Ethiopian	290	0%
Other	201	0%
Nakivale Total	**68 406**	**100%**

Source: Data received from UNHCR internal statistics March 2013, not published

South Sudanese refugees in Kyangwali and Congolese, Rwandan, and Somali refugees in Nakivale.[3]

The demographic data for both settlements, however, cannot be taken at face value due to the difficulty of accurately counting these mobile populations. For example, some refugee households send family members to Kampala, mainly for socio-economic reasons. Our interviews revealed that almost none of these 'divided' households reported this to the UN refugee agency in order to maintain their larger food ration.

Not all settlement inhabitants, furthermore, are refugees. Though not included in the UNHCR statistics in Table 6.1, a number of Ugandan nationals live inside both settlement sites. Ugandan staff members of UNHCR implementing partners (IPs) indicated that most of these Ugandan villagers were already residing in the settlement before its foundation or have since moved into the area despite prohibition by the Ugandan government.[4]

Over decades of prolonged exile, some groups of refugees have also moved out of the settlement and integrated into neighbouring host communities. We learned from interviews with officials of the local district council in Nakivale that many Rwandan refugees who came into the settlement during the early phase decided to move out of the camp and establish an independent economic base outside the settlement area. Some of them were intermarried

---

[3] Ibid.

[4] Interview with a UNHCR officer in Kyangwali settlement, personal communication, 25 February 2013.

with the local Banyankole people and are no longer identified as Rwandan refugees.[5]

Both settlements are administered by an on-site settlement management team reporting to the Office of the Prime Minister (OPM), and are led by the Ugandan Settlement Commander. Under the auspices of OPM, each settlement is officially represented by selected members of the refugee population, who form the settlement's Refugee Welfare Councils.

Refugees in the settlements have a considerable degree of freedom of movement, provided that they obtain prior travel permission from the settlement authority. One OPM officer whom we interviewed in Kyangwali settlement explained this process.

INTERVIEWER: Do refugees have freedom of movement?

OPM: Yes, they do. The only thing they need to do is to get a written permission from OPM, which can be issued immediately upon request. They normally need one day in advance.

INTERVIEWER: Why do they need a permission letter to go outside the settlement?

OPM: This is not to restrict their movement but to protect them. Refugees can be harassed or troubled outside the settlement. We don't want them to face such problems. Also, if refugees miss verification or food ration while they are out, with this letter, they get a second chance to access them.

INTERVIEWER: Can refugees go outside Uganda?

OPM: No, they cannot. The permission letter from OPM applies only inside Uganda with specified date and place for specific purpose.[6]

As discussed in Chapter 5, Uganda's Refugee Act of 2006 establishes that refugees have the right to work just like 'aliens in similar circumstances'. In principle, this also applies to settlement-based refugees. In both settlements, OPM's understanding that refugees can work without a permit appears to have prevailed, and almost all their commerce activities are informal and non-registered. While the Kampala municipality patrol was a constant threat to refugees doing business informally in the city, our research found no analogous entity constraining their activity in the settlements. Instead, local districts paid little attention to whether or not refugees' business activities in and around the settlements were formally registered with local government.

---

[5] Interview with the local district council near Nakivale settlement, personal communication, June 2013.

[6] Interview with an OPM officer in Kyangwali settlement, personal communication, 23 February 2013.

We also observed that this attitude appears to be changing gradually across Uganda and will come back to this issue in Chapter 7.

Compared to Kampala, where refugees are granted very little aid, refugees in both settlements usually have better access to support from aid agencies. UNHCR and the Ugandan host administration employ a so-called Self-Reliance Strategy that aims to encourage rural refugees to achieve self-sufficiency in food acquisition within five years.[7] This approach involves a gradual reduction in the volume of food rations that refugees are entitled to over a period of five years, with each household progressively matching the short-fall by establishing their own sustainable food acquisition strategy.[8] One senior UNHCR officer in Kyangwali described the process for us: for the first two years after arrival, refugees receive the full 100 per cent of a food ration, which will be reduced to 60 per cent from the third year and 50 per cent from the fourth year until the food ration is completely withdrawn in the sixth year.[9]

In addition to free food rations, some livelihood assistance is provided by UNHCR's various Implementing Partners in both settlements. During our fieldwork in 2013, the Nsamizi Training Institute for Social Development and the American Refugee Committee were the two main IPs providing livelihood support in Nakivale. At the time of the study, Nsamizi was tasked with providing technical assistance for refugee farmers to enhance their own agricultural productivity, particularly raising livestock and cultivating honey. Nsamizi also provided training in non-agricultural income generation skills, including phone repair, catering, tailoring, and soap making. However, this type of vocational training was small in scale and had not yet achieved much progress in diversifying refugees' income sources.[10] By comparison, African Action Help (AAH) was the sole UNHCR IP operating in Kyangwali settlement as of 2013. The head of the livelihood and environment unit of AAH explained that as one of the central livelihood assistance providers, the organization was running an agricultural support programme to enhance refugees' food security.

Importantly, within these livelihood support initiatives, no UNHCR IP in either settlement provides any type of loan facility for refugees. This was confirmed in our interview with the same Nsamizi Training Institute officer:

[7] Interview with a UNHCR officer in Kyangwali settlement, personal communication, 25 February 2013.

[8] Refugees who fall into the category of 'vulnerable', however, are except from this policy and receive full rations regardless of the years spent in the settlement.

[9] Interview with a UNHCR officer in Kyangwali settlement, personal communication, 25 February 2013.

[10] Interview with a Nsamizi Training Institute officer in Nakivale settlement, personal communication, 20 March 2013.

> There is no microfinance support in the settlement . . . Refugees are mobile people who are not expected to stay in Uganda for good so it is hard to give loans to them . . . This is a big challenge for refugees who want to start new business or expand their existing business.[11]

In turn, this would have a powerful impact in shaping the Kyangwali and Nakivale settlement economies as refugees turned to informal or communal mechanisms to meet their financial needs.

Over decades of hosting new waves of refugees, the geography of both settlements has been gradually transformed, taking on increasingly 'city-like' features. Among Nakivale's three large zones, Base Camp Zone acts as the settlement's 'administrative capital', being home to a concentration of central offices including UNHCR, its IPs, and OPM. A commercial district has also established itself within Base Camp and includes several trading hubs. These are the Isangano trading centre, the larger Rwandan commercial area known as 'Kigali', and a Congolese hub for business known in the settlement as 'New Congo'. The vibrant Somali refugee population living in Base Camp plays an especially important role for economic activity in this area, as we will explore further. Sizeable markets also exist in Juru and Rubondo zones, although both are served by Base Camp's central markets.

Among Kyangwali's fourteen villages, Kasonga village—located at the entrance of the settlement—serves as an administrative area with offices maintained by OPM and other refugee-supporting agencies. On the other hand, Kagoma village, which hosts the largest weekly market, functions as Kyangwali's most vibrant business area. Here, like in Nakivale's trading hubs, refugees from diverse nationalities sell their own crops, goods, and services to one another, as well as to Ugandan nationals.

We found that most other zones and villages in Nakivale and Kyangwali are largely considered residential and farming areas. In contrast to the 'town-like' administrative and commercial areas situated along major roads close to the markets, these agricultural and residential areas include farmland with structures made mostly of wood and mud, often covered by UNHCR tarpaulins and decorated throughout with colourful doors made from USAID food ration packaging. We observed that economic activities here predominantly included small-scale commerce, such as selling surplus agricultural produce from a wooden table.

With the emergence of demarcated residential/agricultural and business areas within the settlements, our research found that many refugee residents have moved from one area of the settlement to another. Our qualitative research strongly suggested that refugees have undertaken this type of 'intra-settlement migration' in order to access better economic opportunities and

---

[11] Ibid.

more favourable institutional spaces. While refugees are assigned a residence by OPM on arrival, the personal preferences and economic backgrounds of refugees are not taken into account during the allocation process.[12] We found that refugee business people and traders who have been allocated land in farming or residential districts have therefore often moved to the commercial districts.

Emebo, a male Congolese refugee research assistant in Nakivale, is one such example. Although given land in a rural village, he moved to the Base Camp Zone in order to be closer to the Congolese commercial district known as New Congo. As he explains:

> When I came to Nakivale, my family was allocated a land in Nyakando village. It is very far from Base Camp and very bushy. People are scattered. There are no major markets or trading centres [inside the village]. It is OK for farming but our family has never done farming…So we moved to New Congo last year and now live there. I have a small retail shop dealing with daily merchandise. There are many more customers here [in New Congo].[13]

Many other Congolese refugees whom we interviewed in Nakivale indicated that Emebo's experience is by no means unique. Our interview showed that New Congo—with a sizeable market, location close to the road, and proximity to Ugandan traders—frequently attracts Congolese refugees from urban backgrounds who do not have farming experience.[14] Many of these refugees are educated to secondary level and beyond, including teachers, medical doctors, and government officials in the DRC.

Intra-settlement migration is common. Many of those who are given a plot in remote and rural villages relocate towards Kasonga and Kagoma, where there is greater economic activity and availability of customers, including Ugandan villagers and staff members working at aid agencies. From our interviews in Kyangwali, we learned that two distinct patterns define this intra-settlement type of movement. Like Emebo in Nakivale, some families may relocate an entire household into a commercial zone. Alternatively, we found that some refugees rent a shop space in a business area and commute to their place of work from a home in an assigned village. This is a viable option only for those whose assigned residences are relatively closely located to a commercial district.

In other words, a relative form of urban–rural migration is observable even within refugee settlements, with business districts in Nakivale and Kyangwali

---

[12] Informal communications with UNHCR officer in Nakivale settlement, personal communication, 11 March 2013.

[13] Interview with Emebo, a Congolese refugee in Nakivale settlement, personal communication, 15 November 2013.

[14] Informal communications with Congolese refugee research assistants in Nakivale settlement, personal communication, 1 December 2013.

attracting influxes of refugees who are seeking better economic opportunities. This demarcation of economic areas within the settlements, in turn, indicates the growth of an internal settlement economy, where some refugees living in distant villages travel to the commercial districts and buy items to sell in their own villages.

Somali Exceptionalism

Faced with limited international assistance, refugees in both settlements still create their own means of income generation through a wide diversity of livelihood strategies. Figures 6.1 and 6.2 show the five most frequently pursued livelihoods among refugees of each major nationality in Kyangwali and Nakivale settlements during our study period.

Given access to arable land, commercial farming is the most common economic activity for all refugee populations. The crops grown by refugees consist primarily of maize, beans, sorghum, cassava, and potatoes. This concentration of commercial agriculture as a primary livelihood is higher in Kyangwali than in Nakivale, which may relate to the better accessibility of fertile land in the Kyangwali area. Many refugees have also pursued farm work as employees of Ugandan farm owners or wealthier refugee neighbours. In both settlements, our team frequently observed that Ugandan large-scale farmers have employed refugees as temporary workers within and outside of the settlement boundaries.

Despite some variation, the dominant livelihood activities for the Congolese, Rwandans, and South Sudanese are agricultural. The exception to this is

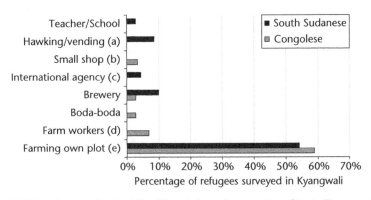

Figure 6.1 Most frequently cited livelihoods by refugee nationality in Kyangwali

Notes: Percentages refer to the ratio of those people engaged in the specific livelihood out of the total surveyed households.
(a) not owning any shops; (b) petty trading of household merchandise; (c) working for UNHCR, an implementing partner, or NGO; (d) works for another's plot for money; (e) for selling

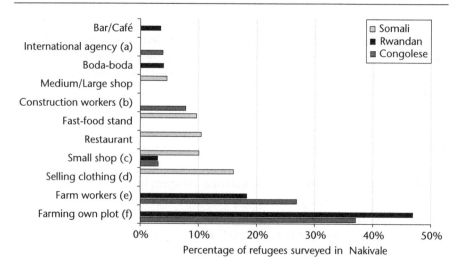

Figure 6.2 Most frequently cited livelihoods by refugee nationality in Nakivale

Notes: Percentages refer to the ratio of those people engaged in the specific livelihood out of the total surveyed households.
(a) working for UNHCR, an implementing partner, or NGO; (b) or brick makers; (c) petty trading of household merchandise; (d) including textiles, shoes, or accessories; (e) works for another's plot for money; (f) for selling

Somali refugees, who refuse to engage in farming activities. The Somalis regard agriculture to be a culturally foreign concept.[15] Most Somali therefore tend to rent out their allotted farm plots to other refugees and instead engage in other forms of commercial activity—in particular through operating small shops, restaurants, and fast-food stands.

This Somali exceptionalism has an impact on the economic geography of Nakivale. The 'Somali Village' of Base Camp 3 represents a hive of commercial activity, attracting refugees from across the settlement. As in Kisenyi—a Somali-concentrated area in Kampala which is discussed in Chapter 5—an informal Somali governing body monitors much of this activity. While the Nakivale Refugee Welfare Council is an official representation of all refugees in the settlement—and is recognized by UNHCR and OPM—the Somali refugee community's 'Committee of Elders' consists only of senior Somali refugees. As with the Somali Community Association in Kampala, the Committee serves a mediation function when any tensions within Nakivale's Somali communities emerge. Like its counterpart in Kampala, the Committee also serves as a key gatekeeper to the Somali community in Nakivale: our research on Somali

[15] It is important to note that even within the Somali community, not all refugees pursue business over agriculture: the exception is 'Bantu Somalis', a distinct ethnic group descended from Central African Bantu migrants who moved to Somalia several centuries ago, and who today primarily pursue agricultural livelihoods in Nakivale.

refugees in the settlement required not only official permission by the OPM, but also necessitated the Somali Chairperson's personal authorization.

The presence of distinctive Somali institutional structures, nevertheless, does not necessarily mean their complete segregation from the rest of the settlement's refugee populations. Mr Abdi, one of the Somali community leaders whom we interviewed in Nakivale, was keen to emphasize his community's amicable relationship with other refugees:

> We [Somali refugees] concentrate in Base Camp 3. But we are not isolated from other refugees. We participate in the Refugee Welfare Council and other events in the camp. We also buy food from other refugees. Other refugees buy goods and items from Somali shops. There are a lot of interactions and interdependence between us. We are living in harmony with other people here.[16]

Base Camp 3 is replete with specialized commercial activities that are not as readily available in other business districts throughout Nakivale. These include shops selling electronics, pharmacies, and FOREX bureaus. Our team noted that some Somali-owned shops in Base Camp 3 tend to be noticeably larger and more sophisticated in terms of the range of merchandise they sell by comparison to equivalent shops run by non-Somali refugees elsewhere in Nakivale. We discovered that partnerships between Somali refugees have played a significant role in facilitating this level of organization. In one example, Amina is one of the 'shareholders' of perhaps the biggest retail shop in Nakivale. She commented on how she had initiated this enterprise:

> I began this business with four other Somali people in 2012. They are all refugees living in Nakivale... We put together our money to start this shop. I am responsible for running the shop. Others take care of buying things from Kampala... It is an equal partnership so we divide all costs and profit by five of us.[17]

This type of shareholder system, where a business is owned by several Somali refugee investors, provides advantages in terms of scale, resources, and diversification of risk. We found that these arrangements go beyond the physical boundaries of Nakivale—some include investors not only from Base Camp 3 but Somali refugees living in Kampala and even members of the diaspora in the West.

As this example suggests, the Somali refugee population in Nakivale routinely seems to negotiate an identity that includes both 'rural' and 'urban' characteristics. During our research, we came across Somali refugee households that had divided themselves between Kampala and Nakivale to

---

[16] Interview with Abdi, a Somali refugee in Nakivale settlement, personal communication, 14 March 2013.
[17] Interview with Amina, a Somali refugee in Nakivale settlement, personal communication, 18 November 2013.

make the most of economic opportunities, often sending economically active
male members to Kisenyi in Kampala to benefit from interactions with the
wider Somali economy. Conversely, the more vulnerable members of the
household, such as the elderly, children, and disabled and ill, remained in
Nakivale, where they could access the humanitarian assistance that UNHCR
only offers in the settlement. The following interview with Mohamed illustrates this type of decision-making. He is a Somali refugee who owns a retail
shop in Kisenyi, Kampala, but is formally registered as a resident in Nakivale
settlement. We interviewed him at his retail shop in Kisenyi:

INTERVIEWER: Are you living with your family now?

MOHAMED: No, my wife and a daughter live in Nakivale. I myself am registered there.

INTERVIEWER: Where do they live?

MOHAMED: Base Camp 3.

INTERVIEWER: Why did you leave Nakivale?

MOHAMED: In Kampala, I have much better access to markets and business
opportunities. Nakivale is too small with too few people.

INTERVIEWER: How is your family in Nakivale?

MOHAMED: They are doing OK. They receive food ration.

INTERVIEWER: How often do you meet them?

MOHAMED: I only go there once in a while. But I remit some money from my
sales here every 1–2 months.

INTERVIEWER: Why don't they come and join you in Kampala?

MOHAMED: Rent! And other living costs! Living in Kampala is expensive![18]

These 'split households' are navigating and leveraging two institutional
spaces—Kampala and Nakivale. Mohamed continues to explain why not all
Somali refugees venture to Kampala:

> In Kampala, everything is on your own. Food, house, electricity, school . . . Not all
> Somali can afford them in Kampala on their own . . . But if you keep some of your
> family members there [in Nakivale settlement], at least they can benefit from free
> support. Others can go to Kampala for work and send back some of their salary to
> the camp. There are many families like us.[19]

We also encountered a significant number of Somali refugees registered in
Nakivale, especially young men, who work for large-scale Somali oil enterprises
in Kampala such as City Oil and HAAS. For all of these families, their primary
income-generating means is not inside the settlement but in Kampala.

---

[18] Interview with Mohamed, a Somali refugee in Kampala, personal communication, 24 June
2013.
[19] Ibid.

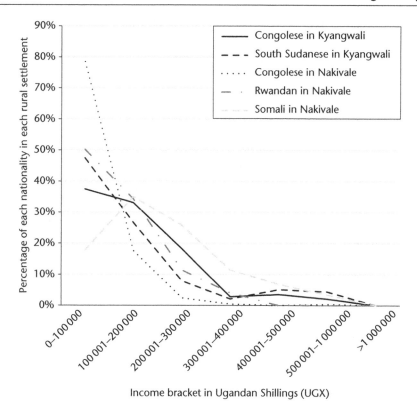

Figure 6.3 Monthly total household income in rural settlements by nationality

Note: Percentages refer to the ratio of those in the income category out of the total surveyed households.

These different types of economic strategies across nationality groups in turn appear to translate into variation in average household incomes across nationality, with Somalis in Nakivale having significantly higher average monthly income levels (Figure 6.3).

Import and Export Economies

Refugee camps or settlements do not exist in a vacuum. Both Kyangwali and Nakivale are far from economically isolated sites. There is almost constant movement of goods and services in between the settlements, to the surrounding villages, local cities, and Kampala.

The settlements frequently attract Ugandan traders and 'middle men' who play an important role in facilitating these exchange networks. For example, farmers living in neighbouring villages bring and sell their fruits or vegetables at commercial markets inside the settlements. Ugandan fishermen bring fish from Lake Albert to sell in Kyangwali.

However, as well as selling products, Ugandans also visit the settlement markets to purchase products or services that are not available in their home villages. Mary, for example, is a Congolese refugee who came to Uganda in 1999 and runs a bicycle repair shop in Kagoma village in Kyangwali:

INTERVIEWER: Who are your main customers?

MARY: Both Ugandans and refugees.

INTERVIEWER: How many customers do you receive per day?

MARY: About ten customers per day. Half of them are locals.

INTERVIEWER: Where are these locals from?

MARY: They come from Bukinda and Rugashari villages [local villages near Kyangwali settlement].

INTERVIEWER: Why do they come to your shop?

MARY: These villages don't have similar shops like mine. Bicycles are important transportation means for some locals but they cannot buy these items in their villages.[20]

Mary's comments suggest that local villages near Kyangwali settlement may be scarcely populated, offering little commercial activity beyond farming and animal husbandry. In the absence of lively local economies, a significant number of Ugandan villagers rely on markets and businesses operating from inside the settlements to procure their everyday products and services.

Many of the well-established shops in both Kyangwali and Nakivale buy goods from existing supply chains run by businesses in Hoima, Mbarara, and Kampala. Ugandan wholesalers regularly come to the settlements and sell goods to satellite shops, which in turn sell them on to other refugee residents across the settlements.[21] Peter, a Congolese refugee who runs a major beverage business in Kyangwali, describes his relationship with his key suppliers, which include well-known Ugandan beverage companies such as Nile Brewery and Pepsi:

I am mainly selling beer and soda inside the settlement. For soda, I buy from Pepsi branches and for beer, I buy [from] an agent of Nile Brewery in Hoima . . . In every month, I normally buy about 600 crates (1 crate = 25 bottles) per month . . . I sell to both locals and refugee retail sellers in the settlement. In this [settlement] area, there are very few wholesalers of beverage like me. Many Ugandans living in and around the settlement come here to buy from me.[22]

[20] Interview with Mary, a Congolese refugee in Kyangwali, personal communication, 17 May 2013.

[21] See Brees (2008) for similar findings in Thailand.

[22] Interview with Peter, a Congolese refugee in Kyangwali, personal communication, 17 May 2013.

When we interviewed a sales manager working for the local Nile Brewery agent in Hoima, he emphasized the importance of his company's links with the Kyangwali settlement market:

> We distribute Nile Brewery items to more than 200 contractors in Kyangwali district. Kyangwali camp is one of our important selling points. In Kyangwali, we have seven refugee shops that we sell our items to. Twice a month, we go to the settlement and distribute 300–400 crates of beverage to these shops.[23]

We also observed similar commercial arrangements between Ugandan wholesalers and refugee shop owners for a wide range of household items, such as drinking water and stationery. The Ugandan wholesale suppliers whom we interviewed confirmed that they usually sell goods to refugee retailers at the same price as to Ugandan retailers.

Our study yielded further evidence of refugees' economic activities being embedded in much wider Ugandan networks and economies outside the settlements. Kyangwali settlement, nicknamed 'the food basket of Hoima', is widely known among Ugandan crop traders for its good-quality maize. Ugandan trucks and minivans regularly travel out of Kyangwali's main road during the harvest season, loaded high with sacks of maize purchased from refugee farmers. Ronny, one Ugandan crop wholesaler in Hoima, spoke to us about his business and the interactions between Ugandan buyers and refugee famers in Kyangwali:

> Since 1998, I have been buying crops from Kyangwali settlement. During the harvest season, I visit Kyangwali frequently...My main trading crop is maize and 60 per cent of my maize stock is from Kyangwali...Last year, I think I bought 500 tons of maize and beans from Kyangwali.[24]

These Ugandan buyers transport maize for sale in district markets in Hoima, further on to Kampala and other Ugandan cities, and even into neighbouring countries. Ronny continued:

> I re-sell maize to many people. Inside Uganda, I sell to traders in Kampala, Arua, Gulu, and Nebbi...Outside Uganda, I sell it to traders in Tanzania and South Sudan. I have twenty regular customers in Tanzania and ten in South Sudan...[25]

In addition to Ugandans travelling to the settlements to buy and sell goods, a significant number of refugees take advantage of relatively permissive

---

[23] Interview with a sales manager of a local agent of Nile Brewery in Hoima, personal communication, 16 May 2013.

[24] Interview with Ronny, a Ugandan crop wholesale trader in Hoima, personal communication, 16 May 2013.

[25] Ibid.

regulations governing their freedom of movement, entering neighbouring villages or towns to seek income generation opportunities.

During our research in Nakivale, we stayed in Kabingo, the small local village located directly in front of the main settlement entrance. Here, we occasionally encountered groups of young refugees (mostly in their later teenage years or early twenties) who had left Nakivale to engage in ad hoc work for Ugandan employers. These refugee 'commuters' had very little financial capital, and as such they were not able to afford long-distance mobility from a remote settlement area to larger cities such as Mbarara, let alone Kampala. Silva, a Congolese refugee youth leader living in Kabingo, describes one such arrangement:

> In Kabingo, there are a number of [young] Congolese refugees. Most of us work as casual labours, mainly for Ugandan farmland owners. Sometimes, we do construction work here. I also worked as a teacher at some elementary schools. We often get better cash payment here [than working inside the settlement].[26]

We also observed refugees in the settlements who seek business opportunities further afield, travelling several hours by road to the nearest largest commercial centres from Nakivale and Kyangwali. In Mbarara and Hoima (the district hubs of Mbarara and Hoima, respectively), daily economic life for rural refugees displays some similarities to the dynamics of urban livelihoods explored in the preceding chapter. On some crowded streets near major markets in Mbarara, for example, refugee hawkers sell colourful *bitenge* fabrics and gold jewellery that catch the eyes of pedestrians. As in Kampala, the *bitenge* merchants do not have permanent business stalls or shops, but sell their products on foot throughout the town. Emma, a Congolese refugee registered in Nakivale, has been living a mobile life between Mbarara and Nakivale since 2011.

> Nakivale is not easy. I have five children to feed but there are few profitable business chances inside the camp...I buy jewellery from Ugandan traders in Kasese and sell it in Mbarara...All of my customers are Ugandan nationals. I receive around ten people in one day...There are so many Congolese refugees selling jewellery like me in Mbarara.[27]

During our research in Mbarara, we also encountered many mobile Congolese refugee vendors who had ventured from Kampala to escape KCCA patrols on 'sales trips' to this largest commercial hub in Western Uganda. We spoke to one such vendor, Fatima, a female Congolese refugee registered in Kampala, who explained this reasoning:

---

[26] Interview with Silva, a Congolese refugee in Kabingo, personal communication, 14 March 2013.
[27] Interview with Emma, a Congolese refugee in Mbarara, personal communication, 4 December 2013.

INTERVIEWER: When did you start selling jewellery in Mbarara?

FATIMA: I started coming to Mbarara around 2012.

INTERVIEWER: Why do you come and sell in Mbarara?

FATIMA: In Kampala, KCCA is always on patrol to catch street vendors. But here [Mbarara] is much more relaxed.

INTERVIEWER: Where do you purchase your jewellery?

FATIMA: Gazaland, near Owino.

INTERVIEWER: How often do you come to Mbarara?

FATIMA: Usually twice a month.[28]

Despite a formal prohibition against crossing the Ugandan national border, we also encountered refugees from the settlements who moved back and forth between their settlement and country of origin in the pursuit of business. James is a Congolese refugee who has been in Kyangwali since 1997 and sells clothing in Kagoma village.

INTERVIEWER: Where do you buy clothing?

JAMES: I buy them from Kampala and DRC and sell in the settlement.

INTERVIEWER: What clothing do you buy from DRC and Kampala?

JAMES: I buy *bitenge* from DRC and other clothing from Kampala.

INTERVIEWER: How do you buy *bitenge* from DRC?

JAMES: I go to DRC every month. I buy them from Congolese traders in Bunagana, North Kivu. I was born in this village and it is also a border town between DRC and Uganda. It is a two-day trip.[29]

Among these types of trade networks, Somali economic networks were frequently more organized, systematic, and extensive than those of other refugee nationalities. Nearly half of the Somali business owners would regularly 'import' products including milk, canned food, pasta, camel meat, clothing, cosmetics, and medicines to Base Camp 3 in Nakivale from relatives living in Kampala. Similarly, Somalis in Kampala would buy products from their network contacts in Nakivale, including *digir*, a lentil favoured in Somali cooking, and some food products provided by UNHCR/WFP (World Food Programme) as free food rations. Maize, a staple food in East Africa, is unpopular among Somalis, who prefer pasta and rice. As a result, maize rations received by Somalis are routinely sold to Somali distributors or 'middlemen', who in turn sell them to their business counterparts in Kisenyi. When the food ration is sold, Somali refugees whom we interviewed explained that they might use the cash earned for some other investment, or to buy other products or services.

---

[28] Interview with Fatima, a Congolese refugee in Kampala, personal communication, 13 December 2013.
[29] Interview with James, a Congolese refugee in Kyangwali settlement, personal communication, 17 May 2013.

We also encountered evidence of the extensiveness of Somali trade networks from rural Nakivale to international locations both in surrounding East African countries and far beyond. As discussed in Chapter 5, Somalis are particularly engaged in transnational business compared to other refugee nationalities in Uganda. In line with this, our team observed that Somali shops in Base Camp 3 deal in a wider diversity and quality of goods, from basic kitchen goods to hard-to-find luxury products, perfumes, and electronics, which are imported from Kenya and as far as from Dubai, Pakistan, India, and China.

The owner of one such shop in Base Camp 3 provided us with a particularly illustrative example of the global reach of Somali trade networks. Demand for tuna, his best-selling product, is high among Nakivale's Somali population who enjoy fish but do not eat the species caught in nearby Lake Nakivale. To meet this demand from his community, the shop owner purchases tuna that is produced in Thailand and imported to Dubai. From Dubai, the cans are transported into Kenya by Somali trade networks, from here they make their way across the Kenyan–Uganda border from Mombasa into Kampala. Finally, the cans are brought from Kampala to this small mud-and-daub shop in rural Southern Uganda.

Just as we observed in Kampala, Somali refugees in Nakivale also benefit from the transnational connections that Somali refugees maintain with the diaspora in the West. Our survey highlighted that while non-Somali refugees in the settlements have almost no access to overseas remittances, nearly 30 per cent of Somali refugees in Nakivale are consistent beneficiaries of overseas money transfers.

Overcoming Market Failures

Compared to living in urban settings, one of the major advantages of living in designated refugee camps is better access to humanitarian assistance provided by aid agencies. Often, this leads to a public notion that refugees entirely depend on external support—commonly referred to as 'aid dependency'. The following comment from a senior staff member of UNHCR in Uganda is illustrative:

Nakivale is a very old settlement. It has been in care and maintenance stage for many years. Refugee's mind setting is fixed in dependency! They are spoiled and addicted to receiving aid from UNHCR and other agencies![30]

[30] Interview with senior staff of UNHCR in Nakivale settlement, personal communication, 6 June 2013.

Our research findings, however, show how refugees' relation with external aid is much more nuanced than the statement above. Refugee aid recipients incorporate, rather than depend on, humanitarian assistance as part of broader resource maximization strategies. As the example of Somali refugees' resale strategy of food rations suggests, refugee households shrewdly incorporate humanitarian assistance as part of broader household economic strategies. Although selling food rations is prohibited by UNHCR and perceived as 'cheating behaviour', this can be also understood as a sign of refugees' agency to capitalize on whatever resources are available to them to pursue economic opportunities.

Enforcing Contracts

In order for economies and markets to function, the enforcement of contracts is fundamental. To uphold the rules of the game, the state needs to provide a control and regulatory mechanism underpinned by the authorities and a coercive enforcement apparatus (Furubotn and Richter 1998: 268). For refugees whose activities fall outside of state protection, however, this basic underpinning is not always guaranteed. One such example is the case of Kyangwali Progressive Farmers Limited (KPF), a cooperative company with over 500 members founded by refugees in 2010. Its aim is simple: to provide a basis on which sorghum farmers can collectively bargain in the sale of their crops, rather than being bid down below market rates by Ugandan 'middlemen'.

The KPF's founder, Gregory, is a Congolese refugee who has been in Kyangwali since 1997. As the first chairperson of KPF, Gregory describes the early days of the enterprise:

> Our motivation was simple. We want to improve the living standards of refugee farmers in Kyangwali. To do this, we need to make a formal contract with improved price with crop wholesalers ... In 2010, we approached a beverage company named Nile Brewery Company Ltd. This is a giant Ugandan enterprise producing beer. To make beer, they need sorghum. Nile Brewery has many contracted sorghum producers. We wanted to be one of contractors of this business. We have been producing good quality of sorghum.[31]

In his dialogue with Nile Brewery, Gregory realized that individual farmers would need to work together in order to produce a large volume of sorghum collectively and secure formal registration status as a corporation.

> To have a contract with Nile Brewery, it must be a formally registered enterprise. This is understandable because it is the largest beverage company in Uganda. So we

---

[31] Interview with Gregory, a Congolese refugee in Kyangwali settlement, personal communication, 15 May 2013.

launched the KPF initially with 161 refugee farmers and registered it with local municipality. Everyone was so excited at that point.[32]

However, refugee-led businesses faced significant constraints in terms of being able to enter into and enforce contracts. Indeed, a direct business deal with Nile Brewery never materialized as the company refused to make such an agreement with a refugee enterprise despite its having achieved the formal registration. The beverage giant instead used a Ugandan subcontractor to buy KPF's sorghum. We were able to interview an employee of this subcontracting company in Kampala, who agreed to speak anonymously about the risks involved in direct agreements with refugee enterprises such as KPF:

> Well, there are many reasons why it is hard for Nile Brewery to make a direct business deal with refugees. In case refugee farmers cannot produce enough amount of sorghum, they need to somehow secure missing amount by themselves with their own money. I think this is difficult for refugees. Also, refugees do not have any collateral such as land. Further, refugees are mobile people. They may disappear from Uganda at any time! From Nile Brewery's view, it is risky to make a direct deal with KPF. This is why we work as an in-between.[33]

Shortly after entering into an agreement with the Ugandan subcontractor, KPF was troubled by a breach of contract. Christopher, a Congolese refugee living in Kyangwali since 2000, is another founding member of KPF and was the incumbent Director of the organization at the time of our discussion. With an apparent look of frustration, he explained KPF's unpleasant experiences:

INTERVIEWER: How did this subcontract go?

CHRIS: Not well. In 2011, we made a subcontract with a Ugandan enterprise because Nile refused to make a direct contract with KPF. But this subcontractor didn't respect the contract! In 2012, we stopped working with this company and made a new subcontract with a different one. But again our contract was not respected! This company used refugee middlemen and bought sorghum from refugee farmers directly at a lower price!

INTERVIEWER: What was the price agreement with KPF and farmers?

CHRIS: On the agreed contract, KPF was supposed to buy 1 kg of sorghum at 650 UGX from refugee producers and sell it to this Ugandan subcontractor at 750 UGX. Then this Ugandan company was supposed to sell sorghum to Nile Brewery at 1,050 UGX.[34]

---

[32] Ibid.

[33] Interview with a Ugandan subcontractor of Nile Brewery in Kampala, personal communication, 13 December 2013.

[34] Interview with Chris, a Congolese refugee in Kyangwali settlement, personal communication, 12 May 2013.

The Ugandan subcontractor had mobilized refugee middlemen and began purchasing sorghum for an immediate exchange of cash. At this point, KPF was struggling to raise sufficient cash to pay all of its farmers at once. Many of the farmers were living hand-to-mouth and needed money in hand for their daily survival. To meet their needs, they had decided to sell the sorghum they had grown for KPF to the confederation of middlemen for immediate income instead. Refugee crop brokers in Kyangwali readily joined in this chain of supply and were quick to purchase this sorghum yield for the Ugandan subcontractor at a lower price. For these refugee middlemen in Kyangwali, who have been making profits by capitalizing on market distortions among refugee small-scale farmers, the birth of this refugee cooperative was fatal to their business. Sensing a threat to their own income-generating means, the middlemen found ways to bypass the KPF and manoeuvre to buy from refugee farmers. Christopher continued:

> For refugee brokers, KPF was not a welcome initiative. We can potentially take away their business opportunities...So refugee middlemen cooperated with the subcontractor and started buying grown maize from our farmers. It was a fierce battle among refugees themselves too.[35]

In the face of breach of contract, the executive members of KPF intended to settle this conflict through a legal challenge, but effective legal recourse was not possible. Christopher continued to explain his view on the accusation of breach of contract:

INTERVIEWER: Did you do anything against this breach of contract?
CHRIS: We tried to make a lawsuit against this company but didn't work out. We were advised by OPM not to pursue such a legal action. They told us that a lawsuit will make a situation worse. Also, some refugee religious leaders advised us not to go too harsh against Ugandans.
INTERVIEWER: Did you negotiate with Nile brewery?
CHRIS: No. As I said, Nile doesn't directly deal with refugees. We contracted with the Ugandan enterprise as an in-between.
INTERVIEWER: Do you have a strategy to improve negotiation?
CHRIS: This year, we are trying to involve OPM as a witness of contract. Also, we are still trying to make a direct contract with Nile Brewery. We could avoid this problem if we didn't have a subcontractor.[36]

Refugees have very little recourse to appeal to the public to illuminate the injustices they may be facing in their business transactions—a reality that KPF discovered. As illustrated, KFP offers a number of insights into how

---

[35] Ibid.   [36] Ibid.

refugeehood shapes refugees' economic lives in ways that are very different from local host communities.

Property Rights

A central feature of the Ugandan settlement model is the allocation of plots of land to refugee householders for subsistence and commercial farming. According to OPM in Kyangwali, for example, refugees' access to land is organized as follows:

> We give a portion of land to refugees. For a household with 1–7 members, the size of land given is 50×100 m (one plot). A household with 8–12, we give 100×100 m (two plots). A household beyond thirteen is granted 150×100 (three plots). They can build their own house, latrine and use the rest for farming.[37]

However, while refugees are allocated plots, they cannot own or purchase them. As the OPM officer in Kyangwali continued:

> The land is free but of course the ownership still remains with the Ugandan government. Refugees cannot purchase the given land regardless of how many years they stay in the camp. The Ugandan government is helping refugees to become self-sufficient by letting them to use the land for farming while they are in Uganda.[38]

Refugees in Nakivale and Kyangwali spoke of having had their allocated land sub-divided or of being forcibly relocated to new plots when new influxes of refugees arrived in the settlement. A Congolese refugee male farmer in Kyangwali commented as follows:

> The size of camp never gets bigger so whenever we have big influxes of new arrivals of refugees, we were forced to give up part or sometimes entire land. For example, I recall that in 2008, many Congolese refugees were asked by OPM to be relocated to a different village to accommodate new arrivals. They also had to give up their farmland.[39]

Without tenure or secured ownership, refugees inevitably employ short-term land use strategies. For those who are given the land but are not allowed to claim its ownership, they have very little incentive to maintain it in good condition, let alone improve it. According to the Congolese refugee farmer interviewed above, refugees will prioritize achieving as much harvest as they

---

[37] Interview with an OPM officer in Kyangwali settlement, personal communication, 23 February 2013.
[38] Ibid.
[39] Interview with a Congolese refugee in Kyangwali settlement, personal communication, 2 March 2013.

can in the current year, rather than investing in long-term measures to maintain land to which they do not have any legal entitlement.

Seen through the lens of property rights, such behaviour is not uncommon for people of any background who have no rights or sense of ownership over the property they are being asked to manage. On the ground, however, aid workers mandated with improving refugees' farming practices often see this as irrational or absurd. We encountered this tension in many discussions with UNHCR, its IPs, and OPM throughout fieldwork. The following excerpt of our interview with a livelihoods officer in one of the UNHCR IPs provides a useful illustration. When we asked the officer to describe key challenges in promoting refugees' livelihoods and economic well-being in the settlements, the officer gave this emotive response:

> Mentality of refugees! This is the biggest challenge for us! After harvesting crops, refugees burn their farmland but it really damages the quality of land! We have been telling refugees not to do that again and again. Instead, we have been instructing them in new agricultural skills such as modern planting and line planting but they refuse to employ these methods![40]

When asked why refugees might not be following the IP's instructions, the same officer gave the following opinion.

> Refugees always want quick results. These new [agricultural] skills take more time for refugees to plant their seeds. Refugees don't want to invest in long-term strategies. They are more concerned with their immediate future.[41]

When assistance programmes fail to achieve intended outcomes, 'blaming refugees' (Verdirame and Harrell-Bond 2005) has been observed among UNHCR staff and their partner organizations. However, in the face of uncertain futures, refugees' rational decisions may well differ significantly from those of local populations who have permanent residence and a secure legal status. The precarious status of exile will inevitably affect refugees' economic choices and activities, and this necessitates taking into account the unfolding uncertainty of their specific institutional and personal contexts (Magill and Quinzii 2002: 2).

At the same time, limited land ownership poses a practical challenge to refugee farmers' economic survival and a policy challenge for Uganda's 'self-reliance' approach. With the limited availability of land to cultivate in the settlements, refugees need to cultivate the same plot over years without fallow periods. Both UNHCR and its partner agencies have admitted that the land given to refugees has also become less fertile as a consequence due to over-cultivation.

---

[40] Interview with a livelihoods officer of UNHCR IP in Nakivale settlement, personal communication, 20 March 2013.
[41] Ibid.

In response, a good number of refugee farmers are gradually shifting their livelihood strategies away from farming to non-agricultural livelihoods. Daniel, a Congolese refugee who resides in Kyangwali, is a typical example of such a case:

> We [his household] have a land for farming. We used to spend more time in the farmland but no longer. Soil is getting poorer and poorer so it no longer yields good amount of crops...Now I am busy running my shop. If I only do farming, I will not be able to sustain my family.[42]

With the land's decreasing fertility being exacerbated by refugees' immediate-term agricultural methods, Uganda's self-reliance approach—which relies on farming by allocating plots to refugees—is gradually being undermined. Although it has been generally admired by the international refugee regime, the self-reliance approach may be coming to a point where it requires rethinking as a result of these types of environmental pressures.

Imperfect Information

Neoclassical economics assumes that market participants hold perfect information. Information in the real world, however, is almost always incomplete; as a result, transaction costs arise because of asymmetrical information held by the parties to an exchange (North 1995: 18). This issue of access to information is particularly relevant to refugee camp economies. As highlighted earlier in this chapter, refugees living remotely may be hindered in accessing market and business information. The location of refugee camps may therefore lead to 'isolation distortions' (Werker 2007) with negative impacts for refugees' economic activities.

Our research revealed that refugees in camps are increasingly utilizing information and communication technologies (ICT) in their daily and economic lives as a means of overcoming this information deficit. We found that ICT, and especially mobile phones, are indispensable tools for refugees to facilitate the communication necessary to carry out income generation strategies and business transactions over longer distances. Our survey data show that in both settlements—while there are variations between nationalities—a good number of refugees regularly use mobile phones in their main livelihood or business (Figure 6.4). Many refugees—regardless of nationality—use mobile phones to communicate with suppliers and customers, rely on their phone to find out market information, and employ the device to transfer money.

---

[42] Interview with Daniel, a Congolese refugee in Kyangwali settlement, personal communication, 13 May 2013.

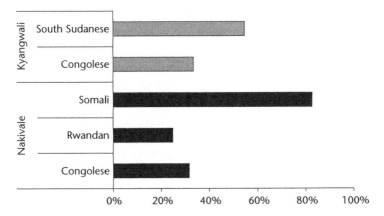

Figure 6.4 Percentage of refugees from different nationalities in Nakivale and Kyangwali using mobile phones in their primary business

In Nakivale, in particular, more than 80 per cent of Somali refugee households use their mobile phones in their primary livelihood activity. This particularly high rate of mobile phone usage makes sense when considering their significant levels of communication with partners in their wider ethnic and clan trade networks across Uganda and East Africa. Our survey also found that in addition to mobile phone usage, a smaller number of Somali refugees use the Internet to purchase products from their Somali trade counterparts in Kampala, Kenya, and other countries. These advanced communications tools are indispensable for Somali refugees who are involved in transnational economic activities.

We also observed that refugee farmers and agricultural distributors registered in Nakivale and Kyangwali seem to be making use of mobile phone technologies in increasingly sophisticated ways. We have highlighted the degree to which refugees' farming activities are closely nested within a national and subregional network of crop trading. Here, mobile phones play a critical role in helping to facilitate and sustain the agricultural trade networks. Most Ugandan distributors live in district capitals such as Hoima, Mbarara, or Kampala.[43] When they want to purchase crops from refugees, they use their phone to call a refugee supplier and specify the amount and type of crops they would like to collect. These intermediaries then telephone their network of refugee farmers to check on each partner's current level of stock in the requested crops. Meanwhile, the farmers themselves telephone other refugee farmers, checking their pricing. Once a deal is fixed between all parties, the Ugandan crop distributors send a partial payment to their refugee

---

[43] Interview with Henry, a Ugandan crop trader in Kampala, personal communication, 11 December 2013.

counterparts via mobile money transfer services. As soon as intermediaries collect and deliver the crops in the requested amounts, the Ugandan traders again transfer their final payment using the same mobile phone services.

This extensive use of mobile phones in the refugee settlements to support financial transactions has recently attracted the attention of several of the largest telecommunications corporations. One such example is the recent arrival in Nakivale of Orange Uganda, a national franchise of the global telecommunications giant France Telecom, which has erected a transmission tower in Base Camp Zone in order to launch its Orange Mobile Money service in the settlement. While the corporation's motives for investing in Nakivale's communications infrastructure derive in part from a self-described commitment to corporate social responsibility, it also stands to gain business from refugees. As one Orange representative put it:

> Nakivale is a busy market. There's always communication going on there, and we thought it was a good space for a match with our services... In Nakivale, our international call bundles are also popular. I know many refugees call US, Canada, UK, Kenya, and India.[44]

This Ugandan representative appeared to know a great deal about how refugees use ICT in the settlement, and about meeting the demands of the Nakivale market. In a subsequent discussion, we learned that Orange had negotiated an informal partnership with a refugee-led community organization in Nakivale for the express purpose of gathering information about the communication needs of refugees in the settlement. According to this Orange representative, this community partnership had helped Orange to confirm strong levels of demand among refugees to be able to make international calls and transfer money on a mobile phone. Indeed, Orange had confirmed that there was a much higher demand for mobile ICT in Nakivale than other places in the local district, and invested resources accordingly.

The Provision of Public Goods

In Kampala, self-settled refugees access the same social services that are available to the surrounding host populations, whether provided by the state or by the private sector. In a refugee camp, by comparison, the UN refugee agency provides fundamental services such as water, medical services, and education. In reality, however, the agency is not always able to meet these goals. In the face of gaps in services, entrepreneurial refugees in Nakivale and Kyangwali

---

[44] Interview with Orange representative in Mbarara, personal communication, 4 December 2013.

create their own solutions, sometimes providing public goods through innovative business models.

For example, we found that some refugees in the settlements provide informal medical services to supplement those of UNHCR. In refugee camps, UNHCR usually sets up medical facilities for refugees, and even for local communities, but the capacity of these clinics is often inadequate to serve all the camp's inhabitants. In Kyangwali refugee settlement, there were only two UNCHR clinics for the entire settlement, and they were located at a substantial distance from some peripheral refugee villages.

Several refugees in Kyangwali had sought to fill this gap and capitalize on demand by establishing their own private clinics. We interviewed one of them, Francesca, a Congolese refugee who started her own pharmacy and clinic in Kasonga village in 2005. Her shop includes a treatment room annexe with a small bed, where patients can receive injections, have blood drawn, or receive intravenous medication.

INTERVIEWER: Where did you acquire your medical knowledge?

FRANCESCA: I was a nurse in Congo.

INTERVIEWER: Where do you buy drugs?

FRANCESCA: In Kampala.

INTERVIEWER: Who are your customers?

FRANCESCA: Refugees and [Ugandan] nationals. On a busy day, I receive almost 100 customers.

INTERVIEWER: I thought there are UNHCR clinics in the camp and they provide free medical services for refugees and locals. Why don't they use them?

FRANCESCA: Yes, that is true. But treatment from the clinics is often not enough. Especially, towards the end of every month, these clinics often run out of medicines so many refugees end up buying their medications on their own. Also, the clinics don't give blood test for malaria. In my clinic, I also provide blood test.[45]

Francesca's comment hints that such private, refugee-owned clinics also serve Ugandan customers living in and around the settlement area. As Kyangwali is located in an area very remote from the district's commercial hubs, which is serviced by very few pharmacies and clinics, this should not be surprising. While locals are allowed to access medical services offered by UNHCR clinics, they confront exactly the same challenges as refugees and they seek medical services from the same refugee providers.

---

[45] Interview with Francesca, a Congolese refugee in Kyangwali settlement, personal communication, 28 February 2013.

When we interviewed the owners of clinics in Kyangwali, we found that they all had a background of working in medicine before their displacement. However, the Ugandan government does not recognize their previous credentials and degrees obtained in their country of origin, and their private clinics must operate informally (i.e. illegally). Nevertheless, we found that refugees and locals welcomed the provision of additional, private medical care in the settlement area. In other words, refugees are filling in gaps in common goods, even in local hosting villages where social services are thinly provided.

Refugee entrepreneurs were also observed providing social services in other areas. As noted in Kisenyi in Chapter 5, a number of Islamic religious schools, madrassas, have been established in Nakivale by Somali refugees and are run as a service for the community.[46] Another entrepreneurial Somali refugee whom we interviewed had initiated shuttle bus services between Nakivale, Mbarara, and Kampala. This transportation service is open to everyone, and many non-Somali refugees use it when they need to travel to Kampala and Mbarara.[47]

In both settlements, refugee innovators were running electricity supply businesses using generators to produce their energy. Some purchased commercial generators and ran wires to paying households; others constructed their own generators out of adapted parts, such as maize-milling machines. Rose, one such electricity provider in Kyangwali, explained why and how she launched and ran this innovative business model:

> I am used to using power. I cannot tolerate life without electricity. Also, I thought there is huge demand for power in the camp. Many of us were using candles and there were many fires as many people fell the candles. I use a generator to provide electricity. I attached long wires that are branched further to contracted houses. I have seventy-seven contracted customers including both refugees and locals. I differentiate the price depending on the number of electronic items in their house. For heavy users, I charge 50000 UGX per month but I only charge 10000 UGX for less users. For instance, someone with laptop and other electronic gadgets can spend more electricity so I charge him 50000 UGX.[48]

Crucially, refugee businesses that supply electricity create spillover impacts on other types of economic activities in the settlement. Some of Rose's major customers included the owners of restaurants and bars, who are able to use the electricity to power refrigerators for their food and beverages.

---

[46] Participant observation by our researcher in Nakivale settlement, March 2013.

[47] Interview with Abdi, a Somali refugee in Nakivale settlement, personal communication, 14 March 2013.

[48] Interview with Rose, a Congolese refugee in Kyangwali settlement, personal communication, 28 February 2013.

We also found that refugee economic activities facilitate another important public good: the commercial marketplace. Both settlements host commercial markets that have emerged spontaneously to facilitate trade exchanges. They have since been approved by OPM and are now regulated by local municipalities. These markets are open to everyone, both refugees and non-refugees, as long as a participant pays fees in the form of a market levy. Each market has a 'regulator,' usually a refugee resident who is responsible for collecting the levy and administering the market's operation.[49] The amount of market tax varies according to the value and quantity of items being sold. For example, in Kyangwali settlement's largest market, Kagoma, the market tax for one market day ranges from 500 UGX (0.25 USD) to 5000 UGX (2.5 USD). The collected tax is paid to the local municipality by a market committee comprising of several refugee volunteers.

In contemporary economics, markets are understood as places where buyers and sellers interact, exchange goods and services, and determine prices. The refugee markets we observed in Nakivale and Kyangwali link different economic actors from a range of different economies. While refugees contribute to these markets as traders and consumers, local Ugandan villagers also buy and sell items and services that are not available in their own villages. The significant economic presence of the refugees, with all its supply chains and demands, has created a public good that provides clear benefits for otherwise scarcely populated areas surrounding the settlements.[50]

Conclusion

Two main differences stand out between the situation of refugees in Kampala and those in the two settlements. The first is the availability of land for farming. Access to arable land, albeit decreasing in fertility, is not available in urban areas. The second is the greater degree of regulation by the state and international organizations in the settlements. Reflecting this, most settlement households engage in some form of farming activity on government-provided plots of land.

However, there is significant diversity in refugees' income generation strategies.

---

[49] Interview with Daniel, a Congolese refugee tax collector in Kyangwali settlement, personal communication, 13 May 2013.

[50] These research findings, of course, do not mean that all social services or goods are provided by refugees themselves. During the research, we observed that a Ugandan utility company is planning to extend its electricity services to the refugee settlements.

A significant number of settlement residents engage in a range of non-farming commercial activities to supplement or replace small-scale income earned from agriculture. This is especially the case for Somali refugees. Given their nomadic and merchant backgrounds, they almost entirely refrain from engaging in agricultural activity, building economic lives that are based on commerce and a range of non-agricultural activities.

Although geographically remote, both Kyangwali and Nakivale have complex economies. Not only is there significant and diverse economic activity within the settlements but their economies are embedded in wider economic structures that extend beyond the geographical boundaries of the settlements. Mainly through a combination of refugee and Ugandan 'middlemen', the settlements are connected to surrounding villages, the respective district capitals, and Kampala. Goods and services are imported and exported to and from the settlements, with refugee entrepreneurs playing an active role in these supply chains. From maize to dairy farming to the *bitenge* trade, the settlement economies are nationally and transnationally networked.

Uganda's Self-Reliance Strategy has played an important role in enabling these economic structures to emerge in the refugee settlements, particularly by allowing refugees to work and to move relatively freely. In both Kyangwali and Nakivale settlements, these refugees' basic rights are in principle respected by the government authority.

On the other hand, the economic lives of refugees in both settlements are not entirely exempt from the constraints that arise from 'refugeehood'. Settlement refugees' economic lives remain regulated and they face an institutional context that creates a distinctive set of economic distortions, with implications for the enforcement of contracts, property rights, access to information, and the availability of public goods. While these distortions impose constraints, they do lead to opportunities for adaptation, entrepreneurship, and innovation.

Nakivale and Kyangwali are by no means representative of refugee camps around the world. They are long-standing communities with vibrant economies. But they do serve to illustrate the complexity of refugees' economic lives in refugee settlements with relatively high levels of socio-economic freedom and market development. In contrast, Chapter 7 shows the limitations of economic life in the more recent and more restrictive emergency camp environment of the Rwamwanja refugee settlement—a recently opened refugee settlement in Western Uganda.

7

Emergency refugee camps

This chapter examines the economic lives of refugees in an emergency context. While refugees living in both emergency and protracted camps confront similar regulatory and environmental factors, they are distinguished by the duration of exile and by the length of time for which the settlement has been in existence. The prevailing policy assumption in 'emergency' situations is that the only available interventions come from the 'humanitarian' toolbox. Development approaches or market-based approaches have traditionally been seen as far less relevant to this 'emergency' phase.

Yet, whether or not there is scope for 'emergency development' approaches is to some degree an empirical question. It relies in part on asking whether, and to what extent, those who are recent arrivals living within newly formed camps are able to engage meaningfully in economic activity. This is a question that is almost entirely unexplored within the existing literature and yet one with far-reaching implications. It matters because it potentially calls into question the assumption that development-based approaches to displacement are only relevant at a certain phase of exile and as part of a 'transition' from humanitarian assistance to development.

If we can understand how refugees engage in economic activity early during their period of exile, we may be able to identify opportunities to support self-reliance from the very start of exile and begin to promote the market-based development of refugee settlements at an early phase. Indeed, such an understanding has implications for the very way in which refugee settlements might be designed in order to offer better enabling environments for the early-stage creation of viable and integrated markets that can benefit both refugees and host communities.

Uganda offers a methodologically rare opportunity to explore the role that time—both in terms of length of exile and also longevity of settlements—plays in shaping refugees' economic lives. This is because Uganda also has a relatively new settlement—in addition to the protracted situations that can be found in settlements like Kyangwali and Nakivale—that was created to protect and assist recent arrivals from the Democratic Republic of Congo. Between 2012 and 2014, violence related to the so-called M23 rebel group led to a significant exodus from North Kivu across Lake Albert. In response, the Ugandan government and the international community created the Rwamwanja refugee settlement in Western Uganda.

The fact that Rwamwanja is a 'new' settlement represents a unique opportunity to study refugees' economic lives at an emergency stage. Not only are these Congolese new arrivals in Uganda, but Rwamwanja itself represents a 'blank slate' economic environment, as opposed to long-established refugee settings in Kyangwali and Nakivale. As a result, this new refugee settlement provides an excellent opportunity to explore the nascent emergence of new refugee economies.

Our research took place some eighteen months after the start of the exodus, when people were still arriving, and most were at the beginning of their time in Uganda, and likewise when the settlement was in an early phase of development. Given that refugee flight is often associated with dispossession and loss of economic assets, the research enabled us to examine economic development within a community at an early phase of socio-economic rehabilitation. Here, we present our findings on Rwamwanja, engaging in comparative analysis with the protracted contexts of the Kyangwali and Nakivale settlements.

Contrary to common expectations, our research reveals that despite the short duration of exile, refugees in Rwamwanja have nevertheless begun to develop economic strategies. We show how the economic lives of the Congolese in Rwamwanja exhibit both similarities and differences in comparison to both Congolese and refugees of other nationalities in the longer-term settlements. We argue that despite significant constraints, the presence of refugees in Rwamwanja has gradually led to the development and diversification of a 'new' refugee-induced economy within an underdeveloped region.

In order to make this case, the chapter divides into three main sections. First, it provides a contextual description of refugees' economic lives in Rwamwanja settlement. Second, it explains the emergence of economic life in Rwamwanja. Finally, we assess the role that governance plays in shaping the evolution of the emergency camp economy.

'Blank Slate' Economy

Rwamwanja settlement is not an entirely 'new' settlement, having been first established in 1964 in order to host Tutsi refugees fleeing Rwanda (Stein 1990). However, the mass repatriation of this same Tutsi population prompted the settlement's closure in 1995. After the departure of the original Rwandan residents, the next seventeen years saw settlement land gradually encroached upon by nationals, who used the unoccupied territory for cattle grazing and farming. In 2012, fighting between M23 militia and the government of the Democratic Republic of the Congo (DRC) brought a large influx of Congolese refugees over Uganda's south-western border. Rwamwanja settlement was reopened by the Ugandan government in April 2012 to host them. The predominantly Congolese refugee population in the settlement totalled 54 287 registered refugees at the time of this study in 2014.[1] In terms of its demographic composition, the single-nationality structure of Rwamwanja resembles Kyangwali, where 85 per cent of residents are Congolese refugees.

The settlement is located in Kamwenge district in south-western Uganda, a drive of 320 km from Kampala. The approach to Rwamwanja through the rural landscape is notably similar to Kyangwali and Nakivale. The winding road to the settlement is unpaved, wandering through bushes and trees covered with bananas, cassava, palm, and jackfruits. Occasionally, large maize fields appear on the horizon. Although a local driver was keen to emphasize that there had been improvements in road conditions since the opening of Rwamwanja in 2012, clouds of dust fly up continuously, stinging visitors' eyes and making for precarious driving. During rainy seasons, the dusty road turns into a sea of mud that impedes entry and exit into the settlement.

Rwamwanja itself occupies around 50 square miles and consists of a total of thirty-six villages (UNHCR 2013b). According to OPM, around 80 per cent of the settlement land is considered suitable for crop cultivation. The settlement's topography is defined by hilly terrains with mild slopes and a mixture of fertile arable land and light tree cover. The settlement's soil and climate are generally hospitable for growing maize, beans, and cassava, with the exception of some steep slopes in rocky terrain areas.

In Chapter 6, we discussed how Nakivale and Kyangwali settlements have taken on 'city-like' characteristics over time. In Rwamwanja, however, even the most basic demarcations between commercial areas and residential villages have scarcely emerged. The so-called Base Camp area lies at the entrance of the settlement, comprising an administrative zone where most OPM and UNHCR offices are located. The settlement's other villages are a mixture of residential, farming, and small business clusters.

The immediate region surrounding the settlement is mainly populated by Bankyankole and Batooro ethnic Ugandans. These indigenous communities traditionally (and predominantly) derive their livelihoods from agriculture and animal husbandry. Interviewing Ugandan villagers who have lived in this region for a few decades, we learned that the area has long been

---

[1] According to UNHCR data, as of June 2014, only twenty-eight Rwandese refugees lived in the settlement.

underdeveloped, particularly in the years before the recent influx of refugees. The availability of basic goods and services is very limited, both inside and outside the settlement. As of early 2015, the region still had no electricity. There is very little access to water in and around the settlement area. Inside the settlement, we observed small ponds filled with muddy water where refugees were washing clothing. UNHCR has set up a limited number of boreholes, which refugees also rely upon. Transportation linking Rwamwanja and other cities is also scarce. Some private taxis and minibus services transport passengers from Rwamwanja to other locations, but all of these services are ad hoc and small scale, placing restrictions on refugees' mobility.

During the camp's closure between 1995 and 2012, Ugandan nationals encroached on settlement land. On reopening the settlement in 2012, the Ugandan government evicted these villagers, resulting in acute tensions between the Ugandan government and the dislocated population. At the time of our fieldwork, however, tensions between Rwamwanja's refugee population and the host community appear to have lessened, mainly due to the growing levels of economic engagement between the two groups. When asked about this relationship with local Ugandan villagers, refugees in the settlement generally agreed that there had been a substantial improvement.

Despite the current settlement's short life span, several markets and trading centres have already emerged both in the settlement and in bordering host community villages. These markets have developed spontaneously but are regulated by OPM once they grow beyond a certain size. One of UNHCR's implementing partners (IPs) whom we interviewed in the camp indicated that when trading centres reach a large enough size, the refugee community must ask for permission to expand from OPM. In markets in neighbouring villages, refugees are permitted to sell goods alongside Ugandan merchants, provided that they pay a set sales tax to the council district. The amount of sales tax varies according to the items being sold. For instance, in one local market, a participant is required to pay 500 UGX (about 0.25 USD) for 10 kg of tomatoes, 1000 UGX (about 0.5 USD) to sell a bag of maize, and 9000 UGX (about 4.5 USD) to sell a cow.

'No one chose to come to this camp.' 'We were forced to come to Rwamwanja.'—We heard these types of phrases repeatedly from Congolese refugees in Rwamwanja when we asked how they are finding their life in exile in this settlement. Their comments reflect that refugees crossing the border between Uganda and the DRC are assigned to, rather than choose, Rwamwanja as their place of settlement.

With the limited availability of camp accommodation across host countries, assigning refugees to a specific camp or settlement when they first arrive is normal practice for refugee-receiving states. In Uganda, the vast majority of refugees were assigned to Kyangwali and Nakivale by OPM. New arrivals to

Rwamwanja are first hosted at the settlement's reception centre, receiving hot meals for several days. Here, they are also provided with relief supplies, including saucepans, spoons, plates, cups, plastic sheeting, a hoe, soap, blankets, jerry cans, mats, and *panga* (machetes). As noted previously, they are entitled to a monthly food ration, including maize, cow peas, salt, beans, and cooking oil, for the initial period of their exile.

After the registration process is completed, arriving households are allocated a plot of land, normally 50 × 50 metres, for their use both as a residence and for cultivation. However, we also observed that OPM is subdividing certain plots in order to accommodate newer arrivals. Within Rwamwanja, as in both Kyangwali and Nakivale, OPM allocates refugees to settlement villages without taking refugees' own preferences and skills into consideration. Despite this, our team only rarely observed any intra-settlement mobility in Rwamwanja.

Like Kyangwali and Nakivale settlements, Rwamwanja is governed by an on-site management team and led by a Ugandan Settlement Commander under the auspices of OPM. The OPM in Rwamwanja generally employs the same regulatory principles as observed in other settlements, allowing refugees to work and issuing them with permits to move freely within Uganda for specific journeys outside the settlement boundaries. However, in practice, there are greater restrictions on economic activity beyond the settlement. The following is an excerpt of our interview with an OPM officer in Rwamwanja.

INTERVIEWER: Can refugees move out of the settlement?

OPM: Yes, they can. They just need to submit a request letter specifying the place they are going and duration of their trip in advance.

INTERVIEWER: Why do they need a permission letter to go outside the settlement?

OPM: This is for refugees' own security. In case of any trouble they face outside the settlement, this letter will protect them.

INTERVIEWER: Can refugees go and do businesses outside the settlement?

OPM: Well, that might be a bit difficult...Refugees came to Uganda for protection but not for economic reasons...[2]

The government officer equivocated when asked if refugees are permitted to conduct economic activities outside of the settlement area. Later interviews with refugees confirmed that OPM is generally reluctant, or at least does not actively encourage, refugees to engage in income generation activities outside the settlement.

As in Kyangwali and Nakivale, we found that OPM maintains a policy that refugees can work without a permit in accordance with the Refugee Act 2006.

---

[2] Interview with an OPM officer in Rwamwanja settlement, personal communication, 2 February 2015.

Inside Rwamwanja, some refugees run commercial activities, albeit at lower levels than in the other settlements studied. From the beginning of 2015, however, the local Ugandan municipality has begun to register refugee businesses inside the settlement and even collects business licence fees from refugees as they do from local Ugandan villagers. This taxation is a contentious issue for the refugees, and is provoking negative repercussions that we will discuss later in the chapter.

Uganda's Self-Reliance Strategy for refugees also applies in the new Rwamwanja settlement. Over a period of five years, refugees are expected to achieve self-sufficiency in their food acquisition with a corresponding, gradual reduction in the volume of the free food rations they receive. However, we learned from officers working for UNHCR and its IPs that the strategy is not necessarily working well in Rwamwanja, as a considerable number of refugees arriving in the camp have no agricultural skills. The officers we interviewed acknowledged this lack of farming skills as an issue, but they have not taken any action to offer meaningful support for those who wish to pursue non-agricultural economic livelihoods. We will come back to this important issue in a later section.

As of 2014, there were four UNHCR IPs and six operating partners (OPs) working in Rwamwanja. Of these organizations, the Lutheran World Federation (LWF) and Adventist Development and Relief Agency (ADRA) carried the primary responsibility for livelihood assistance in the settlement. LWF's livelihood support activities included, for instance, distributing agricultural inputs, such as seeds and farming tools; community sensitization on soil and water conservation; and training on modern agriculture techniques and non-farming business skills such as baking and tailoring. ADRA provided similar forms of assistance to newly arrived Congolese refugees both in agriculture and other related types of income-generating activity.

In Rwamwanja, refugees are treated more as 'temporary guests' than in the prolonged settlements. For example, the construction of any type of permanent or longer-term residence is disallowed, or at least strongly discouraged, by OPM. Refugees are not permitted to plant perennial crops, such as bananas, tea, and coffee, inside the settlement because these crops take many years to grow. Refugees are also disallowed from using tin as a roofing for their homesteads. The vast majority of dwellings are therefore made mostly of wood and mud, and covered by plastic sheets provided by UNHCR. However, our team noted that while many of these plastic covers are already torn, no replacements have been made available. During an interview with one refugee family at their hut, we were hit by a heavy storm. Pouring rain immediately penetrated the leaky roof and swamped a small living space in the house. Until this incident, we had not realized that refugees are officially prohibited from using metal roof structures for their housing, as this conveys an aesthetic of 'permanence'.

The robust police presence inside Rwamwanja settlement is a second major contrast to Nakivale and Kyangwali: we learned from OPM that there were a total of eighteen police stations inside the settlement, and each station was deployed with uniformed policemen. A considerable number of refugees also spoke of their anxieties about the possible presence in the camp of those involved in atrocities, such as former soldiers of M23. We spoke to a number of refugees who expressed concerns about violent behaviour by some of these former combatants, particularly during the early phase of their exile, but this had since subsided when many seemed to have left the settlement.

Another difference that distinguishes Rwamwanja from prolonged settlement contexts is the absence of a refugee representative body. We have described how in both the Nakivale and Kyangwali settlements populations are officially represented by selected members, who form the settlements' Refugee Welfare Councils (RWC). Despite more than two years passing since the opening of Rwamwanja, however, no RWC has been formed for the settlement. Rather, each village sends an executive council member to attend monthly meetings, where a variety of issues are discussed and reported directly to OPM. Refugees are not informed of the content of this report. The lack of representation in the settlement, in turn, means that its refugees have no unified, collective voice, and that there is very limited communication between refugees and the supporting agencies working in the camp. During our research, we found that many refugees spoke of feeling 'distanced' from meaningful communications with the settlement authorities.

The Emergence of an Economy

Refugees in Rwamwanja have not been given the right to decide where they live in Uganda. Regardless of their aspirations and background, they find themselves in this remote, rural, agricultural settlement. Unsurprisingly, our research revealed that the most common livelihood practised in the settlement is commercial farming. A substantial number of refugees also work as farm labourers on commercial farmland. Combined, these two agricultural activities constitute nearly 90 per cent of all respondent households' primary income-generating activities. In contrast, only a handful of households rely on non-farming livelihoods, such as carpentry, small shops, and hawking as a primary income generation strategy (see Figure 7.1).

In comparison to their counterparts in Kyangwali and Nakivale settlements, refugees' reliance on farming-related activities is noticeably higher in Rwamwanja. The diversification of livelihoods, or having a more diverse range of opportunities to generate income, has scarcely begun to emerge in

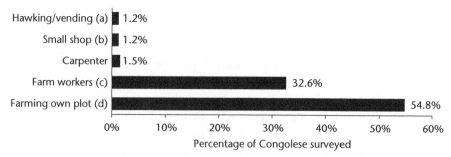

Figure 7.1 Most popular livelihoods in Rwamwanja

Notes: Percentages refer to the ratio of those engaged in the specific livelihood out of the total surveyed households.
(a) not owning any shops; (b) petty trading of household merchandise; (c) works on another's plot for money; (d) for selling

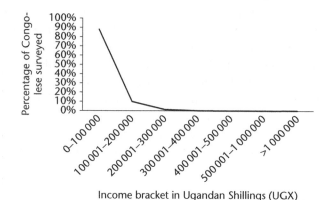

Figure 7.2 Monthly total household income in Rwamwanja

Rwamwanja. With so many refugees concentrating their efforts on similar livelihood activities, many household incomes in the settlement are also at more or less the same level. As our survey data demonstrates in Figure 7.2, nearly 90 per cent of respondents in Rwamwanja earn below 100000 UGX (50 USD) per month, and levels of equality are higher than in the more established settlements but at seemingly lower income levels.

The data in Figure 7.2 indicate a high number of respondents in the lowest income category. This proportion suggests that the economic profitability of small-scale agriculture is very limited. Joshua, a small-scale farmer whom we interviewed, corroborates this point.

I grow maize and beans with my small plot. But farming does not make good money. For the last season [over five months], I made around 350000 UGX [70000

UGX per month]. I sell my crops to Ugandan nationals but they don't give me a good price.[3]

The predominance of commercial farming in Rwamwanja does not mean that all of these refugees were engaged in agriculture before their displacement. During a series of focus group discussions with refugees, we discovered that a considerable number of them had no farming background at all in the DRC, a result which is strongly supported by our statistical evidence.

Refugees whom we encountered and interviewed in Rwamwanja frequently expressed frustration at having been 'forced' to become farmers. In the absence of freedom to choose where they would reside, they were effectively required to become agriculturalists in order to adapt to the rural setting, regardless of whether they were familiar with this type of work. Alain, a refugee with a background in trade, offered the following comment:

INTERVIEWER: Before you came to Uganda, what were you doing in DRC?

ALAIN: I had my own shop in a town.

INTERVIEWER: What were you selling?

ALAIN: Many things like food, matches, charcoal, cell-phone credit . . .

INTERVIEWER: What are you doing now in Rwamwanja?

ALAIN: Farming. That is all I can do here.

INTERVIEWER: Have you done farming before?

ALAIN: No! Never! I was born and raised in a town. I don't like farming!

INTERVIEWER: Why don't you try different work?

ALAIN: No choice! I don't have access to initial capital to begin my own business.[4]

Our research suggests that refugees in Nakivale and Kyangwali are similarly presented with few livelihood options beyond farming. However, unlike refugees in Rwamwanja, they are established enough in their new context to move from agriculture to non-farming livelihoods. This transition appears to have taken place within several years of arrival and may yet begin to appear in Rwamwanja.

Refugee Entrepreneurship

In addition to adjustment to a rural context, a significant number of refugees whom we interviewed found it challenging to function within the new economic, social, and political institutions of their exile. Forced displacement in

---

[3] Interview with Joshua, a Congolese refugee in Rwamwanja settlement, personal communication, 5 February 2015.
[4] Interview with Alain, a Congolese refugee in Rwamwanja settlement, personal communication, 5 February 2015.

most cases entails disruption or discontinuity in refugees' livelihood strategies due to the loss of pre-existing economic assets. These losses, in turn, mean that there will be inevitable shifts in their livelihood strategies (Hammar 2014: 27; Mallett and Slater 2012: 16; Jaspars and O'Callaghan 2010: 169).

As an example, forced displacement often takes away refugees' previous accreditations and licences obtained in their country of origin. Many refugees whom we encountered in Rwamwanja had to abandon their previous economic strategies because an official licence or diploma could not be acknowledged in the Ugandan system. The following comment by Cindy, a former nurse in the DRC, illustrates this particular challenge.

> In DRC, I went to medical school and received a diploma in medicine. After that, I worked as a nurse for three years... now I am farming for a living [in Rwamwanja]. I had never done it before... I want to do the same job [nursing] but I was told that my diploma is not recognized in Uganda.[5]

In addition to losing their qualifications, a significant number of refugees are unable to bring key commercial assets with them into exile, and are thus unable to continue in their previous professions. For example, we came across several commercial drivers who managed to keep their driver's licence with them but were unable to bring their motorbike or vehicle. Similarly, we met tailors who had to give up their sewing machine while fleeing from the attacks of a rebel group. These material livelihood assets can in theory be purchased in Uganda, but none of the newly arrived Congolese yet had adequate savings or the means to borrow financial capital to purchase replacement products.

Transitioning to unfamiliar systems was also a challenging process for many refugees. Refugees who used to work as teachers in the DRC spoke about the difficulties of moving from a Congolese (French language) education system to the Ugandan (English language) system. The schools established in Rwamwanja are part of Uganda's education system and are taught in English, the ordinary language of instruction, of which the vast majority of newly arrived Congolese refugees have little command at the time of their arrival. Jacques, one of these refugees and a former secondary school teacher, explains:

> In DRC, I was teaching accounting and business at a secondary school. It is very hard to get teaching work here... In DRC, we have a different educational system—it is a French system. Our diploma is not accepted in Uganda... I applied some teaching posts in the camp but did not get any of them. They always recruited Ugandan teachers.[6]

---

[5] Interview with Cindy, a Congolese refugee in Rwamwanja settlement, personal communication, 3 February 2015.

[6] Interview with Jacques, a Congolese refugee in Rwamwanja settlement, personal communication, 2 February 2015.

Jacques also spoke about the challenges of working in English or Ugandan local languages. Even if he were to apply for teaching posts outside Rwamwanja, he thinks his chance of getting a job is slim because of his limited communication skills in English and other local languages.

> I can speak French and Swahili but not much in English. I cannot speak any Ugandan local languages. I think it will be difficult for me to teach the Ugandan curriculum in English.[7]

We interviewed a number of field officers working for UNHCR and their IPs, who were aware of these adaptation challenges in the Rwamwanja context. One of the Ugandan livelihood officers working at one of UNHCR's IPs gave us the following response.

> I know that there are refugees with professional qualifications like doctors, nurses and teachers but it is very hard for them to get a formal position in Uganda. How do we utilize their existing skills? Or should they pursue farming instead? These are big challenges for us.[8]

While refugees are resilient and can gradually restore their economic strategies over their exile period, we observed that this recovery process has not yet taken place for the vast majority of Congolese refugees living in Rwamwanja. In the face of loss, disrupted livelihoods, and a new institutional framework, many of them found themselves depending on the cultivation of farmland, which is one of the few resources available to them in Rwamwanja.

In comparison to the longer-term settlements, the range and diversity of refugees' economic activities in Rwamwanja are much more limited. This does not mean that all Rwamwanja-based refugees are engaged only in farming: despite few livelihood options and only a short period of exile, a small number of outliers have pursued non-farming economic strategies.

Located just outside the entrance of the settlement is the Katalyeba market, where a handful of refugees sell goods and services. One of them, Nicholas, provides tailoring services to customers with a sewing machine which he has brought with him from the DRC. Without any farming background, he describes how he has persisted with his prior occupation:

> Tailoring has been my business for many years. I learned it at a vocational training school in DRC. I also had a shop selling used clothing but the rebel soldiers looted all of them ... When we escaped, I gave up many things but I carried this machine with me. It was heavy but this is my lifeline.[9]

---

[7] Ibid.

[8] Interview with the livelihood officer of UNHCR IP in Rwamwanja settlement, personal communication, 6 February 2015.

[9] Interview with Nicholas, a Congolese refugee in Rwamwanja settlement, personal communication, 5 February 2015.

Nicholas's decision to maintain his occupation as a tailor despite the obstacles of his displacement echoes the findings of other recent studies on refugees' economic activities in an emergency context. Desert Rose's (2012) study of the Kobe refugee camp in Dollo Ado, Ethiopia also found that refugees prefer to pursue livelihood activities in the same sector as prior to their displacement, rather than to acquire new vocational skills.

> Their skills are those that they have brought from Somalia. So traders in the camp were traders in Somalia, tailors were tailors, teachers were teachers, farmers were farmers and blacksmiths were blacksmiths. If there is no market for their skills, they usually do not work. (Desert Rose Consulting 2012)

One of the most difficult challenges for those who intend to go beyond the limitations of farming livelihoods is to secure start-up capital. As we have explored in previous chapters, refugees in Ugandan camps have no access to seed money from aid agencies, nor to formal banking facilities, and must acquire their own sources of capital. One of our interviewees in Rwamwanja, Sango, is a 30-year-old male refugee who arrived in Rwamwanja in mid-2013. Within a few months, he started up what is now a booming business dealing in hardware products and construction materials. Because of the continuous influx of refugees to Rwamwanja, these new arrivals need construction materials for their housing, and many need the tools to make essential repairs to their makeshift tents. With so few shops selling construction materials, Sango's business is in significant demand. At the first interview, we asked how Sango had managed to launch this relatively capital-intensive enterprise in such a short time:

INTERVIEWER: How did you get the start-up capital for your business?
SANGO: I sold my motorbike in Uganda.
INTERVIEWER: Did you bring your motorbike with you?
SANGO: Yes, I was planning to leave DRC anyway so I carried some items to a border town.[10]

A modest number of refugees have also managed to bring their own savings to Uganda. These fortunate households were normally wealthier in the DRC and, like Sango, were preparing in advance for their flight to Uganda. James's household is one such case. His family were the owners of several grocery shops in eastern DRC and fled the DRC in early 2014. They had begun to plan their flight several months earlier. James never revealed how much money his family had carried to Uganda in savings, but their lifestyle was telling. In Rwamwanja, he and his sisters were making a living by running retail shops

---

[10] Interview with Sango, a Congolese refugee in Rwamwanja settlement, personal communication, 4 February 2015.

within and outside of the settlement. Having become fed up with the 'inconvenient and dirty camp life', and though formally prohibited from doing so by OPM, his household was renting a two-bedroom house just outside the settlement, paying around 60000 UGX a month (about 30 USD) in rent.

The comments of these entrepreneurial refugee outliers highlight some clear commonalities. First, almost all have previously pursued the same or very similar livelihoods while living in the DRC and are now continuing in the same occupation from within their new institutional context. Second, their livelihoods do not normally require an official licence or diploma, as opposed to former doctors, nurses, or teachers who are unable to transfer credentials to Uganda. Finally, all of these exceptional households made 'anticipatory movements' (Kunz 1973, 1981) before their exile. Being better prepared, these households have usually managed to bring their key livelihood instruments or sources of capital with them. These combined conditions have enabled them to start to apply non-farming economic strategies within a relatively short period of exile.

In addition to these cases, some refugees have also taken a more patient approach to starting a non-agricultural business. Such people initially work as farmers for one or more seasons to accumulate financial capital, launching their business with their accumulated savings. For example, one Congolese refugee whom we encountered running a phone charging business explained how he accumulated savings from a successful crop harvest and invested the income into a solar panel, which provides him with the energy he needs to charge mobile phones for his customers. He also indicated that there are several other refugees who have duplicated this business model in their own villages.

At the time of our research, Rwamwanja's economy was just beginning to take shape. Before April 2012, this economy did not exist. Yet our interviews reveal that economic activity began almost as soon as the current refugees arrived, triggered by the presence of international assistance.

According to refugees who have been living in Rwamwanja since 2012, economic activity inside the settlement emerged almost immediately. The first visible economic activity was refugees' beginning to exchange UNHCR/ WFP (World Food Programme) food ration products. Soon, this bartering took on additional dimensions through the involvement of Ugandans from neighbouring villages. Refugees exchanged bags of maize or cooking oils for Ugandan crops such as bananas and cassava. They also began to sell non-food products to local villagers, including such items as *pangas*, saucepans, hoes, and seeds, which were given to refugees by UNHCR as a form of emergency aid. As food rations were distributed by UNHCR/WFP, new ad hoc 'markets' began to emerge throughout the settlement. While the refugee and host populations had very little pre-existing ethnic or cultural affinity, they still managed to initiate these economic relationships using simple sign language to communicate with one another.

These initial trading activities have since transformed into more organized and regularized refugee markets. Kaihora market is one of the largest market-places to be formally approved thus far by the OPM Settlement Commander. This weekly market opens every Sunday between 8 a.m. and 7 p.m. in Kaihora village—one of thirty-six villages in the settlement. Adam, the Congolese refugee chairperson of Kaihora market, explained to us how the market emerged as a way of providing a structure that would promote economic activities for refugees:

INTERVIEWER: When did Kaihora market start?
ADAM: February 2014.
INTERVIEWER: Who started this market?
ADAM: It is hard to tell who started. Even before 2014 February, there were business activities in the village but they were all individual. We thought having an organized market would be beneficial to all camp residents.[11]

According to Adam, Kaihora market currently attracts about 2000 sellers and customers per market day. These figures include a significant number of Ugandan national traders, who come from nearby villages or larger economic hubs in the local districts and sell their items or services to refugee residents. During our research period, Kaihora market was not collecting any market duty from participants, unlike other local markets—an attractive incentive for thousands of local traders.

We interviewed refugees who recalled that the scale of the settlement economy began to grow significantly after the first harvest season, when refugee farmers sold their crops to local merchants and some of them used their capital to invest in other businesses. One livelihood officer working for a UNHCR IP in the settlement told us that around mid-2013—about one year after the reopening of Rwamwanja—he began to see the buds of non-agricultural commerce inside Rwamwamja. In Kaihora village, for instance, one of the first of these non-farming businesses was a makeshift bar. Andrew, its owner, described the early days of his business:

I came to Rwamwanja in June 2012. First I did farming and made small money. I also worked for Ugandans as a farmworker. [With the money earned] I went to Katalyeba market and bought beer and soda. In 2013, I opened this mini-bar in the camp...I was running a bar in DRC so I know this business well.[12]

---

[11] Interview with Adam, a Congolese refugee in Rwamwanja settlement, personal communication, 5 February 2015.
[12] Interview with Andrew, a Congolese refugee in Rwamwanja settlement, personal communication, 5 February 2015.

The influx of refugees and aid workers into this scarcely populated rural village has also contributed to stimulating and expanding local economies in the surrounding areas. According to Ugandan villagers who have been living in the area for several decades, the area was originally bushy and underdeveloped, with very few major industries or economic sectors. Ugandan villagers in the region traditionally engage in farming and animal husbandry for their principal livelihoods. However, many new businesses began to appear after the influx of refugees, including restaurants, bars, guesthouses, and retail shops. We interviewed the Ugandan chairperson of one host village who has been residing in the area for more than three decades. He offered this description of the transformation of the Rwamwanja area:

> Things have changed so much since the arrival of refugees here. The population of course increased. Not only refugees but many Ugandans moved to this area because of economic reasons ... I think food production level increased as many refugees are doing farming. Also, a lot of aid came to the area. Schools, boreholes developed, and nationals are also using these facilities.[13]

As the comments of the local chairperson indicate, a significant number of Ugandan entrepreneurs have set up businesses in response to the new demands and opportunities generated by Congolese customers. Henry, a Ugandan owner of a popular restaurant located at the entrance of the settlement, migrated from Kampala to Rwamwanja and established his food business in January 2014:

> I used to run a small restaurant in Kampala. My friend [who was doing construction works at the inception of the camp] told me that there are many business chances in this area. I came and checked the area and found no good restaurants. There were also many aid workers inside the camp so I decided to move here ... currently, I receive about 200 customers per day. Many of them are working for these agencies but some of them are refugees and Ugandan business people visiting the camp.[14]

In addition to these new enterprises built after 2012, we found that owners of pre-existing businesses in the host area have benefited significantly from the presence of refugees and humanitarian workers. For example, following the arrival of many refugees in 2012, one local family renovated their bar to target the growing population. The female owner of the enterprise told our team that the business grew rapidly, and in 2014 her family expanded the business, creating a lodge with a restaurant just outside the entrance of the settlement.

---

[13] Interview with the Ugandan chairperson of a hosting village in Rwamwanja, personal communication, 5 February 2015.

[14] Interview with Henry, the Ugandan owner of a popular restaurant located at the entrance of Rwamwanja settlement, personal communication, 4 February 2015.

These and other comments from the local host population seem to high-light that the internal camp economy has attracted external economic actors and even contributed to the revitalization of the host economy in the surrounding area. In Kyangwali and Nakivale, Ugandan merchants also explained to us how they were attracted to set up shop in the settlements' initial days by the emerging business opportunities and potential market demands of newly arrived refugees.

The Emergence of Networks

In Rwamwanja, the extent of refugees' mobility and networks was far more limited than in our other research sites. While some refugees do venture outside the settlement to purchase products that are unavailable inside Rwamwanja, they rarely go beyond the immediately neighbouring Ugandan villages. The largest economic centre near Rwamwanja is a town called Kyenjojo, with an estimated population about 350000 people. With very little means of transportation to and from Rwamwanja, we came across very few refugees who could travel regularly to this major commercial hub, let alone to Kampala or Mbarara.

Similarly, our team found that the business connections of refugees whom we interviewed in Rwamwanja were also largely confined to the immediate surrounding area. This contrasts strongly with Kyangwali and Nakivale, where a significant number of refugee farmers sell their crops to Ugandan brokers who come from much further afield, and where refugee-grown crops have become part of much wider trade networks. Our research results indicated that the density and frequency of such business transactions are both much lower in Rwamwanja. For example, we did not come across any refugee households that drew upon transnational networks for their day-to-day economic activities, and almost no overseas remittances were being received by the refugees we surveyed in Rwamwanja.

On the other hand, we found that some refugees who possess greater resources are already beginning to move out of the settlement into larger economic centres, predominantly to Kampala. Our interviews in Rwamwanja revealed that these richer refugees have rented their land to other refugees but have moved out of the settlement. In fact, we encountered some of these refugee households in Kampala. Arnold, a 34-year-old refugee, came to Rwamwanja in October 2013 but left the settlement for Kampala within a few months. He agreed to an interview with us in a café in the capital and explained:

INTERVIEWER: Why did you leave Rwamwanja?

ARNOLD: I didn't like the camp life. The camp is very underdeveloped. Also, I am not a farmer.

INTERVIEWER: In DRC, what were you doing for living?

ARNOLD: I was running many businesses. Most recently, my main business was trading minerals.

INTERVIEWER: What are you doing in Kampala now?

ARNOLD: I am running a brokerage business with some traders in DRC. I deal with construction materials. My wife and sisters are selling *bitenge* and jewellery here.

INTERVIEWER: Are there any other refugees who left Rwamwanja and now live in Kampala?

ARNOLD: Yes, many. They left the camp for similar reasons like me.

INTERVIEWER: Do you prefer to live in Kampala to Rwamwanja?

ARNOLD: Absolutely! It is expensive here but I have many more opportunities here.[15]

Arnold's story highlights that on the one hand, a certain number of refugees have migrated to pursue an institutional environment that promotes greater economic opportunities. On the other hand, we were intrigued to find that some Congolese refugees have actually migrated to Rwamwanja from other settlements or cities in Uganda. Peter, a 26-year-old Congolese refugee, left Nakivale settlement, where he is officially registered with OPM, and moved to this new settlement with his wife and two children in late 2012. Here is an excerpt of our interview with him in Rwamwanja:

INTERVIEWER: Why did you come to Rwamwanja?

PETER: My land in Nakivale was no longer fertile. I heard from my [refugee] friends in Rwamwanja that there is better land and more business chances here [in Rwamwanja].

INTERVIEWER: What were you doing before you came to Uganda?

PETER: Farming.

INTERVIEWER: How are you finding your life in Rwamwanja?

PETER: My life is better here. Land is not necessarily fertile but there is more demand for business in Rwamwanja.

INTERVIEWER: What are you doing now?

PETER: Middleman business. I am working for three Ugandan traders in Kampala, Mbarara, and Kamwenge.[16]

Peter's perspective was that Rwamwanja's economy is still at an embryonic stage, and competition is consequently less intense compared to the relatively more developed markets in Nakivale. He explained that within Nakivale, the number of crop brokers has reached saturation point. With such fierce competition

---

[15] Interview with Arnold, a Congolese refugee in Kampala, personal communication, 9 February 2015.

[16] Interview with Peter, a Congolese refugee in Rwamwanja, personal communication, 6 February 2015.

among refugee middlemen in Nakivale, his household had to rely on a range of income sources for day-to-day survival. In Rwamwanaja, by contrast, he can deal with a much larger volume of crop trade and make more profit. In Peter's case, the institutional constraints of Rwamwanja offered an attractive opportunity to his farming background and experience as a crop broker.

How Governance Shapes Markets in Rwamwanja

In Chapter 3, we discussed how refugee economies are distinctive in part because they lie at the intersection of the formal and informal sectors. In long-term settlements like Kyangwali and Nakivale, the commercial activities of refugees fall almost entirely within the informal sector. In Rwamwanja, however, the local district municipality and OPM are actively trying to 'formalize' economic activity in order to impose taxes on commercial activity.

The district government and OPM have imposed a settlement entry fee on Ugandan business people—mainly crop brokers—who come to the settlement for commercial reasons. Ugandan middlemen whom we interviewed indicated that as of early 2015, each of these national traders has been required to pay 10000 UGX (about 5 USD) whenever she or he enters the settlement. The entry cost has clear implications for trade activities between refugees and Ugandan middlemen, as it is passed on to the purchase price for agricultural crops. As a result, local traders are forced to lower the price at which they buy crops from refugees, creating a market distortion.

While the entry tax is mainly targeted at Ugandan traders, the local municipality in the Rwamwanja area is also working to formalize refugee enterprises and collect business taxes from refugees who own shops inside the settlement. In the Ugandan Refugee Act 2006, the clause 'Duties and Obligations of Refugees' states that 'a recognised refugee shall (f) if engaged in gainful employment or fully integrated and has a source of income, pay taxes in accordance with the applicable tax laws of Uganda.' While this clause is difficult to impose on informal commerce inside the settlements, the taxation of refugees has continued to emerge as a trend in Uganda since early 2015.[17] An OPM officer whom we interviewed in Rwamwanja went so far as to advocate tax collection from refugees:

I think refugees should pay tax. Refugees are part of the Ugandan economy. They are treated in the same way as Ugandans so they should meet the obligations like us.[18]

[17] Commercial farming was excluded from imposition of tax.
[18] Interview with the OPM officer in Rwamwanja settlement, personal communication, 7 February 2015.

A senior OPM official in Kampala also supported the imposition of business taxes on refugee commerce taking place inside the settlement:

> We are aware that the local government is collecting annual trading tax from refugee businesspeople in the camp. We are fine with it. In Uganda, refugees have access to gainful employment and economic opportunities like us. They are getting a lot of benefits in Uganda.[19]

It is not surprising that almost all refugee business owners whom we interviewed strongly resisted this taxation. One refugee shop owner emotionally expressed his frustration at the emerging policy.

> I refused to pay the tax. Tax collectors said to me that they collect levy from everyone regardless if they are refugees or nationals because refugees are given equal status. But I don't think so. Nationals can access loans but we cannot borrow money from anywhere. They can go to any markets they want to sell but we cannot. We are not given equal status at all![20]

The shop owner above managed to refuse to pay the tax, but such cases are rare. The process of tax collection has been undertaken by members of the local municipality and has usually been accompanied by uniformed policemen. Most refugees whom we interviewed have ended up paying the required tax.

One of the major advantages of maintaining an informal or unregistered enterprise is to avoid paying tax and other official fees. In Rwamwanja, however, refugees are losing out on informal economic space by being required to operate with formal status. The limited duration of refugees' exile also means that substantial taxation significantly damages the cash flow, capital, and health of refugee-run businesses. We will discuss the legitimacy of tax collection from refugees further on in this chapter.

During our focus group discussions, one of the most frequent complaints raised by refugees was the difficulty of reaching and communicating with settlement authorities such as OPM and UNHCR in order to convey the challenges they are facing. A refugee youth leader from one village deplored how removed these governing bodies are from the everyday life of refugees:

> OPM is a 'big boss' in the camp. It is hard to meet OPM officials. The security guards will stop us and ask why we need to meet OPM...UNHCR is also not accessible either. We cannot go to the UNHCR office randomly. Thursday is the day we can meet UNHCR officers but they are not always available.[21]

---

[19] Interview with the senior OPM official in Kampala, personal communication, 10 February 2015.

[20] Interview with a Congolese refugee shop owner in Rwamwanja settlement, personal communication, 6 February 2015.

[21] Interview with a Congolese refugee youth leader in Rwamwanja settlement, personal communication, 7 February 2015.

This estrangement is even acknowledged by the national staff members of NGOs working inside the settlement. When we conducted a focus group with these officers, the participants agreed that communication lines between refugees and the Rwamwanja camp authorities are 'fractured'. Refugees do not have a collective political voice to make their agendas known to OPM and UNHCR, in part because of the absence of a Refugee Welfare Council in the settlement.

We found that the distance between refugees and the settlement authorities has been the cause of a series of serious miscommunications and misunderstandings between the groups. For example, a large number of refugee farmers firmly believed that the OPM is fixing the purchase price of maize and beans for Ugandan middlemen and taking the profits into their own pockets. George, a 34-year-old Congolese refugee who came to Rwamwanja in 2013, was emotively expressive of his suspicion of the Ugandan administration as follows:

> All national brokers buy 1 kg of maize at 300 UGX. But outside the camp, the price is much higher! I heard in external markets, 1 kg of maize is more than 500 UGX. Our maize deserves that [500 UGX]! I am sure that OPM is controlling the price of our maize! I think OPM does not want refugees to earn a lot of money here.[22]

While George was correct about the uniform price of 300 UGX for 1 kg of maize, at the time of this interview this reflected the current market price. We managed to interview some local crop middlemen who were buying from refugee farmers in Rwamwanja. Anthony, one of these agricultural brokers, expressed his frustration at this type of thinking among farmers in Rwamwanja:

INTERVIEWER: At what price do you buy 1 kg of maize from refugees?
ANTHONY: 300 UGX.
INTERVIEWER: Is that the market price?
ANTHONY: Yes. Refugees complain and negotiate the price but this is the current market price. They are so ignorant!
INTERVIEWER: How do you evaluate the quality of refugee-made maize?
ANTHONY: Very diverse. Some are OK but many are not good. This is another reason why we pay only 300 UGX. Their maize is not as good as they think.[23]

Communication between refugees, UNHCR, and UNHCR's IPs left much to be desired. For example, a deep misunderstanding seemed to have emerged among aid organizations regarding some of the livelihood difficulties that refugees were facing. We frequently heard livelihood officers comment that

---

[22] Interview with George, a Congolese refugee in Rwamwanja settlement, personal communication, 4 February 2015.
[23] Interview with Anthony, a Ugandan agricultural broker in Rwamwanja, personal communication, 6 February 2015.

'refugees are not patient so they sell crops at a cheaper price' or 'refugees mishandle crops after harvest so their crop quality is low'. When we shared these comments with one refugee farmer, he gave us the following response.

> I don't think it is a matter of patience. Many of us including my family need daily cash for our survival so we have to sell crops as soon as we harvest. Also, we don't have storage facilities for crops. This is why we put them on the ground or inside our house. I know it is not good for the quality of crops [because mud and sand are mixed with crops] but what can we do? We have no alternatives.[24]

In the previous chapter, we discussed a clash of perspectives that had emerged between refugees and aid organizations. During our interviews with employees in humanitarian agencies in Rwamwanja, we often heard aid workers 'blaming refugees' in ways that were similar to what we had observed in the protracted settlements:

INTERVIEWER: Are there any challenges when you work with refugees?

IP OFFICER: Refugees are generally receptive but some are not obedient.

INTERVIEWER: What do you mean 'not obedient'?

IP OFFICER: They don't come to our community agriculture demo. Many of them are [those who don't come to the agricultural demo] not involved in farming so they are not interested in our initiatives. Also, they complain a lot.[25]

This conversation with a UNHCR IP officer supports the assertion that there are gaps in communication between aid agencies and refugees, or people whom these agencies are mandated to assist.

The guiding principle of Uganda's self-reliance policy is to 'help refugees help themselves', particularly in terms of their daily dietary needs. Given the rural and remote locations of the settlements, the Ugandan government and UNHCR have promoted commercial farming as a means for refugees to become economically self-sufficient. In Rwamwanja, however, we found that the absence of virtually any other livelihood options was a cause of acute frustration for the refugees. When we asked a Congolese refugee whether he knows the self-reliance policy in Uganda, he replied as follows.

> I understand what self-reliance is. It sounds like a good policy. But if UNHCR and OPM want me to become self-sufficient, why don't they let me choose where to stay and leave it to me? I like to choose my own way of pursuing self-reliance.[26]

---

[24] Interview with a Congolese refugee farmer in Rwamwanja settlement, personal communication, 6 February 2015.

[25] Interview with a livelihood officer of a UNHCR IP in Rwamwanja settlement, personal communication, 6 February 2015.

[26] Interview with a Congolese refugee in Rwamwanja settlement, personal communication, 5 February 2015.

In an informal conversation with UNHCR officers in Rwamwanja, some of them offered frank opinions about the challenges of encouraging self-sufficiency among refugees in the settlement. One of these officers sympathized with refugees.

> Current support is almost entirely designed for farmers. As the emergency phase is ending, we now have to start looking into non-farming activities. But the budget is decreasing as it enters the care and maintenance stage. It is a big challenge for us to empower refugees who want to pursue commerce.[27]

In Rwamwanja, we worked extensively with Robert, a Congolese refugee research assistant on our project who lives in Kampala. Robert assisted our data collection in Rwamwanja as a translator of Swahili, which is the mother tongue of refugees in Rwamwanja. Since his arrival in Uganda in 2007, he has been self-settled in Kampala and has never lived in any of the refugee settlements. Every evening at our lodge, we sat together and discussed refugee life in Rwamwanja over dinner. One night, Robert expressed his own perspective on the apparent challenges that this emergency context presents for Uganda's Self-Reliance Strategy. As he noted:

> Personally, I think self-reliance is a good policy. Refugees should be encouraged to become independent. But in Rwamwanja, I am not sure whether refugees are given adequate conditions to become self-reliant. Especially, it is hard for refugees who don't know farming.[28]

One high-ranking expatriate UNHCR officer in Kampala was aware of the limitations of the self-reliance policy in the country. In particular, the officer pointed to the lack of a bridging strategy to transfer refugees' economic lives from an emergency context to a longer-term development phase.

> In an emergency phase, first and foremost, our focus is on refugees' physical survival. We don't want any refugees to die of hunger or malnutrition. So food security is an absolute top priority in an emergency. But the issue is after the emergency situation. We have few options to assist different types of livelihoods of refugees. For instance, in a single refugee population, we have farmers, pastoralists, merchants, and white-collar workers. It is not easy to meet all of their livelihood demands or needs at once.[29]

In our survey, we asked the recipients of aid to describe the extent to which they are dependent on external aid. Approximately 80 per cent of respondents

---

[27] Interview with a UNHCR officer in Rwamwanja settlement, personal communication, 7 February 2015.
[28] Interview with Robert, a Congolese refugee assistant in Kampala, personal communication, 10 February 2015.
[29] Interview with a high-rank expatriate UNHCR officer in Kampala, personal communication, 10 February 2015.

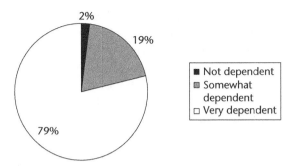

Figure 7.3 Refugees' perceptions of dependency on external aid in Rwamwanja

answered that they felt 'very dependent' on support from UNHCR and other organizations (see Figure 7.3).

Nonetheless, our qualitative interviews suggested that the high dependence on aid among refugees in Rwamwanja is not necessarily a sign of their lethargy, but may rather be derived from the limited access to livelihood opportunities described throughout this chapter. For instance, a common explanation that refugees give for their perceptions of dependency on aid is the inadequate size of farmland to produce a sufficient volume of crops. As already mentioned, the land given to them for both living and farming has been occasionally subdivided by OPM to accommodate new arrivals to Rwamwanja. This, in turn, deprives households of their primary means of production and income generation, inevitably increasing their levels of reliance on food rations.

For some refugees involved in non-agricultural businesses, the livelihood support provided by aid agencies has been found irrelevant or unhelpful. Jonathan, a Congolese refugee salon owner, commented as follows.

> UNHCR's support is targeted at farmers but I am not [one]. I am running a small salon and UNHCR did not help me build this business. I still receive a food ration but I only use cooking oil and sell the rest of the ration to locals.[30]

Self-reliance and aid dependency are often perceived as polar opposites in the global refugee regime. Yet, as these comments indicate, they can interact with one another in complex ways that may contradict these perceptions.

Rwamwanja has presented a challenging environment for its Congolese refugee inhabitants. Most refugees have had to discontinue familiar livelihood strategies, arriving dispossessed of their economic assets. They have been obliged to settle within a remote rural settlement, without their specific abilities

---

[30] Interview with Jonathan, a Congolese refugee salon owner in Rwamwanja settlement, personal communication, 7 February 2015.

and aspirations being taken into account. Most have been forced to adopt agriculture as their primary livelihood, whether or not they were farmers in the DRC. Meanwhile, they have also been subjected to restrictive local interpretations of national legislation. Understandably, these restrictions have translated into a noticeably higher concentration of refugee households earning lower incomes in comparison to the more established settlements. Despite the unfavourable context and the relatively short duration of their exile, however, refugees have gradually begun to transform the economy of the settlement and the surrounding area. This case offers a series of important analytical implications.

The government's approach to refugees in Rwamwanja is characterized by contradiction. On the one hand, specific restrictions are placed on refugees' daily lives, including restrictions on their mobility, their use of metal roof structures, or perennial planting. On the other hand, the local municipal government (and OPM) are formalizing and imposing a tax on refugees based on a claim of 'equal treatment to nationals'.

While the municipal authorities' practice of formalizing refugee commerce promises to increase taxation revenues for the district, the benefits for refugees of formally registering their status in Rwamwanja are still unclear. Despite being expected to be taxpayers, they have not received the guarantees of enforceable commercial contracts, or legal ownership of their place of business and means of production, that one might expect from participation in the social contract.

Furthermore, refugees continue to be deprived of the means to organize collectively even through the simple representative structures found within the longer-term settlements. While UNHCR and OPM were not readily accessible by refugees in Nakivale and Kyangwali, refugees did at least have formal representation through the RWC as an avenue to consolidate their collective voice, and to convey it to the settlement administrations.

The administrative controls exercised by the authorities, especially the OPM, have been much stronger in Rwamwanja than elsewhere with restrictions on mobility and agricultural activities being far more tightly regulated. These tighter regulations have placed refugees in the liminal position of being partly integrated into and party excluded from the economic life of the surrounding region and host country.

The empirical findings of this chapter pose some fundamental questions for Uganda's Self-Reliance Strategy. As already discussed, Uganda's promotion of refugees' self-reliance is widely known as an exemplary model. The strategy is underpinned almost solely by a subsistence farming model, within which refugees are given access to a plot of land of a certain size, 'transforming' them into farmers. This approach has functioned well for many refugees with a farming background and has led, for example, to Kyangwali settlement becoming known as the 'food basket of Hoima' because of its high levels of agricultural productivity.

In Rwamwanja, however, this same approach is creating significant challenges for refugees without farming experience. Considerable numbers of refugees have come from non-farming backgrounds as traders, drivers, teachers, and nurses. However, given the rural location of Rwamwanja and the lack of other residential options, these refugees have had to pursue self-sufficiency through agriculture. In other words, they had to abandon their main profession in order to survive in their new context. The result of this transition has been a loss of human capital, and with it the potential to contribute in diverse ways to the host economy.

The case highlights how, even in the most restrictive circumstances, economic diversity should be more strongly promoted within livelihood interventions. Assuming that any one income-generating activity (such as farming) offers a suitable fit for the skills and talents of the population is to diminish the potential both of those individuals and of their communities to contribute to the host economy. We maintain that interventions should build upon existing skills. Indeed, in some cases, Congolese refugees forced to become farmers possessed skills—such as being doctors, nurses, and language experts—that were already in demand in Uganda.

Conclusion

Refugees in Rwamwanja have begun the process of building a 'new' economy. With little pre-existing infrastructure, the settlement represents a 'blank slate' in contrast to the more established settlements. The case therefore offered a rare opportunity to examine the dynamic emergence of a refugee economy immediately following a mass influx of refugees.

Despite being deprived of economic resources and needing to adjust to a highly restrictive institutional environment, Congolese refugees have nevertheless exercised the necessary agency to develop their own livelihood strategies. In some cases, a few entrepreneurial outliers have encouraged the gradual diversification of the economy through the establishment of new businesses, driving the development of new markets in a previously underdeveloped region.

As in the two more established settlements, agricultural activity offers the most viable economic opportunity, and most refugee households resort to farming-related activities despite many not even having agricultural experience prior to displacement. In contrast to the more established settlements, however, refugees with non-farming backgrounds have had extremely limited access to alternative livelihood strategies, having fewer opportunities to use non-farming skills, experiences, and qualifications.

Refugees' economic activities in Rwamwanja have therefore been less heterogeneous than in our other research sites in Uganda. Rwamwanja is also not as well networked to the more established settlements, lacking the density of local, national, and transnational economic connections to Kampala, Kyangwali, and Nakivale. Indeed, only a handful of survey respondents in Rwamwanja were engaged in specialized enterprises dealing with commercial goods and items beyond agricultural products.

Perhaps the most noticeable difference between Rwamwanja and our other research sites was the more stringent enforcement of regulations on refugees' lives. While some of these regulations are national regulations, they have been interpreted, implemented, and enforced more stringently within the more remote Rwamwanja settlement. The local authorities have, on the one hand, wanted to benefit from taxing refugees, but on the other hand, have made every attempt to limit refugees' opportunities for long-term economic or social integration.

Nevertheless, Rwamwanja reveals how, even under restrictive conditions, economic activity still takes place. The case highlights the dynamic process through which a new economy emerges following a mass influx of refugees even in an area with little pre-existing market activity. Out of initial aid delivery, informal barter creates the green shoots of economic diversification within which a small number of entrepreneurial refugees and nationals develop new businesses that transform constraints into opportunities. While this trend is embryonic in Rwamwanja, it offers important insights into the need for international actors to consider ways in which market-based activities can be supported at the earliest possible stage following a refugee influx.

8

The role of innovation

When people flee conflict and persecution, they have to adapt to changing contexts. They face new regulatory environments, new markets, and new social networks. These new circumstances present challenges and opportunities for refugees to survive and, occasionally, to thrive. The ways in which refugees are regulated leads to significant constraints on economic activity. Yet, despite this, many refugees develop highly innovative responses. Sometimes this can be transformative for the individual and the wider community.

Until recently, there has been little focus on innovation by refugees. Although there has been a growing debate about the role of 'humanitarian innovation', it has generally focused on ways in which innovation can be used to improve the response of humanitarian organizations. Although important, this work has tended to neglect the role of innovation by crisis-affected communities themselves. Put simply, the 'top-down' focus of humanitarian innovation has often neglected 'bottom-up' innovation by displaced populations themselves.

Innovation is an important part of everyday life. It occurs whenever people engage in creative problem-solving and make changes in how they respond to challenges. The scope of individual innovations can vary across a very broad spectrum from the incremental to the transformative. Within refugee populations, a small but significant minority engages in transformational innovation.

As has been recognized since the work of Joseph Schumpeter (1934), innovation has implications for an economy. It is the means through which individual agency dynamically drives economic change and growth within an economy. Following this logic, we argue that innovation similarly lies at the heart of refugee economies. In this chapter we explore this relationship. First, we conceptualize the relationship between refugee economies and innovation. Second, we examine the conditions that enable particular forms of innovation, and look at their wider economic impact. Third, we explore the kinds of enabling environments that are likely to support refugee innovation.

Innovation and Refugee Economies

Innovation is the way in which individuals or organizations create change by introducing new solutions to existing problems. Contrary to popular belief, these solutions do not have to be technological and they do not have to be transformative; they simply involve incremental adaptation of a product or process to context (Bessant and Tidd 2009).

In the private sector, the concept of 'innovation management' has existed for over a century (Tarde 1903). Although there are different ways to conceptualize the innovation process, it can broadly be considered as a four-stage process involving: (1) specifying a problem; (2) identifying a solution; (3) piloting and adapting a solution; (4) scaling the solution if and where appropriate.[1] In practice, this is not necessarily a linear process and frequently involves iterative feedback across the stages. A burgeoning literature on innovation suggests it often emerges from a number of sources, including cross-fertilization across sectors (Johnson 2011) and iteration through learning from success and failure (Babineaux and Krumboltz 2014).

In recent years, innovation has been integrated into humanitarian work. Since around 2009, there has been an identifiable 'innovation turn' across the humanitarian system. United Nations agencies, NGOs, governments, businesses, and even the military have begun to engage with the idea of humanitarian innovation, including creating special labs, funds, and partnerships to enable untapped ideas and solutions to be drawn upon (Betts and Bloom 2014; McClure and Gray 2014; Ramalingam et al. 2015). Innovation has also been applied for the purpose of rethinking organizational cultures and behaviours, and to improve response practices within particular sectors of humanitarianism, such as shelter, water, sanitation, energy, or logistics.

However, what has generally been missing is a recognition that humanitarian innovation is not just about improving organizational response. Around the world, communities affected by crisis are often at the forefront of response. Faced with significant constraints, they adapt to find solutions. This is particularly the case in relation to livelihood activities. Even faced with vast constraints, displaced populations sometimes develop a range of creative and entrepreneurial responses (Betts and Bloom 2013; Betts et al. 2015).

However, in addition to helping refugees and other crisis-affected communities to help themselves, innovation also plays a dynamic role within refugee economies. Economics has also long recognized the wider role that innovation plays in enabling economies to diversify and grow. Within both micro- and

---

[1] The process of innovation here has been adapted from existing literatures such as Garud, Tuertscher, and Van de Ven (2015) and observed as a broad trend in innovation management by Tidd and Bessant (2009) and Rothwell (1994).

macroeconomic theory, innovation serves as a means to stimulate markets, to drive efficiency, and increase productivity. Building on Solow's (1957) observations that technical progress can play a role in economic growth, endogenous growth models (Arrow 1962; Romer 1986) have shown how efficiency gains can drive growth in the ways actors use existing inputs. Indeed, the implication of this is that creative individuals add value not only for themselves but also for their wider communities.

As Joseph Schumpeter (1934) recognized at an even earlier stage, individual 'innovators' are central to any economy:

> ...every individual can accomplish by adapting himself to changes in his economic environment, without materially deviating from familiar lines. Therefore, too, the carrying out of new combinations is a special function, and the privilege of a type of people who are much less numerous than all those who have the 'objective' possibility of doing it. Therefore, finally, entrepreneurs are a special type. (Schumpeter 1934: 81)

Schumpeter describes an individual who is able to navigate markets and spot opportunities to exploit them as an 'entrepreneur'. When an entrepreneur succeeds in exploiting opportunities, she will undercut others in the market. Schumpeter termed this 'creative destruction', since old ideas and businesses fall with the onset of others. These new profits and improvements in the market enable an economy to grow. As a consequence, innovation has come to be a trait directly associated with individuals and entrepreneurs (Drucker 1985; Bessant and Tidd 2015). The term 'intrapreneur' has also emerged in the literature to identify entrepreneurial individuals who drive forward new ideas within large organizations (Antoncic and Hisrich 2003; Kolchin and Hyclak 1987).

For Schumpeter, the entrepreneur plays an essential role in preventing an economy's stagnation by challenging the status quo. Development is therefore 'defined by the carrying out of new combinations' (Schumpeter 1934: 66), and it follows that '[t]he carrying out of new combinations [is what] we call "enterprise"; the individuals whose function it is to carry them out we call "entrepreneurs"' (Schumpeter 1934: 74).

Schumpeter's ideas have an application in the role of innovation within refugee economies. As we laid out in Chapter 3, being a refugee is to occupy a distinctive institutional position. It creates particular forms of market distortions. These distortions, including the creation of artificial scarcity and abundance, lead to both constraints and opportunities. Innovation represents the process through which refugees adapt in these environments, maximizing opportunities and mitigating constraints. In this sense, innovation can be understood to represent the ways in which refugees are able to apply their agency—their skills, talents, and aspirations—in order to transform their structural situation into new sets of opportunities, which create value for themselves and for others.

Within refugee economies, innovation represents an analogous concept to Giddens' (1984) notion of 'structuration': individuals' opportunities are shaped by their structural environment; however, people also have the agency to act upon and change their structural environment. For us, 'innovation' is a process through which refugees can exert the agency to dynamically transform the economies in which they participate.

Lessons and corrections will occur throughout the four-stage process of innovation in response to opportunities or constraints that emerge in the surrounding environment. Once an innovation has taken place, it can in turn become the groundwork for others to build upon. The economic activities that we have seen in our research in Uganda have to a large extent been made possible by individuals who have engaged in innovation to transform their structural constraints.

Despite a range of constraints discussed in previous chapters, a number of features make the refugee context auspicious for innovation. When people flee to new countries, they face new markets, regulatory environments, and social networks. However, they may bring with them ideas and practices that may be new to the host country context. The continual arrival and transition of multiple refugee communities within the same host country therefore means that 'new combinations' and interactions emerge in this context. In turn, this interaction creates opportunities for new innovation and entrepreneurship.

Refugee Innovation in Uganda

Our research highlights a number of ways in which refugee entrepreneurs transform structural constraints into opportunities, creating new combinations of ideas and products that in turn shape the growth of their economies. As Schumpeter recognizes, innovative entrepreneurs have unique personalities and find a 'joy of creating, of getting things done, or simply of exercising one's energy and ingenuity' (1942: 93):

> ... the carrying out of new combinations is a special function, and the privilege of a type of people who are much less numerous than all those who have the 'objective' possibility of doing it ... entrepreneurs are a special type.
>
> (Schumpeter 1934: 81)

In our qualitative research in Uganda, we discovered that some of the intrinsic traits of innovative entrepreneurs, as identified by Schumpeter, may be encouraged by the particular context of refugee life. Our survey and interviews demonstrated that refugees independently sought new solutions in the radically new contexts they found themselves in during exile. Refugees utilized their existing skills and experiences, as well as new skills learned after arrival, to create social or economic change for themselves and others. Additionally, we found that refugees embarking on a process of innovation worked hard at maintaining a future-focused mindset, despite the hardships they had previously endured, taking on risks within their economies.

Here, we draw upon the conceptual framework of 'innovation processes' by following individual refugees through their own processes of innovation. Analysis of this process allows us to understand how certain problems encountered by refugees are defined, solutions found, adapted, and scaled. This highlights a number of factors beyond individual traits which influence and restrict refugees' opportunities for innovation in the urban, protracted, and emergency camp settings.

In an urban setting, refugee innovation leverages existing infrastructure, which enables refugees to navigate the complex networks of activity. In this sense, refugees are engaging in incremental innovation to build on the economy that already exists. In protracted settlements, innovation is responsible for diversifying the economy as it grows. And in an emergency, refugees use more transformative innovation to create a functioning market from a 'blank slate'. Consequently, in each setting innovation provides benefits at three levels: for households, for local surrounding communities, and for the national economy. This section explores these different economic settings in turn, from urban to emergency.

In Kampala, those who stood out as doing something different formed the basis for our analysis. Refugees are engaging in two aspects of innovation: as creators of businesses and in social innovation to support other refugees. Urban refugees are nested within broad economic structures, where densely populated areas broadly have access to electricity, water, road networks, educational institutions, healthcare facilities, and an abundance of shops and trade. These services offer refugees an existing platform from which to innovate.

The four-stage process of innovation provides a useful framework to examine how innovators have both succeeded and struggled with new ventures in an urban environment. Eugenie's story provides a good example as we follow her through her problem definition, solution identification, adaptations, and finally scaling. Eugenie is a Rwandan refugee, and unlike many Rwandans she does not work in the second-hand clothes trade, nor the dairy industry. Eugenie's unique path led her to become one of the only refugee employees working in the specific office of an international NGO in the city—where she teaches other refugees arts and crafts. Eugenie has also established her own business to trade the artistic items she produces—breaking into a market not commonly frequented by refugees. 'Before being a trainer, I learnt how to innovate myself,' Eugenie told us.[2] She was a teacher by profession, and in Rwanda worked in marketing for a large company; however, she arrived in Uganda in 2006 with no options for work at the start. Eugenie's problem definition was to find a source of income to support herself and her family—a starting point from which many of our interviewees also began in their process of innovation.

In the city, Eugenie was surrounded by many Ugandan craftspeople and she took an interest in art and design herself—an attractive alternative to begging, something in which Eugenie refused to partake. In 2008, she approached a Ugandan woman who crafted jewellery by hand and ran a shop in the centre of the city selling necklaces made of paper and manufactured beads. Eugenie discussed her interest with a friend who provided Eugenie with a small amount of money to pay the Ugandan woman 300000 UGX (150 USD) in exchange for training in jewellery making. This second stage of innovation was made possible through the informal financing and the fact that Eugenie's native Rwandan language of Lingala was also used in Kampala.

Following the training, Eugenie's Ugandan mentor gave Eugenie 70000 UGX (45 USD) worth of materials, which included pliers and raw materials. She began selling her own necklaces door-to-door and slowly saved small amounts of money left over after buying food for her children and paying her rent. At the time of our interactions, Eugenie used these skills to work as an arts and crafts trainer for an NGO, supporting the livelihoods of other refugees. This was an opportunity that Eugenie had found through her community work with a refugee-led human rights group. The group's founder had personal contacts with the NGO which was seeking a trainer to join their team. In this sense, new opportunities had occurred later in the process of innovation—through Eugenie's urban social networks.[3]

Eugenie continues to expand her skills even further, learning new craft techniques through her networks of craftspeople in the city, and she offers valuable opportunities for learning to other refugees. Eugenie has also registered her own business to sell refugee crafts in national and international markets. Eugenie's process of innovation started small but over several years has become an important part of other refugees' lives as well as her own. In addition, this incremental innovation also has potential knock-on effects for the national economy through sales of craft goods to, for example, hospitals and the tourist trade.

Innovation, such as Eugenie's, is common among refugees in Kampala. A different initiative led by Congolese refugees provides a deeper example

---

[2] Interview with Eugenie, a Rwandan refugee in Kampala, personal communication, June 2013.
[3] Social networks were also documented as a strong attribute for other refugees in an urban economy in Chapter 5.

of how social initiatives also follow a process of innovation, and what this looks like in an urban environment.

Young African Refugees for Integral Development (YARID) is a community-based organization creating an independent institutional space for fellow refugees to learn skills and foster their own innovative ideas. During the first stage of innovation (problem definition), the founders of YARID were clear that they wanted to tackle the issue of unemployment among their fellow Congolese refugees in Kampala. YARID started in 2007 using the limited resources available to them, including a public football playing field in the area of Nsambya, where many young Congolese resided. YARID convened a weekly football match, which unexpectedly started to attract over 100 people each week. Many of the participants stayed to chat after the game, forming a community that often spoke together about their problems, including unemployment. The YARID founders discovered that a key challenge to accessing employment in Kampala for many refugees was a lack of English speaking skills, leading them to organize informal English lessons each morning in a local church building.

For YARID, the second stage of the innovation process (solution finding) was extremely democratic and focused on social benefits. This ethos continues to be important as their social enterprise expands. YARID's Director, Robert, explained 'Without the community we couldn't have done this. We come together, we think together, we decide what to do.'[4] Being embedded within the community not only gives YARID the ability to understand what people are asking and need, but also enables local Congolese and other refugee communities to trust the work they do. Rather than providing free handouts like many charities, YARID instead has focused on creating a 'safe space' where refugees can gather and develop skills that are useful for the Kampala economy. YARID now runs a women's tailoring workshop, business planning classes, computer training, and social media classes, among others. One refugee in Kampala, James, explains how he has made use of the English and computing classes provided by YARID to launch his photography business:

> English classes helped [me] to talk with customers and computer classes helped too. There are no other photo shops here. I tried at the start and didn't know it would be successful.[5]

Although financing has been a challenge for YARID, Robert is adamant that 'financial resources are not the only thing. Some people say we can't do things because of money. But when you have an idea there are many ways you can

---

[4] Robert Hakiza, YARID Director, presentation on 'facilitating bottom-up innovation' held at the Humanitarian Innovation Conference 2015, University of Oxford.

[5] Interview with James, a Congolese refugee in Kampala, personal communication, 27 June 2013.

find to start something.'[6] YARID's use of the local football pitch in their early days, and the generous donations of time by their many activity volunteers provide ample evidence for this claim.

Of course, access to finance remains necessary for material activities. In many instances, the ad hoc expenditure necessary to keep the organization running often comes from the pockets of the YARID founders and volunteers. Robert explains that volunteers often buy or bring the chalk needed for the daily English classes, which also helps to create a sense of ownership among volunteers and participants. YARID is currently trying to enter the 'scale-up' stage of its innovation process, but has faced challenges in finding larger sources of financing for rent and equipment. They have also struggled with negative attitudes from large organizations in the city, which are unwilling to support them as they are unaware of the existence of refugees in Uganda.[7] Recently Robert has engaged in several international conferences and, at the time of writing, began to win internationally competitive funds for innovation towards growing YARID's work.

As we see from these cases, the challenges of enterprise in an urban setting, as cited in Chapter 5, are also applicable to the process of innovation. Access to financial capital was the most commonly cited challenge for urban entrepreneurs, mentioned by 32 per cent of urban refugees in our survey, compared to an average of 19 per cent in Nakivale and Kyangwali.

Although economic constraints were a problem, the urban context also offered a far greater number of opportunities for innovators. With perseverance and ingenuity, some innovators were eventually able to access existing institutions and services that were available in Kampala.

A well-established Congolese film-maker, John, made the most of the urban landscape by approaching the national film institute for training when he arrived in Uganda. Film-making was a passion John had discovered in his youth when a television first came to his village in the DRC. However, unlike Eugenie, language was a significant barrier for John upon his arrival to Kampala. He described the difficulties he faced when he tried to enter the *bitenge* fabric trade in the city: 'I did not speak English, so just had to trade with prices written on paper. Ugandan traders took advantage since I couldn't speak the language.'[8]

After several visits to the film institute John found a lecturer who spoke French and who allowed him to take the courses at an affordable price. John taught himself English whilst at the school, and went on to become a

---

[6] Robert Hakiza, YARID Director, presentation on 'facilitating bottom-up innovation' held at the Humanitarian Innovation Conference 2015, University of Oxford.

[7] Ibid.

[8] Interview with John, a Congolese refugee and film-maker in Kampala, personal communication, 20 June 2013.

successful film producer in Kampala. His acquired skills have enabled him to have one of the more successful film companies in the city.[9] John also trains other young refugees who have gone on to produce films and music of their own, something he has in common with Eugenie and Robert—an interest in providing opportunities for other refugees. For John, however, urban opportunities not only support his business, but also pose personal challenges. Although discrimination is not reported as an acute issue for refugees' economies in Kampala,[10] John has experienced threats from Ugandans and has been the target of break-ins, which has stifled the viability of his business in certain parts of the city. He speculates that his direct competition with Ugandan film-makers may be a source of this discrimination.[11]

In this active urban environment, the greater number of resources and markets are key for enabling innovation. Still, for refugees, being able to exploit and take advantage of these resources usually requires personal risk and uncertainty. Beyond income generation, many innovations in Kampala are also driven by a strong sense of social responsibility, and strive to support other refugees through skills transfer or directly through the delivery of needed goods and services. Although often at a small scale, innovation can begin to incrementally influence the urban economy over time by creating new initiatives that are attuned to the interests of the refugee population.

Compared to Kampala, innovation in the protracted refugee settlements can look very different. In Nakivale and Kyangwali, refugees rely on international agencies for assistance and for the maintenance of public services such as water, education, health, and energy. In informal economies, innovation is often a response to different constraints, hardships, or absence of services (Fu et al. 2014). In Chapter 6 we already met Francesca, a nurse, and Rose, an energy provider, both of whom exemplify refugee innovators who are filling in for gaps in provision of essential services in the protracted settlements.

In Kyangwali, the formation of another group, COBURWAS International Youth Organization to Transform Africa (CIYOTA), demonstrates how social innovation in public services can diversify and go beyond financial economic gains. CIYOTA is run by a strong group of dedicated refugee volunteers who are seeking to improve the education facilities and opportunities available in the settlement. Because Kyangwali lacks sufficient educational resources, CIYOTA built a new primary school in the settlement, and secured the right for Kyangwali refugees to attend a Ugandan secondary school in Hoima town. To provide further support, CIYOTA also runs a hostel in Hoima for refugee students. A few years after starting, the organization had set its sights beyond

---

[9] Ibid.   [10] As noted in Chapter 5.
[11] Interview with John, a Congolese refugee in Kampala, personal communication, 20 June 2013.

Kyangwali and cultivated a leadership curriculum with the goal of nurturing future leaders of Africa. CIYOTA has scaled several of these innovative approaches, and has since opened offices in other parts of Uganda and also in the DRC.

The case studies demonstrate the ways in which innovative solutions often stem from individual refugees' own experiences of frustration or deprivation in the settlements. For example, Rose recognized her own need for electricity and the danger of using candles for lighting, which led her to begin her energy business.[12]

In Nakivale, innovation is helping to expand the diversity of the local economy. Demou-Kay is a young Congolese man who learned to make films in the DRC and came to Nakivale only two months before our meeting. After connecting with other young Congolese refugees upon his arrival who helped him to navigate the settlement, Demou-Kay sought to earn an income, but he also strongly wished to maintain his existing skill set in film-making. Demou-Kay was able to hire camera equipment and a laptop from other refugees within the settlement and would use the Internet connection at the UNHCR-founded Community Technology Access (CTA) centre to download new software for editing films and to learn new technical skills. With this expertise and equipment, he was able to advertise his skills and now occasionally finds work filming at weddings and concerts around the settlement. However, Demou-Kay has been unable to turn his business into full-time work, as the demand for filming in Nakivale is still relatively low, and is further constrained by the limited expendable income of most residents.[13]

However, this has not dampened Demou-Kay's enthusiasm for other technology projects. Through experimenting with new skills and odd electrical parts he found in the settlement, Demou-Kay used his self-taught technical expertise to build a radio transmitter. After some experimentation, the radio transmitter he created transmits sound via radio waves up to a 10 km radius. The radio is used to transmit a regular radio programme run by Demou-Kay and his fellow Congolese church youth group. The radio station offers a way to radically diversify life for residents as a source of information sharing, entertainment, and a platform for dialogue about issues that affect the settlement. During our visit we were shown the small mud-and-daub radio studio, provided to the group by the church. Here the team was starting to earn a modest income from charging for song requests played on their regular broadcasts.[14]

---

[12] See Chapter 6 for more details of the interview with Rose, a Congolese refugee in Kyangwali settlement, personal communication, 28 February 2013.

[13] As seen in Chapter 5, income distribution is lower in protracted settlements compared to Kampala.

[14] Interview with Demou-Kay and his youth group at the radio studio, Nakivale, personal communication, May 2013.

The radio replaced an old megaphone that had previously been used to communicate information in this part of the settlement and has arguably brought more efficient information sharing to the camp. As we noted in Chapter 6, imperfect information in the market acted as an opportunity for innovation—in this case the radio offered a unique platform for public information about markets and broader life in the settlement. One of the young people running the station explained:

> The radio station is better than the old megaphone. It sends messages up to 10 km around the settlement. The radio transmits information like details of lost ration cards, and lost children. So far one person has already found their family through an announcement on our radio show.[15]

At the time we met the youth group, Demou-Kay and his colleagues were in dialogue with the government authorities to obtain a radio licence, and they had aspirations to scale the station to Kampala in future.

Looking at another example of innovation in a settlement economy, we go to the heart of Base Camp, Nakivale's largest market district. Here there is a diverse array of services available, but the more unusual shops stand out. A few shops have small solar panels rigged to roofs made of plastic sheeting and bound wooden branches. Below the solar panels are hand-painted signs displaying lists of technical and electronic services such as printing, Internet services, music copying, and phone repair.

James is the owner of a long, narrow shop with a printer, computer, phone repair tools, and car battery. The equipment is ready to be used and is linked by visible wires to the solar panel on the roof above. James described the development of this innovative shop as part of a longer struggle to find work when he arrived in Nakivale five years ago.[16] Unable to continue in his former profession as a nurse, he started life in Nakivale in a similar way to many other Congolese refugees we met, working in the construction trade.[17] Predominantly driven by his passion for technology, and seeking to pursue new business opportunities, he saved his earnings to purchase his first computer and solar panel, and pursued technical training in the nearby town of Mbarara to learn how to repair mobile phones. Recognizing a gap in the market for efficient phone repair, he purposefully cultivated new skills under constraining circumstances and regularly travels outside of the settlement for the materials he needs.

[15] Interview with a Congolese refugee in Nakivale settlement, personal communication, 3 May 2013.
[16] Interview with James, a Congolese refugee in Nakivale settlement, personal communication, 3 May 2013.
[17] See Figure 6.2 in Chapter 6 for most frequently cited livelihood activity by refugees. Construction is listed third most common for Congolese refugees in Nakivale.

The training was not easy...As far as I know, I am the only one using computers for phone repairs here. People are interested in me and this business, many bring their phones here. My only regret is that I didn't start this technology business sooner.[18]

James explained that he aspires to scale his innovative business by expanding into new and updated technologies. It was clear that James had developed his business acumen over several iterations of learning and trying new things. In a setting where electricity and mobile internet coverage are sparse, James has succeeded in creating a unique innovation that contributes to the local economy and other businesses in new ways. In fact, within the settlement there were several other businesses that specialized in music and computing services that had followed James's lead, expanding the local market for these services.[19]

Material resources are the basic inputs for any material economy, but in a resource-constrained and rural environment, innovation has an important role to play in introducing new goods and services. In another small mud-and-daub building, this time in the back streets of Base Camp, a discreet computer game shop has been set up, solely resourced from used goods. Inside the shop, second-hand computers and games consoles are lined up against the walls with a bench for customers to sit and play from. The Somali owner, Abdi, explained how he has been able to make improvements to his equipment in order to maintain his business.

I make some adjustments to make the equipment last longer, this one is better than Sony [pointing to one of his games consoles]...Spare parts are important. I never overlook something I find on the ground. I take any old electronics or metal parts I find from the street, such as old torches.[20]

Abdi proudly revealed to us his large box of spare parts that he had collected from people and from waste around the settlement; these were important assets to his business. But he still has some challenges, primarily issues with keeping his generator maintained and running, as well as concerns about theft in his shop at night. His thin tarpaulin roof offers little security, and yet investment in a more permanent roof would be costly. To manage these risks, Abdi uses his collected spare parts to carefully maintain his generator, and at night he moves his expensive games from the shop to minimize the risk of robbery.

Despite these challenges, his business has already started to scale locally in the settlement due to his own success as an innovative entrepreneur:

---

[18] Interview with James, a Congolese refugee in Nakivale settlement, personal communication, 3 May 2013.
[19] Ibid.
[20] Interview with Abdi, a Somali refugee in Nakivale settlement, personal communication, 4 May 2013.

Instead of waiting for donors I wanted to make a living...I talked to friends in Kampala who run similar businesses and so I decided to start one here...There's one other guy here who also charges money for games, who learned from me. But I'm the pioneer. This guy sometimes comes for advice, and I occasionally give him spare parts.[21]

Abdi's decisions about his business are also tied to his precarious position as a refugee, as he was reluctant to make larger or long-term investments given his lack of ownership over his shop building and the knowledge that he might either choose or be forced to leave the camp.[22] The precarity of life in exile as well as expectations of aid affect the ways in which refugees choose to innovate and come up with new solutions. One shop owner started his shop in collaboration with other refugee families, hoping that they might receive support from humanitarian organizations in Nakivale. His shop is running well, but the families' hopes for scaling it up lie in a long-awaited donation from international agencies.

Inevitably, innovation involves risk, and some experiments with new livelihood activities encountered failure. The former Somali owners of a bakery eventually closed their business down due to low sales and respiratory health problems from oven smoke fumes, rendering their investments in the handmade bespoke baking trays and ovens useless. However, the family risked a new business venture following this initial failure, and have now found success cooking and selling *samosas* outside of their small grocery shop. The *samosas* are cooked on a mud-stove which Salima, the wife, constructed after watching a neighbour receive training from an NGO-hired community-based worker. The stove was built from free and naturally available materials, and she had adapted the design to suit the needs of their shop. This new venture successfully exploits a new and more fruitful market opportunity which incorporates their existing skill set (baking) and locally available resources.

Innovation in the settlements demonstrates that despite limited access to public services, educational opportunities, and raw materials, markets can still expand as innovators introduce new and important activities to settlement economies. Diversification of the settlement economies can be attributed to those who are willing to take risks and who bring new skills not otherwise available in the local economy.

In Rwamwanja, an emergency refugee situation, innovation again takes a different form. Here, resources and services are even more restrictive than in the protracted settlements. As many residents of this camp are new to Uganda and relatively recently uprooted, their resources for innovative business endeavours are limited. Looking at the innovation process in an emergency

---

[21] Ibid.
[22] As discussed in Chapter 6, land rights are not provided to refugees living in camps.

setting, it is apparent that most refugees are only able to reach the first few stages of innovation during their first years of exile.

However, the 'outliers' mentioned in Chapter 7 spotlight how increased innovation is beginning to emerge over time. For innovators like Nicholas,[23] innovation in its earlier stages is made possible by previous material assets, financial savings, or a strong desire to continue prior professions rather than embark on a livelihood of farming. These outliers often must take personal risks to start new ventures and businesses, but are able to offer new skills and resources not previously available.

A social innovator in Rwamwanja, Matthew, describes motivations similar to YARID's founders in starting a youth organization to take action in response to a community-wide issue that many of his peers were facing:

> When I came to Rwamwanja settlement, I saw many young people doing nothing. They were idle. No job, no education opportunities. Many young refugees were not seeing any hope in the settlement. Many of them started negative behaviour—drinking, smoking, fighting...I wanted to do something to change the desperate situation. In DRC, I was involved in a youth group so I wanted to do the same here.[24]

As a former youth leader, Matthew was able to capitalize upon his experiences bringing people together for activities such as music and drama. Although many were uninterested at first, Matthew continued to test new ideas, and the group has gradually expanded to eighty-nine members.

Although the group focuses on social mobility, they are also beginning to have a small impact on the local economy. Matthew designed and constructed musical instruments from old jerry cans and oil tins distributed as part of food rations from the UNHCR to form a music band which now plays at ceremonies and other events in the settlement:

> These are not mainly for income generation but we are invited to events often and play music in various ceremonies. Sometimes, we get volunteer donations. Or sometimes people give us some money to organize a social event or concerts.[25]

The group hopes to continue its expansion, which is both enabled and constrained by the small amounts of excess expenditure that residents in the settlement can contribute. Although new to the market, Matthew has played a small part in contributing to the entertainment options within the economy.

---

[23] Chapter 7 describes how Nicholas carried his sewing machine with him to Uganda to continue his tailoring trade.

[24] Interview with Matthew, a Congolese refugee in Rwamwanja settlement, personal communication, 8 February 2015.

[25] Ibid.

Most of the non-agricultural economic activities that took place in Rwamwanja could be considered part of an innovation process, but importantly were also connected to agricultural livelihoods and industry. People like Andrew, the bar owner, quoted in Chapter 7, started his business from savings initially earned through farming. This was the first bar opened in Rwamwanja and was a transformative innovation at the time, since it offered a small alternative to the aid-dependent lifestyle and charity-based systems in the settlement.

Another refugee we met was also determined to continue a livelihood that he loved, rather than farm. Luke, a sculptor from the DRC, described art as his vocation. He faced many challenges, including limited market access to customers and access to tools, as well as trauma from his life in the DRC:

> I can only approach customers in and around the camp area. Also, it is not easy to buy necessary tools for sculpture. I could not bring all necessary items for sculpture from DRC. I have to travel to Kampala to buy specific tools because they are available only in Kampala.
>
> Also, it is not easy to keep mental composure now. This type of artistic work requires good mental composure. But my mental peace has been destabilized since my departure from DRC. I feel like draining my heart. Whenever I remember what happened to me in DRC, my mental composure is disturbed. I am afraid to be sent back to DRC.[26]

Despite these challenges, Luke is pursuing his love for sculpting and sits each day outside his home carving ornate statues out of large blocks of wood purchased from Ugandans nearby. Luke sells mainly to Ugandan customers, entering directly into the national economy. In these early stages of innovation Luke has not tested many different formations of his business, nor scaled, but he is trying something radically new in his context.

In emergency contexts, there are larger number of gaps and opportunities in the market, but innovation is hugely constrained by the lack of resources available. When transformative innovations do take place, they can act as accelerators for the rest of the economy and offer opportunities from which others can build.

Across all of the contexts, 'knowledge exchange' among refugees is crucial throughout the innovation process. Exchange of skills and information enables people to identify problems or opportunities during the first stage of innovation, as well as to create appropriate and technical solutions based on an understanding of the specific types of needs and markets available. This knowledge accumulation occurs through personal or shared experiences as

---

[26] Interview with Luke, a Congolese refugee in Rwamwanja settlement, personal communication, 5 February 2015.

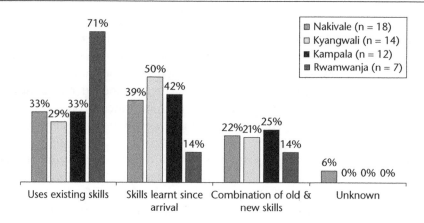

Figure 8.1 Source of skills obtained for current livelihood

Source: Data based on 51 qualitative interviews conducted with refugees identified as conducting unique initiatives in their economies

well as drawing upon or developing new skills in exile in ways that contribute to innovation.

In Rwamwanja a greater percentage of innovators were able to use existing skills, as less time spent in exile meant that less money was saved and spent on new training. In protracted sites and in the urban context, many of the interviewees had saved up financing and spent several years seeking new skills which they then applied to their new initiatives.

Figure 8.1 shows the distribution of this descriptive data in terms of percentage of innovators interviewed and the source of the skills they used to create their innovation.

Additionally, our data also demonstrates that refugee innovation varies across different economic settings. Incremental innovation through small changes is most common in an urban environment, where refugees' innovations plug into a wealth of existing resources, actors, and networks. This makes entirely new or transformative ideas rarer, given the greater numbers of resources and innovators that exist in urban spaces. However, in an emergency setting, the economic 'blank slate' provides fertile ground upon which innovation can have knock-on effects for other new types of initiatives, businesses, and production. In a newly emerging economy, refugee innovators serve as the catalysts who help accelerate economic activity and create transformative innovations. Meanwhile, in a protracted settlement context, refugee economies are already diverse, yet understandably underdeveloped in comparison to the capital city, leading to a combination of incremental and transformative innovations that are able to exploit remaining gaps.

Figure 8.2 depicts the frequency of incremental and transformative innovation occurring across the different economic settings.

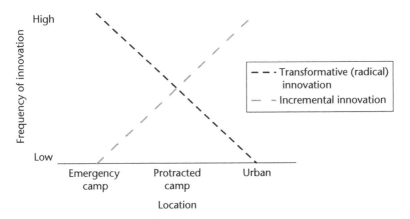

Figure 8.2 Type of innovation by economic setting

Facilitating Refugee Innovation

Innovation exists among refugee communities. The capacity to innovate, however, is shaped by the enabling environment within which innovation takes place. One endemic challenge for refugee innovation is the omnipresent disparity between what international refugee assistance offers, and the lived experience, agency, and preferences of refugees themselves (Barbara Harrell-Bond 1982; Kibreab 2004).

There are many well-known examples of well-intentioned international agencies trying to develop projects that inevitably are poorly adapted to what refugees want or need. One Congolese refugee, Dan, reflected on these gaps:

> [T]hey [international agencies] don't always give the best type of help... the best would be for example to help me buy a generator. There is fuel and I can do the calculation and add my savings to see if it is possible to make a business. I could write a business plan... It's been difficult to plan for long term since I may be told to go back, but I would like to get a generator to power a machine or expand my goat rearing.[27]

Dan also explained that many construction workers used mosquito nets distributed by international agencies as rope in their buildings, instead of their intended use.

> Mosquitoes are not as big as food or unemployment—if these problems were solved then people could buy their own mosquito net. People would be self-reliant. But

---

[27] Interview with Dan, a Congolese refugee in Kyangwali settlement, personal communication, 10 May 2013.

instead they [the NGOs] give mosquito nets—some houses have ten mosquito nets and so they use them as ropes.[28]

A Congolese beekeeper in Kyangwali, Jon, highlighted a series of problems he had encountered with international assistance. He explained to us that last year, staff from one international NGO visited him to learn more about his beekeeping business. They indicated that he would benefit from identifying other local beekeepers in the area so that they could start a group together. After making these arrangements, the group was given some overalls to prevent bee stings and tools for making beehives, as well as ten modern beehives to share. However, Jon had not expected any new hives from the NGO when they arrived in early 2013. As he described it, '[the NGO] just brought it, they didn't ask if we needed it'. The shared new hives were installed on his land because he had space alongside his many handcrafted hives. When we returned to see Jon five months after our initial visit, we learned that the new beehives had not yielded much honey in comparison to the traditional hives, and many of the new hives had become infested with an insect that drove the bees out of the hive. These hives were now waiting in the forest to see if any bees would return to them.

In addition, the newly formed beekeeper group was a failure, and did not collaborate beyond occasionally sharing the original equipment that the NGO had given them. As Jon explained:

> We [in the group] only share tools and overalls. The overalls are good for stopping stings from the bees when we clip the wings and we collect honey. I don't use the overalls often, as others are using them. They don't live near here.[29]

Through the NGO Jon did teach a group of new beekeepers how to build handcrafted beehives as part of a broader training course on beekeeping; however, he found that his interaction with the NGO was limited and non-consultative, and few useful outputs emerged from the relationship.

This example highlights the complexities and challenges that NGOs face in supporting livelihoods and innovation, and the critical necessity of paying close attention to existing cultures, capacities, and ideas of refugees. More successful interventions have involved the creation of facilities that refugees can adapt to support their own choices and livelihood innovation activities. In Nakivale, for example, UNHCR has created a Community Technology Access (CTA) Centre focused on improving IT skills and access to online learning (UNHCR 2015b). Nakivale's CTA Centre is refugee-led and refugee-managed, located in the centre of the settlement, and runs computer training

---

[28] Ibid.

[29] Interview with Jon, a Congolese refugee in Kyangwali settlement, personal communication, 9 May 2013.

classes and an open Internet café where customers pay an hourly fee to use the facilities. The CTA has become a hub for refugees in Nakivale—out of the 11 per cent of refugees in the settlement who accessed the Internet daily, 58 per cent of them did so at the CTA.[30]

During a meeting with the refugee committee that directs the CTA, committee members mentioned examples of refugees who use the space to support their livelihoods.[31] One woman used the Internet to find out the price of goods in the markets outside of the settlement, and another man had sold his car using sales contacts he made via the Internet. It was here at the CTA that Demou-Kay, the young Congolese man who had built the radio station previously discussed, worked most days to make his films and download software and resources that he would use both for his business and to support the radio station.[32] These diverse and unintended uses of the CTA were of interest to the UNHCR staff supporting the centre, particularly since the CTA was originally designed to facilitate refugee education and online work, rather than innovation (Anderson 2013; UNHCR 2015b). Yet these observations are congruous with data from CTA projects worldwide. A recent study evaluating the impact of these centres globally recognizes the difficulties in supporting refugees' self-reliance, and recommends that the CTA centres could be developed further to support livelihood innovation among refugees (Anderson 2013).

This chapter demonstrates that refugee innovation occurs regardless of international assistance—and sometimes in spite of it. However, there are significant obstacles that prevent refugees from fully scaling their innovations, and which the international community could play a role in mitigating. Recognizing the role of individual innovators and the ways in which they adapt to structural constraints is an important opportunity through which to reconceive dominant aid models. This involves supporting an enabling environment for refugees that provides auspicious regulatory conditions, better business development opportunities, access to capital and banking facilities, improved local infrastructure, and access to electricity and Internet connectivity. It may also involve the international community shifting its focus from being the dominant planner of refugee communities to taking on a facilitation role.

Efforts to facilitate refugee innovation can also take lessons from discussions on participatory development approaches (Chambers 2007). Although beneficiary participation has become a development trope, ongoing debates highlight a diverse array of competing perspectives and critiques (e.g. Cornwall

---

[30] Not using population estimate figures, but calculated using raw figures of households who stated that they use the Internet.

[31] Focus group with CTA committee, Nakivale, May 2013.

[32] Interview with Demou-Kay, Nakivale, personal communication, May 2013.

and Brock 2005; Chambers 2012), including concerns about the coercive influence of external actors, exclusively rhetorical use of 'participatory' as a label, and also the entrenchment of existing power relations within communities (Cornwall 2002; Hailey 2001). Participatory approaches are also often limited during the early stages of humanitarian response (Brown and Donini 2014; Boyden et al. 2002).

A genuinely people-centred approach to innovation would need to go beyond existing participation practices by starting with refugees' own problem identification and working directly with refugees to identify and pilot possible solutions. It would also need to involve not only consultation with and support for individual innovators, but also a deeper understanding of how existing social systems enable innovation within structural constraints. Fundamentally, it requires external actors to recognize that innovation takes place within a pre-existing market context and complex social structure. Rather than assuming that refugees' own adaptation mechanisms do not exist or are irrelevant, external actors would better contribute by building upon and enabling initiatives from within communities.

Conclusion

This chapter demonstrates that refugee-led innovation often takes place despite significant constraints. Furthermore, it shows how processes of innovation are an integral part of refugee economies. Mostly taking place on a small scale, refugees' own ideas and talents are being put to use to create unique businesses and to open up local markets to new goods and services. Regulatory and infrastructural barriers, however, continue to restrict refugees' creative capacities and limit their ability to scale their businesses and social endeavours.

On a theoretical level, refugee 'innovators' play an important role within refugee economies. They may be thought of as the individuals and groups that transform structural constraints into opportunities that in turn benefit the wider economy. This echoes Schumpeter's long-standing recognition of the role that innovation plays within an economy. It highlights the need to recognize and support outlying refugee innovators and entrepreneurs, in part because of the wider social contributions they make. In conceptualizing innovation in refugee economies, we can think about the economic outcome of innovation at different levels. First, it may benefit the individual by providing income for them and their family. Second, it may have a knock-on impact on the local economy—providing, for example, local infrastructure, or community spaces to learn new skills. Third, it may go on to have a wider impact at a national or transnational level, creating positive economic outcomes for host communities or businesses. Cutting across these outcomes, and making them possible, lie the institutional constraints and opportunities that both structure and are structured by refugee initiatives, local, national, and international markets, the international community, and the host government.

Yet, there remains a fundamental gap in understanding refugee innovation, as there has been little systematic research in this area. Our research in Uganda offers a starting point for understanding refugee innovation by drawing attention to its diversity, as well as highlighting some of the factors that contribute to an enabling environment for such innovation. Refugees make use of Uganda's national systems in their innovations—tapping into the infrastructure available, education systems, and formal business regulations. The outcomes of these endeavours have a knock-on impact for the personal life or business of the individual, for their surrounding community, and even the region that they live within. Facilitation is key in thinking about how refugee-led innovation can best be supported to ensure that it is positively leveraged for a humanitarian good.

There is immense untapped potential to facilitate refugee innovation in ways that can contribute to empowering both individuals and communities. International organizations, NGOs, and implementing partners are faced with the challenge of ensuring that such facilitation is participatory and works in a representative way with pre-existing community structures. Too often 'humanitarian innovation' has been approached in top-down ways that risk marginalizing the creativity, entrepreneurship, and resilience of refugees and displaced populations themselves.

9

The role of business

The global refugee regime has generally been thought of as state-centric. This is unsurprising, given that it is by definition based on an intergovernmental framework within which governments reciprocally commit to providing asylum to people whose own states are unable to ensure their protection. The regime is premised upon upholding international refugee law, which relates primarily to the obligations of states, and UNHCR's primary responsibility has been to play a supervisory role in supporting states' implementation of their obligations under that legal framework.

Since the start of the twenty-first century, however, there has been a growing interest among governments and international organizations in the private sector's potential role as an alternative source of funding and delivery of refugee assistance. Initially triggered by recognition of funding shortages in protecting refugees in host countries in the global South, and a desire to diversify its donor portfolio, UNHCR began to explore the role that multinational corporations and foundations could play in philanthropy or corporate social responsibility (CSR), opening its first Private-Sector Fundraising Unit in 2006.

Gradually, UNHCR's view of the role of the private sector has become increasingly nuanced. It has started to recognize a range of ways in which business can play a role in humanitarian assistance, including through social enterprise and through a range of for-profit roles connected to core business interests. Today, its engagement includes recognition of the roles that business can play in innovation, employment creation, skills transfer, and reverse supply chains. UNHCR has begun to recognize the potential diversity of private-sector motives for engagement, including 'triple bottom line' companies that seek to optimize social goals and sustainability as well as returns.

The private sector is especially relevant in the context of refugees and development. Historically, attempts to close the 'relief-to-development' gap have been state-centric. They were premised upon the idea that Northern donor states would provide additional sources of development assistance for refugees, in exchange for which Southern host states would improve refugees' access to self-reliance or local integration. This frequently resulted in an international cooperation problem, in which neither party could be persuaded to make an adequate commitment to their side of the bargain.

An alternative way of conceiving of self-reliance is as inherently related to both states and markets. Refugees' ability to access opportunities is partly a consequence of the policy environment, and is inextricably connected to the right to work and freedom of movement, for example. But it also relies upon opportunities to be producers, consumers, and employees, and interactions with markets within and beyond the particular rural or urban context in which they live. In other words, the way in which business works—whether endogenous or exogenous to the community—and the opportunities it creates are a central and conceptually neglected part of refugees' access to self-reliance and livelihood opportunities.

Until now, there has been limited literature on the role of the private sector in the global refugee regime. This is in contrast to the vast literature that now exists relating to the role of the private sector in other areas of global governance. It has been widely recognized that private actors may play important roles in global governance through, for example, lobbying, CSR, private rule-making and standard setting, the development of voluntary codes of conduct, public–private partnerships, philanthropy, innovation, and the role of expert knowledge, among other examples. It considers how business often plays a role across the different levels of global governance: agenda-setting, negotiation, implementation, monitoring, and enforcement (Abbott and Snidal 2009).

Most of the existing literature relates to aspects of global governance focusing on the international political economy in areas including international trade, the environment, and health governance (Hall and Biersteker 2002; Brown and Woods 2007; Cutler et al. 1999; Fuchs 2007; Ruggie 2007; Clapp 2009; Faulkner 2005; Levy and Newell 2005; May 2006). In contrast, there has been only limited work on the role of the private sector in global humanitarian governance (Weiss 2013; Zyck and Kent 2014). Although some work has been done on the role of the private sector in migration—examining its role in facilitation, control, and protection—it has not considered the refugee regime in detail (Hernández-León 2008; Gammeltoft-Hansen and Nyberg Sørensen 2013).

As Zetter (2014: 5) has suggested, the private sector offers 'enormous, yet untapped, potential to improve the lives and livelihoods of both the displaced and the host'. However, with a few notable exceptions, empirical and theoretical work on this topic remains limited. There have been a few case studies developed on Jordan, for example (Zyck and Armstrong 2014), Kenya (Drummond and Crawford 2014), and Uganda (Omata and Kaplan 2013). However, there remains limited understanding of the diverse motives underlying private-sector engagement with the refugee regime (Kaplan and Rozeboom 2015).

The existing literature on the role of business in the refugee regime suffers from a series of weaknesses. First, it fails to recognize the diversity of the private sector. In policy debates, business is all too often seen as synonymous with multinational corporations (MNCs) and foundations at the global level. This fails to take into account diversity in terms of types of firm (e.g. multinational corporation or small and medium-sized enterprise), scale (e.g. global, national, local), sector (e.g. telecommunications, finance, consumer goods), and motivation (e.g. philanthropy, CSR, core business) (Kaplan and Rozeboom 2015).

Second, the literature often assumes that the role of business in the humanitarian sector is mainly limited to formal public–private partnerships between humanitarian organizations and business. For example, in Zyck and Armstrong's (2014) typology of the private sector, they see business serving uniquely as donors, suppliers, or technical advisers to humanitarian agencies. They also acknowledge that 'the business community directly and indirectly helps refugees meet their needs by selling them goods and services inside and outside of camps', but this offers an incredibly narrow account of the diverse ways in which businesses can and do shape the lives of refugees independently of the formal humanitarian system. For example, this leaves no scope for recognizing that the private sector is not just external to refugees, but that refugees themselves are often an integral part of that private sector.

We attempt to move beyond the limitations of existing literature by offering an account of business that (1) recognizes the different levels at which business operates; (2) diverges from frequent assumptions of business being homogenously motivated by profit and takes account of the diversity and complexity of motives and optimization strategies; (3) transcends simplified judgements of the role of business, which is often judged as either 'good' or 'bad', by offering nuanced ways of understanding the conditions under which it can play a positive role in creating sustainable solutions for refugees.

Reflecting these aims and drawing upon our Uganda case study, the chapter divides into three main parts. First, it offers an overview of the refugee regime and the role of the private sector. Second, it sets out a typology of the different roles and modes of engagement of the private sector in the regime. Third, it explores normative dimensions of how we can think about the ethical implications of private-sector engagement and what this might mean for regulation of the private sector in its engagement with refugee protection and assistance.

The Refugee Regime and the Private Sector

The refugee regime is commonly thought of as comprising the norms and organizational structures that govern states' responses to refugees. Given that this is based primarily upon an intergovernmental treaty—the 1951 Convention—and an intergovernmental organization—UNHCR—the global governance of refugee protection has traditionally been a state-centric regime (Loescher 2001; Betts 2009). This is unsurprising, given that its primary purpose has been to oversee and support states' implementation of their obligations under international refugee law.

However, at the margins, private actors have always played some role in the refugee regime. Private-sector actors were crucial to the inception of the modern refugee regime, since UNHCR had almost no governmental funding when it was created in 1950. The United States did not fund UNHCR until 1955 and chose instead to generously fund rival humanitarian agencies, including its own refugee office, the US Escapee Program, that were closely aligned to American foreign policy interests. UNHCR employed various strategies to overcome these financial and operational restrictions, including seeking funding from private foundations (Betts et al. 2012; Loescher 2001).

With a grant from the Ford Foundation in 1952, UNHCR involved itself for the first time in providing assistance to NGOs to promote the integration of refugees in Western European asylum countries. This funding also enabled UNHCR to take the lead role in responding to a refugee crisis in West Berlin in early 1953. This new area of activity was specifically identified as a moment of strategic opportunity for enhancing UNHCR's profile and ability to fulfil its mandate.

Yet, this early private-sector role was largely forgotten, and for a long time it was assumed that UNHCR's almost exclusive partners were states and NGOs. Within academic work, the private sector has mainly been seen as source of instability and threat within the international political economy in ways that were likely to cause rather than address human displacement (Duffield 2001; Castles 2003; Chimni 1998; Collinson 2011). Throughout debates on 'refugees and development' in which markets were recognized as central, the key actors engaged in the debate and discussed in the resulting literature were states and NGOs (Betts 2009; Bradley 2013; Gorman 1993; Krause 2013).

At the policy level, this began to change in 2006 when, faced with a significant funding shortfall, UNHCR began to consider a growing role for a range of 'non-traditional donors'. The global-policy-level debate on the role of the private sector has since evolved over time. It can be considered to divide into three broad waves: first, engaging philanthropy and CSR (2006–10); second, engaging core business and innovation (2010–13); third, recognizing a multilevel ecosystem (2014–). These areas can each be explained in turn.

The first wave related to *philanthropy and corporate social responsibility*. Following a trend established by other international organizations, UNHCR created a Private-Sector Fundraising Unit in 2006 and, more recently, a Corporate and Foundation Partnerships Unit at its headquarters in Geneva. It has also begun to develop its US Board of Trustees as a basis for building partnerships with multinational corporations in the United States. In 2009, for example, it raised around $50 million in private-sector contributions (Betts et al. 2012).

Firms were prepared to contribute to UNHCR largely on the basis of their CSR initiatives, wishing to be associated with a strong humanitarian brand and sometimes working on particular projects. UNHCR's major private-sector contributors have included Nike, Merck, BP, the Motorola Foundation, and All Nippon Airways, for example (Betts et al. 2012). UNHCR now has a private-sector engagement office based in London that continues to play a strong role in building relationships with the private sector, within which philanthropy and CSR are a major part of its ongoing strategy.

The second wave related to engaging businesses based on their *core business* and on *innovation*. As well as serving as a source of funding, private-sector actors have increasingly become engaged partners, working collaboratively with UNHCR to develop ideas and policies. Since 2010, as part of the 'modernization' remit of the Deputy High Commissioner for Refugees, the Office has increasingly sought to establish public–private partnerships to offer sources of expertise and innovation in areas such as digital media and engineering. Its Private-Sector Fundraising Office in Washington, DC has played an active liaison role, together with the US Board of Trustees, to foster links with firms and entrepreneurs in Texas and Silicon Valley whose role is not confined to philanthropy but extends to being active partners in offering expertise, networks, and policy guidance.

In 2011, the UN Deputy High Commissioner for Refugees, Alex Aleinikoff, commissioned the consultant Ari Wallach and his company Synthesis Corp to undertake a review and make recommendations relating to the 'modernization' of UNHCR. Within the slide deck of recommendations, a series of ideas were presented, notably on how to improve innovation within the organizations. Eventually, in April 2012, UNHCR Innovation was founded out of this process. Its roots were in the organization's private-sector engagement functions at Headquarters.

UNHCR Innovation was built upon an initial private-sector donation from the IKEA Foundation, which out of an overall 110 million Euro grant to UNHCR also provided 50 per cent of UNHCR Innovation's budget for its first two years. By November 2012, UNHCR Innovation had developed its core ideas based on the notion of 'Amplify, Connect, Explore', referring to the three stages of looking inside the organization for good practice, enabling connections in-house, and seeking partners and solutions outside the organization, including in the private sector (UNHCR Innovation 2015a,b).

The initiative established its first field 'lab' in Dollo Ado in Ethiopia in order to undertake a series of pilots. In addition, it established a series of virtual 'labs' in thematic areas such as 'Learn', 'Link', 'Self-Reliance', and 'Energy'. It developed a range of projects over time, most notably the Refugee Housing Unit (RHU) supported by the IKEA Foundation and prototyped through piloting in Iraq, Ethiopia, and Lebanon.

A key part of UNHCR Innovation's work was its strategic use of private-sector funding to bypass internal UN restrictions on, for example, procurement and tender. It was able to develop its in-house knowledge management platform UNHCR Ideas by seeking external funding to buy in the services of the London-based Mindjet, and was similarly able to commission Hyperakt to develop its brand and website through a small private-sector grant. For both of these companies, the opportunity to work with UNHCR offered more than simply a contract; it was a means to expand their business to a new humanitarian market.

UNHCR Innovation also created an advisory board comprised primarily of private-sector actors. Its innovation council, known as the 'iCircle', was established in 2013 and included the UN Foundation, Hewlett Packard, Ashoka, the Vodafone Foundation, IKEA Foundation, Hunt Oil, the Chobani Foundation, and UPS among its private-sector partners. The initiative also listed the Omidyar Network, Google, and Microsoft among its partners. Furthermore, it began to seek other creative forms of business engagement. These included an attempt to develop 'smartsourcing', commissioning Accenture Development Partnerships to examine prospects for micro-work within refugee camps, and exploring 'reverse supply chain' ideas to enable Syrian artisans in Lebanon to sell products to Zara Home.

The third wave is engagement with a *multilevel ecosystem* based on growing recognition that the role of business is not just about UNHCR partners, and—crucially—not just about role of multinational corporations. Rather, it includes the range of businesses that engage with refugees and displaced populations, irrespective of whether they are formally recognized by international organizations. These businesses may exist at the global, national, local, or even transnational levels. They may be for-profit businesses or social enterprises. Their interaction with refugees may involve refugees as producers, consumers, recipients, or employees.

From the refugee shops that line the 'Shams-Élysées' in the Za'atari refugee camp in Jordan,[1] to the *hawala* system of informal remittance transfer among Muslim refugees, to telecommunications companies that provide the handsets and phone credit through which refugees send messages and money, to nationals who buy and sell agricultural produce in and around refugee

[1] The 'Shams-Élysées' refers to the main commercial street that runs through the middle of the Za'atari refugee camp.

settlements, the 'private sector' has gradually been seen in broader terms, and with it so too has the scope for refugee-related entrepreneurship.

Indeed, this conception of the private sector that goes beyond organized partnership with humanitarian organizations has taken off with the development of the World Humanitarian Summit of May 2016, in which it has increasingly been recognized that humanitarian providers go far beyond the 'international humanitarian system', and that there is a wider 'ecosystem' that responds to humanitarian needs including those of refugees and displaced populations.

Gradually, UNHCR has recognized its historical neglect of refugee entrepreneurs themselves. Our Uganda data show that over 20 per cent of refugees in Kampala self-identify as entrepreneurs, and even in the settlements nearly all households have some independent source of income generation. Whether in the formal or informal sectors, refugee entrepreneurship often thrives, and UNHCR is beginning to recognize that one of its roles needs to be to provide the enabling conditions that allow refugee entrepreneurship to flourish. As our Uganda study has revealed, such conditions obviously include the right to work, as well as access to electricity, transportation, telecommunications, and the Internet.

In addition, a growing number of social enterprises, motivated by both profit and social purpose, are entering the humanitarian space. Their potential to contribute to refugee assistance has also often been neglected. They exist on a spectrum, from organizations such as Refunite that support refugee communications to the Ugandan Technology for Tomorrow (T4T) initiative, which has produced its Makapad product based on recyclable sanitary products for both profit and social purpose. To engage with the idea of a multilevel ecosystem is to move beyond a view of 'the private sector and refugees' as exclusively about the public–private partnerships of international organizations.

Business Motives for Working with Refugees

A conceptual starting point for thinking about the role of business in the refugee regime is global public goods theory. The received wisdom is that refugee assistance can only be provided by states, or by organizations that act on behalf of states. This is based on an underlying assumption that refugee protection is what economists call a 'public good'. Public goods are characterized by two properties: the benefits are 'non-excludable' and 'non-rival' between actors. In other words, the benefits accrue to all actors irrespective of who contributes, and the benefits are not diminished by someone else's enjoyment.

An example of a public good at the domestic level is street lighting. An example of a global public good is action to combat climate change. In both cases, it is assumed that without a concerted institutional actor, individuals—or states at the global level—will have a strong incentive to free-ride on the provision of others. The result will be underprovision of those public goods. Even if a group of people (or states) would be better off acting collectively than they would be in isolation, without institutionalized cooperation, there is likely to be collective action failure (Olson 1965).

It is the dominant assumption that refugee assistance is a public good at the national level and a global public good at the global level (Suhrke 1998; Thielemann 2003; Betts 2003). This has led to the widely held belief that it can only be provided by governments at the national level and by intergovernmental organizations, or NGOs funded by governments, at the international level.

However, there is also a literature on the so-called 'private provision of public goods'. If indeed there are private benefits that accrue to being the provider of a particular good, or if some of the benefits are excludable and accrue only to the provider, then it may be possible to encourage private rather than institutionalized provision.

This same logic applies to the refugee context. Indeed, it may well be that rather than being pure public goods, refugee protection and assistance are mixed goods, which confer both private and public benefits. While everyone may benefit from the security and protection afforded by humanitarian support to refugees, there may also be specific private benefits from being the provider of certain kinds of humanitarian assistance. These supplementary benefits are referred to in the public goods literature as 'joint products' (Betts 2003; Sandler 1997). For example, if there are supplementary incentives for a business to work with refugees that relate to for-profit motives, these may motivate alternative sources of provision of the underlying public goods of protection and assistance.

The institutional design challenge then becomes not only about creating collective action to provide public goods through the state and the inter-state system. The challenge is also how to create incentive structures that facilitate the private provision of public goods while mitigating any possible risks that may stem from regulating these alternative, private providers of public goods.

In the case of 'refugees and development', this logic again highlights that development-based approaches to refugees can be about more than simply intergovernmental cooperation to provide development assistance. Instead, they should recognize that a diverse ecosystem of private actors has a complex array of motives and reasons for engaging with refugees, not only as aid recipients, but as consumers, producers, entrepreneurs, borrowers, lenders, employers, and employees. The next step is therefore to examine what some

Table 9.1 Motives for private-sector engagement with refugees

Motive for Engagement	Global	National (e.g. Uganda)
Philanthropy	Chobani Foundation	YARID
CSR	Hewlett Packard	MTN
Innovation	Ikea Foundation	T4T
Labour	Samasource	City Oil
Strategic Positioning	Orange	Owino Market
Supply Chain	Zara Home	Nile Breweries
Social Enterprise	Magdas Hotel	KPF

of these diverse incentives for business to engage as a supplementary provider of refugee assistance might be. Indeed, understanding the motives of businesses is the key to designing institutional structures to influence their behaviour.

There is currently no compelling typology of the role of business in either the refugee regime or humanitarianism more broadly. In Table 9.1, we set out a simplified typology intended to highlight the diversity of motives for private-sector engagement with refugees. It is based upon seven different sets of motives and modes of engagement that emerge from our national-level research in Uganda, and for which there are also parallels at the global level: (1) philanthropy; (2) CSR; (3) innovation; (4) access to labour; (5) strategic positioning; (6) supply chain; (7) social enterprise.

Of course, in each case, no private-sector actor or business fits perfectly under any one of the categories of motives for engagement. In practice, businesses will have a complex mix of motives. However, they offer broad archetypes which subsume at least part of the core drivers behind particular actors' engagement with refugees.

Philanthropy remains a central motivation for some private-sector actors to engage in refugee assistance. A number of actors view their engagement in refugee assistance as altruism and seek to deploy their resources to assist refugees out of a sense of moral obligation. Within Uganda, there are fewer obvious wealthy individuals and families who play this role. The nearest equivalents are community-based organizations that try to provide support to refugees, by means that include applying for sources of external financial support. In Kampala, the nearest thing to philanthropy mainly comes from non-profit NGOs like YARID or InterAid rather than businesses per se. At the global level, Hamdi Ulukaya offers an example of an individual who, having taken the Buffet Pledge to give away his wealth, is contributing to refugee-related causes through his Chobani Foundation.

CSR is a major driver for multinational corporations to engage in social impact activities. Firms operating within oligopolistic industries have the scope to be concerned with brand as a means of product differentiation.

Often, this involves being associated with good causes, including through the establishment of autonomous foundations and trusts. Within Uganda, the telecommunications company MTN has worked with UNHCR to develop an app to enable refugees to be reunited with their families. At the global level, a host of companies are seeking to engage with UNHCR's work, in part to create brand association with an important global issue. Examples include the humanitarian engagement of firms like Hewlett Packard and UPS.

Innovation is a growing motive for firm engagement. Put crudely, if a firm can innovate for the 50 million displaced people in the world, it may effectively be developing products or processes with the possibility of scaling to the bottom two billion people who live on less than $2 per day. Refugee camps offer an environment within which innovation can take place and can lead to scale. In Uganda, national entrepreneurs such as Technology for Tomorrow (T4T)'s Moses Musaasi have recognized these opportunities. After developing his papyrus leaf-based female sanitary product, the Makapad, which is produced in refugee camps and sold to UNHCR to distribute to refugees, Musaasi subsequently sought to scale the product to the wider Ugandan market. At the global level, innovation is a significant part of what motivates the IKEA Foundation in the development of products such as the Refugee Housing Unit.

Access to *labour* is another reason for private-sector engagement with refugees. Refugees have skills, talents, and aspirations. They frequently have a desire to work that may be thwarted by host state regulation or by the remote geographical location of refugee camps. Yet, within the context of globalization, new opportunities are emerging to relocate work to geographically remote areas. In the Ugandan case, one example that stands out of a firm using refugee labour is the Kampala-based oil company City Oil, which is run by ethnic Somalis who privilege the employment of Somali refugees. At the global level, the Silicon Valley-based company Samasource has piloted an attempt to outsource micro-work to refugees in the Dadaab camps in Kenya.

Strategic positioning is another reason why firms might work with refugees. As Michael Porter has highlighted, 'clustering' shapes a significant proportion of business investment decisions. If firms can locate in areas in which there are key infrastructural opportunities to access markets, they will do so. In the case of Uganda, the Owino market in Kampala offers a case in point. As the largest market in East Africa, a significant number of both refugee and non-refugee businesses mutually benefit from being located alongside one another within a space that serves as a transnational hub for the exchange of goods. At the global level, firms may also choose to geographically locate their operations close to refugees, because doing so offers broader market opportunities. The telecommunications company Orange, for example, has a comparative advantage in international dialling and so has chosen to build infrastructure and mobile phone masts in some refugee settlements, including in Uganda.

Inserting oneself into a pre-existing *supply chain* also offers an incentive for business engagement with refugees. In the case of Uganda, Nile Breweries chose to buy sorghum from refugees because it was able to exploit a gap within the existing supply chain, whereby refugees had previously been unable to sell their sorghum to market as efficiently. Nile Breweries was able to insert itself within an existing supply chain in ways that produced efficiency gains and a greater return for refugee suppliers. A similar logic applies at the global level, where UNHCR has piloted the idea of the 'reverse supply chain'. For example, it has tried to encourage Zara Home to buy directly from Syrian refugee artisans in Lebanon.

Finally, *social enterprise* remains an underexploited motivation for engagement with refugees. Based on having motives that go beyond profit maximization to include social goals, social enterprise can take many forms. One such social enterprise in Uganda is the refugee-run Kyangwali Progressive Farmers Limited (KPF), which emerged as a cooperative to enable refugees to sell products to external companies at a higher rate of return by cutting out middlemen and brokers. On a global level, social enterprises are emerging within the refugee space and include, for instance, the Hotel Magdas in Vienna which employs and trains a staff almost entirely comprised of refugees and asylum seekers.

Ethics and Codes of Conduct

Business engagement with refugees and displaced populations is therefore extremely diverse. It offers immense opportunity, but also risk. While many businesses have motives that are more complex than profit maximization, they are also generally motivated by factors that go beyond pure altruism. Yet working with refugees often involves working with vulnerable populations. This means that there is a need to ensure that the role of business is both ethical and compatible with protection standards.

Refugees are often vulnerable because they are in need of international protection, having fled persecution in their country of origin. This usually means that they are in countries in which they have to adapt to new social networks and markets, as well as adjust to different languages and cultures. The regulations of the host state may also place refugees in a precarious position by limiting access to the formal economy.

This context means that businesses working with refugees need to ensure their interventions are informed by ethical practice. This is especially important because although business may have the potential to make significant contributions to refugee self-reliance, it would only take one 'bad case' of humanitarian practice to completely discredit the role of business in humanitarianism.

Consequently, having clearly defined ethical standards and codes of conduct is imperative to avoid an 'entrepreneurial Goma' moment in which the very idea of business and humanitarianism is irreparably undermined. Refugee camps pose a particular challenge for business because of the risks of both exploitation and also simply the perception of exploitation.

To take an example, the Silicon Valley-based company Samasource developed a pilot partnership with the NGO Care International in the Dadaab refugee camps to develop a data-outsourcing project for Somali refugees. Samasource began working in Dadaab in March 2010, focusing on crowdsourcing which included searches for universities, data entry, and making Easter cards. Refugees were paid around $50/month compared to the $100/month that is usual for refugees in the camp. The refugees voiced their dissatisfaction with the rate, but Samasource did not increase the wage rate. One person involved with the project also complained that the company had not done any prior research before beginning the project, and that some of the sixteen workers hired by the project resigned because of a perception of low pay, long hours, and poorly managed expectations. Samasource ended the project after only four months in Dadaab.[2] While there is no suggestion that Samasource acted inappropriately, the example highlights that entrepreneurial engagement with refugees needs to be thought through carefully.

The humanitarian sector lacks a clear code of conduct or ethical principles relating to the role of business. This is in contrast to other sectors—such as many of the extractive industries or forestry, for example, within which voluntary codes of conduct help ensure that firms conform to certain minimum standards in order to be regarded as legitimate. Although it would be almost impossible to stop any company from working with refugees insofar as they complied with municipal law, voluntary codes of conduct can help make clear who is legitimate and who is not in ways that can exert pressure and can empower international actors to highlight and repudiate cases of bad practice. Examples of codes of conduct in other areas include those adopted by the Forest Stewardship Council and the Kimberley Process Certification Scheme, for example.

The development of principles for ethical practice relating to the role of business would need to emerge from a process of ethical reasoning and practice. However, it is clear that in order to be ethical, business engagement should be led by a principle of 'do no harm' to individuals or communities and involve informed consent that is meaningfully given. It must involve mechanisms for complaint and accountability in the event of bad practice. Projects should also be based on principles of fairness and equity in terms of the

---

[2] Information provided anonymously by project partner.

197

distribution of benefits that arise from interventions. In working with refugees, there should also be respect for the principles within international refugee and human rights law (Betts and Bloom 2014).

However, while recognizing these risks, markets still have an important role to play. Despite their constrained circumstances, refugees are capable of making meaningful choices, including between employment opportunities. The aspirational aim of the global refugee regime should ultimately be to promote autonomy. With that in mind, the principle that should arguably guide our judgement of the role of business is a liberal principle: does the role of a particular business enhance or diminish an individual's entitlements and capabilities (Sen 1999)? While many humanitarians remain intuitively suspicious of the private sector, business clearly offers many untapped opportunities to enhance refugees' access to self-reliance. Codes of conduct should be designed to prevent abuse and ensure minimum standards, and not to further diminish refugees' freedom to engage with markets.

Conclusion

There has traditionally been an assumption that the global refugee regime is primarily about states. When a country of origin is unable or unwilling to provide for its citizens' most fundamental rights, people cross international borders to avail themselves of the surrogate protection of another state. To support that host state, other governments may then work collectively, through intergovernmental organizations, to share responsibility with the host state.

In practice, though, that state-centric view of the global refugee regime has never been accurate. Refugees—like many other migrants—engage with markets. In doing so, they frequently come into contact with business. Many refugees are themselves entrepreneurs. They also interact with businesses as consumers, producers, employees, and beneficiaries, for example. Furthermore, globalization is today bringing new opportunities to further enhance the role of business within refugee protection and assistance.

Yet in contrast to many other areas of global governance within which the role of business has been widely recognized and studied, there has been little exploration of the role of business in humanitarianism in general, and the refugee regime in particular. This has been in part due to a lack of detailed empirical research and case studies. Drawing from our Uganda study, this chapter has offered a simplified typology of the range of complex motives that underlie business engagement with refugees.

No longer simply based on philanthropy or CSR, businesses now engage with refugee issues for reasons that directly involve core business strategy, whether driven by innovation, access to labour, or strategic positioning. Furthermore, business exists at multiple levels. It should not be viewed as synonymous with multinational corporations or large foundations working directly with large humanitarian organizations. Rather, business exists at all levels: global, national, local, and even transnational.

It is clear that business brings both risks and opportunities to the humanitarian sector. Ethical standards and codes of conduct are needed in order to mitigate risks and ensure the role of business is compatible with human rights standards. However, if the ultimate goal of the refugee regime is autonomy, then entrepreneurship and business have an important and historically neglected role to play. In order to take advantage of these opportunities, actors like UNHCR need to be better equipped to engage in private-sector outreach but also, and more fundamentally, to build political economy analysis into their own daily work.

10

Conclusion

We began this book with a recognition that, with growing numbers of dis-placed people and declining state willingness to provide protection, we urgently need more sustainable solutions. There has been a long-standing recognition that development-based approaches that support refugee self-reliance might provide a fruitful means to move beyond dependency towards greater autonomy, all while enabling refugees to contribute to the national development of host states.

Yet, as we have seen, the history of development-based approaches to refugees has been mixed. This is in part because most such approaches have been premised upon intergovernmental initiatives, in which Northern donor states have been expected to contribute additional development assistance and Southern host states have been expected to offer long-term local integra-tion for refugees. With few exceptions, mutual mistrust has meant that his-torical attempts to overcome this collective action problem have failed.

Today, however, there are opportunities to take an alternative approach. Rather than seeing 'refugees and development' as only about intergovernmen-tal agreements, we can also look beyond the state to the role of markets. As development practitioners have long been aware, development is about more than development assistance. It is also about the role of the private sector and markets. In the context of displacement, refugees themselves are often a key part of that private sector.

Even under challenging circumstances, refugees have complex economic lives. They engage with markets. If these interactions can be understood, they may be built upon through interventions that better support refugees' ability to help themselves and others. Yet, in order to take advantage of this oppor-tunity, we need better research. Despite pioneering work on the economic lives of refugees, there has until now been a lack of both theory and data.

We have offered a starting point for thinking theoretically about the eco-nomic lives of refugees. Going beyond existing work on 'livelihoods' or 'impacts', the concept of refugee economies has been used to draw attention to the entire resource allocation system governing refugees' consumption, production, and exchange. It represents an attempt to look holistically at refugees' economic lives from the perspective of their own lived experiences.

The premise for our refugee economies approach has been that refugees are not different from other people as human beings; they are simply in exceptional circumstances. What makes refugees' economic lives distinctive is the institutional context of being a refugee. Indeed, we know from New Institutional Economics that the way markets work is shaped by the institutions that regulate them—by property rights, contracts, and governance. Following this logic, we have suggested that what makes refugee economies distinctive is that 'refugeehood' places people within a particular institutional context, generally different from citizens or other migrants.

We have suggested and empirically illustrated three ways in which refugees may be in an institutionally distinctive position. Their economic lives lie, we suggest, (1) between state and international organization authority; (2) between national and transnational geography; and (3) between the formal and informal sectors. While these are not universally applicable to all refugees, and other populations will have some of these characteristics, they offer a starting point for identifying what—following New Institutional Economics— makes refugee economies theoretically distinctive.

Theory is useful insofar as it helps us to answer particular questions. Our driving research question has been: *what explains variation in economic outcomes for refugees?* Such outcomes could mean many things. But one of our many areas of interest has been to explain variation in income levels among refugee populations and, relatedly, dependency levels. Our theoretical answer to this question—like the answer to almost any social science question— involves a combination of structure and agency.

On the structural side, we suggest that the institutional context of being a refugee shapes outcomes. On the agency side, the capacity of refugees to transcend that institutional context both as individuals and as communities also shapes outcomes. Here, we return to our empirical research in Uganda to flesh out what particular variables are doing the work under each of these categories, and what this means for building a testable theory of refugee economies.

Three Different 'Refugee Economies'

One of the methodologically useful aspects of locating our research in Uganda has been that it has enabled comparative research across a number of contexts: urban (Kampala), protracted camp (Nakivale and Kyangwali), and emergency camp (Rwamwanja). Our theoretical contention is that there is not one

Table 10.1 Variation in the institutional context of refugee economies

Context	Authority	Infrastructure	Regulation
Urban	State	Transnational	Low
Protracted Camp	Hybrid	National	Moderate
Emergency Camp	International	Local	High

but several different and overlapping refugee economies, shaped by the different institutional contexts. This is borne out by our empirical research across the sites. Each of these different spaces places refugees in slightly different institutional contexts, along the three institutional spectra outlined in our framework.

Table 10.1 illustrates this variation in the institutional context of refugee economies across the three sites. In each case, the three refugee economies have the characteristics that distinguish refugee economies. However, each particular site leads to an institutional context that is at a different point along each spectrum. Put simply, the urban context is the nearest to being the same institutional context as that enjoyed by citizens; the emergency camp situation is the furthest from what is usual for citizens. The protracted camp situation is somewhere in between these extremes.

In Kampala, the primary authority relevant to refugees' economic lives is the state. International organizations are peripheral to the economic lives of most refugees, insofar as they ensure minimal legal guarantees of non-refoulement, and offer supplementary support to the most vulnerable through an implementing partner, InterAid. The geographical scope of economic life in the capital is also mainly transnational. Refugees are able to use large markets such as Owino, Nakasero, Kikuubo, and Kisenyi to engage easily with transnational trade networks. There are also relatively low barriers to engaging in formal economic activity. The Refugee Act is generally interpreted as giving refugees the right to work, even though the Kampala Capital City Association (KCCA) occasionally harasses refugees to pay licence fees for a work permit.

In Nakivale and Kyangwali, the situation is more mixed. Authority is divided between the state and the international community. Settlements are formally administered by the Office of the Prime Minister (OPM) and led by the Ugandan Settlement Commander. However, in practice this is carried out in close collaboration with UNHCR, which provides assistance through a number of implementing partners. The geographical scope of economic activity is limited for most refugees in these camps. The majority engage in farming activities and sell crops to middlemen. However, for a significant minority, their economic lives are embedded in much wider trade networks that transcend communities, settlements, and often also national borders. Finally, although there are some barriers to formal-sector economic activity in

Uganda—including some restrictions on the right to leave the settlements—the Refugee Act is generally interpreted to imply that refugees can work without a permit.

In Rwamwanja, international organizations more significantly play the role of a surrogate state, with UNHCR and WFP (World Food Programme) providing food assistance and playing a more proactive role in the management of the settlement. While some of the Congolese refugees have brought items with them from home, the Rwamwanja economy is one of the most geographically isolated, with trade and exchange mainly confined to the surrounding areas. Meanwhile, there are significant barriers to economic activity that have been put in place by the government. Tighter restrictions have been imposed on refugee movements in this camp, and the district government has imposed an entry tax on Ugandans who wish to engage in exchange within the settlement. In that sense, Rwamwanja is perhaps the least economically integrated of the three sites, and faces the greatest number of constraints.

Collecting data across all three contexts has enabled us to explore the effects of this institutional variation on economic outcomes. What is very clear from our data is that there is a spectrum of income and dependency levels. Refugees have the highest income and lowest dependency levels in the city, followed by the protracted camp context, followed by the emergency camp context. This statistical association persists even when controlling for variation in nationality, education, and length of exile (see Appendix A). Congolese refugees, for instance, have higher levels of mean income and are less likely to be dependent on aid in Kampala compared to Kyangwali or Nakivale and have lower mean incomes and higher levels of dependency in Rwamwanja than any of the other study sites. The average monthly income of Congolese refugees in Kampala is 120 USD. The average income in Nakivale and Kyangwali is 39 USD, and the average income in Rwamwanja is 17 USD.

In terms of dependency on aid agencies, most refugees in Kampala do not receive any such forms of assistance, and therefore only 9.4 per cent of total respondents consider their households 'very dependent' on support from UNHCR and other aid agencies. Put differently, the self-settled refugees in Kampala are 'doing it for themselves'. In contrast, in refugee settlements where refugees usually have better access to assistance, the percentage of households that feels dependent on institutional aid goes up considerably. In Nakivale and Kyangwali, averaged across different nationalities of refugees, 58.9 per cent of respondents feel that they are 'very dependent' on assistance from aid organizations. In Rwamwanja, the percentage of 'very dependent' respondents goes up to 78 per cent of total respondents.

The findings presented here, with results from quantitative analyses of the survey data in Appendices A and B, provide empirical evidence for the idea that institutional context influences economic outcomes for refugees.

Furthermore, beyond the rather banal observation that being in a city correlates with better economic outcomes, our qualitative research tells us about why this relationship might be observed. It suggests that the greater refugees' opportunities are for integration into the mainstream economy (or the lower the degree of institutional separation), the more positive the economic outcomes are likely to be.

Explaining Variation in Economic Outcomes

In addition to institutional context, the specific characteristics and capacities of individuals and communities also matter for explaining variation in economic outcomes for refugees. Indeed, our data show that there is also considerable variation in economic outcomes between different nationality groups and between individuals with different characteristics.

Survey data reveal significant variation in income levels across nationality groups, independent of institutional context (see Appendix A, Table A.1). On average, there is a clear rank ordering of Somalis as having the highest incomes, followed by Rwandans, followed by the Congolese. Controlling for the effects of context, the average Somali refugee earns 69 per cent to 97 per cent and the average Rwandan refugee 37 per cent more than the average Congolese refugee of the same gender, age, level of education, and length of time in Uganda (Appendix A, Table A.1). In Kampala, 29 per cent of Somalis, 25 per cent of Rwandans, and 15 per cent of Congolese primary earners earn more than 300 000 UGX/month (150 USD). In Nakivale, 21.6 per cent of Somalis, 4 per cent of Rwandans, and 0.9 per cent of Congolese primary earners earn more than 300 000 UGX/month. In Rwamwanja, just 0.4 per cent of primary earners in Congolese households earn more than that amount.

To some extent, these differences may be explained largely through nationality or ethnicity. Indeed, it seems plausible that to some extent there is a 'being Somali' variable that explains part of this variation. Our qualitative research reveals high levels of trust within clan-based networks, as indicated by the presence of informal insurance mechanisms known as *ayuto*, the existence of Islamic alms-giving such as *sadaqah* and *zakat*, and the trust-based *hawala* system for remittance transfer. Across all the sites, Somali economic life is also governed by clearly identifiable informal rule-based structures such as the Somali Community Association—which serves as the official representative body of Somali society in Uganda. Culturally, Somalis are more likely to engage in remittance transfer.

Rwandans often do well in Uganda, likely because many have close cultural ties to Ugandans. Many Rwandans are anglophone and therefore better able to integrate into the national education system and employment markets than other groups, such as the Congolese. Given the long history of Rwandan refugees in Uganda, going back to the late 1950s, there are also relatively well-established diasporic networks within the country. However, the Rwandan community also faces a number of nationality-specific constraints on economic outcomes. These include internal community divisions, sometimes along Hutu–Tutsi lines, and the additional levels of surveillance and risk faced by Rwandans perceived to be aligned with Rwandan opposition political parties.

Congolese have less clearly defined community-based structures for regulating and supporting their economic activity. In Kampala, despite some geographically contiguous residential pockets such as Nsambya, there are greater levels of dispersal across the city. Unlike the Somalis, there is no strong overarching authority for the Congolese community in Uganda. Consequently, there is an absence of organized structures of mutual support, and Congolese in the city tend to engage in small-scale business activities such as buying, selling, and hawking. In the settlements, they have a strong culture of agricultural activity, and hence predominantly focus on farming. This is reflected in the fact that they tend to do better where higher levels of fertile farming land are available; in Kyangwali 8.4 per cent of Congolese earn more than 300 000 UGX/month (150 USD) compared to 0.9 per cent in Nakivale.

However, for the most part, differences in outcomes both between and within nationality groups appear to be attributable to quantifiable variables: notably, education, networks, and entrepreneurship.

Education

Education shapes economic outcomes for refugees. Our dataset shows interesting variation in the returns to education, controlling for nationality and geographical location (see Appendix A, Table A.1). Acquiring an additional year of education is associated with a 3 per cent higher average income. The type of education matters. An additional year of primary education is associated with 1 per cent higher earnings, secondary school 10 per cent, and tertiary education 27 per cent. Finishing primary school is associated with a 30 per cent higher income.

However, these returns vary considerably by nationality. Each year of education is associated with only a 0.1 per cent return for Congolese but a 2.2 per cent return for Somali and 2.4 per cent return for Rwandans (see Tables A.2.1, A.2.2, and A.2.3 in Appendix A). These differences are found even when controlling for institutional context. Differences between nationalities in returns to education may be due to differences in the livelihood opportunities to which they are exposed through the personal networks and community structures discussed previously.

The less cohesive structure of Congolese communities in Kampala means educated Congolese refugees are likely to have fewer personal connections and may therefore be less likely to locate professional positions that utilize their skills. Educated Rwandan and Somali refugees with similar levels of education, however, may be able more successfully to draw on diasporic and ethnic networks and thereby maximize the economic returns to education by finding professional positions.

Education levels also appear to have a significant influence on refugees' choice of where to live. Each year of education is associated with a 22 per cent higher chance of living in Kampala than in the settlement (see Appendix B). Once again, there are differences across nationalities. For each year of education, a Congolese household has a 34 per cent ($p < 0.001$) higher chance of living in Kampala than in the settlement and a Rwandan household has a 42 per cent ($p < 0.001$) higher chance. This reflects that rural–urban refugee selection seems to be correlated with a household's ability to be economically autonomous. In particular, the choice to live in Kampala is determined by a combination of level of education and the number of dependent children. Each child reduces the probability by 21 to 36 per cent (see Appendix B). In contrast, survey data reveal no statistically significant association between location and education amongst Somali households.

In multivariate regression analyses exploring variables predictive of refugee income, a number of other variables were found to be significant in addition to education (see Appendix A). These include experience, employment status, and gender. When all of these variables are controlled for, age is not associated with higher income. Experience in Uganda is, however, found to matter. Each year spent in Uganda is associated with an average increase in income of between 4 and 8 per cent. Primary earners who are not farmers and are self-employed earn 4 to 24 per cent more, on average, than employed refugees and self-employed farmers. In terms of gender, female primary livelihood earners with equivalent levels of education and the same nationality, in Uganda for the same length of time and in the same location, earn an average of 15 per cent less income than male primary livelihood earners.

Networks

Far from being 'enclave economies', refugees' economic lives are embedded in complex networks, that shape their consumption, production, exchange, and access to capital. Yet different households and communities have economic networks that exist to different degrees and scales. Such networks may be local, national, or even transnational. The extent of refugees' networks appears to play an important role in determining economic outcomes. These socio-economic connections exist at different levels.

Locally, refugees have important economic interactions across communities. Even in the Nakivale and Kyangwali settlements, refugees are not simply reliant upon economic interactions with refugees of their own nationality: 33 per cent of refugee businesses have refugees of other nationalities as their largest group of customers; 26 per cent of refugee businesses have Ugandans as their largest customers. Similarly, when it comes to purchasing daily goods, refugee households buy from a range of sources. In the long-term settlements, 69 per cent of households buy goods and services from Ugandans, 93 per cent from refugees of their own nationality, and 88 per cent from refugees of another nationality. In Kampala 96 per cent buy from Ugandans, 78 per cent from refugees of their own nationality, and 48 per cent from refugees of another nationality.

Nationally, refugees' economic lives are connected to other parts of the country. This is especially the case in the long-term settlements. Nakivale is connected to the Mbarara economy and Kyangwali to the Hoima economy, both of which have important exchange links to Kampala. However, it is actually only a minority of refugees who leave the settlements in person. Out of 621 self-employed people in the settlements, less than 10 per cent regularly venture outside the settlements for income-generating activities. Instead, trade in and out of the settlements depends mainly on a small group of 'middlemen', both refugees and Ugandans, who make money from arbitrage activities of buying and selling in settlements at mark-up.

Transnationally, different groups of refugees have different degrees of transnational network connections. Remittances serve as a good proxy measure for transnational connections. Somalis receive a disproportionately higher level of remittances: 51 per cent of Somalis in Kampala received remittances, at an average level of $114/month/household. This compares to just 18 per cent of both Congolese and Rwandans in Kampala receiving any remittances. In Nakivale, 27 per cent of Somalis receive remittances at an average rate of $54/month/household, while remittance receipt by other nationalities in the settlements is negligible.

Another proxy for socio-economic networks is mobile phone use, which also varies by nationality. While mobile phone use is almost universal among urban refugees, in Nakivale, for instance, 83 per cent of Somalis use mobile phones in their primary income-generating activities, compared to 32 per cent of Congolese and 25 per cent of Rwandans. A further variant on the role of networks is connections to host state nationals. In Kampala, many Somali refugees, for example, find employment with Somali–Ugandan enterprises such as City Oil, which employs nearly sixty Somali refugees across the greater Kampala area. The example of tuna fish found in Somali shops in Nakivale, imported from Thailand via Saudi Arabia via Mombassa, stands out as illustrative of their transnational economic ties. Yet, even though Somalis clearly have the strongest transnational networks, other nationalities still have economic lives that are embedded within the global economy. This is perhaps best illustrated by the Congolese *bitenge* trade, which involves importing fabric from as far afield as India and China to Kampala and then on to the settlements.

Entrepreneurship

As we highlighted in the conceptual framework for this book, 'innovators'—outliers who develop businesses that help themselves and their communities—play an important role in refugee economies. While successful and large-scale entrepreneurship is only available to a minority, innovation represents an important and neglected driver of economic change within refugee communities. One important indication of its significance is that our research reveals that in Kampala, 21 per cent of refugee business owners employ others, and among their employees, 41 per cent are Ugandan nationals. In other words, refugee entrepreneurship can create jobs for host country nationals.

However, in addition to this impact on host communities, the capacity of refugees to engage in entrepreneurial activity appears to matter for economic outcomes for refugees. This does not take place in the way one would necessarily expect, as not all entrepreneurship is of equal quality. In Kampala, there is an inverse correlation between the average income levels of a national refugee community and its levels of self-employment: 94.8 per cent of Congolese are self-employed, 78.2 per cent of Rwandans, and just 25.9 per cent of Somalis.

However, what seems to matter is the scale and quality of the entrepreneurship. Somali entrepreneurs are more likely to scale a business to the point at which they can employ others, partly explaining why 74.1 per cent of Somalis are able to find employment in the businesses of others. Our qualitative research highlights the diversity and creativity of many of these highly innovative businesses. In contrast, most Congolese businesses do not employ others but are based on petty trading of agricultural produce, fabrics, or jewellery within competitive markets with very low margins.

In the settlements, the pattern is a little different. Congolese and Rwandan refugees are most likely to engage in agricultural activity, farming their own plots or working as farm workers on the plots of other refugees. In Kyangwali, 65.8 per cent of Congolese are engaged in agricultural work; in Nakivale this figure is 63.9 per cent. For Rwandans in Nakivale, it is also 65.2 per cent. Where Congolese and Rwandans do engage in entrepreneurship, it is mainly through small shops, hawking, or bars and restaurants, and scale is only rarely achieved. Only exceptionally do larger-scale businesses such as the

Somali-run bus service between Nakivale and Kampala or the Congolese cinema in Nakivale's 'little Congo' emerge.

In contrast, Somalis almost entirely shun agricultural work and instead engage in a huge range of entrepreneurial activities. This diversity is best illustrated by the thriving array of businesses within Nakivale's Base Camp 3. Our qualitative research reveals how some of these unique businesses attain significant scale. The greater likelihood of Somali businesses to attain scale is exemplified by the greater standard deviation in incomes for Somalis compared to other nationality groups. In Kampala, for example, 6.3 per cent of Somalis earn over 1 000 000 UGX/month, compared to 3.7 per cent for the next highest income group, the Rwandans. In Nakivale, we found twenty-four Somalis with incomes over 400 000 UGX/month (500 USD) compared to just one person of any other nationality.

This begs the question of what explains variation in entrepreneurship. Our qualitative interviews suggest that one of the greatest barriers to scaling businesses is lack of access to finance and capital, given restrictions on refugees' access to formal banking facilities. This was most significantly identified by self-employed Congolese in Kampala. For Somalis, though, high levels of remittance-sending in addition to collective community-based savings and investment mechanisms provide a means to partly overcome limited formal access to credit and capital. Other reported barriers included the price of government business permits, xenophobia and discrimination, and language barriers.

Implications for Research

'Refugee economies' offer a starting point for a new research agenda focused on explaining economic outcomes for refugees, which is distinct but complementary to existing research agendas focused on refugee 'livelihoods' or 'impacts'. Its purpose is to begin thinking in theoretical terms about the economic lives of refugees, which can guide the collection and interpretation of data and in turn lead to meaningful policy and practice.

The logic of refugee economies is based on the premise that refugees are not different as people, they are simply in exceptional circumstances. We know from basic economic theory that all markets are subject to imperfections and distortions. We also know from New Institutional Economics that institutions and governance shape these imperfections and distortions. It logically follows that what makes 'refugeehood' economically distinctive is the way in which it creates a different set of institutional structures around the economic lives of refugees, compared to those of citizens or other migrants.

Methodologically, we suggested that Uganda offers an especially interesting context for exploring the effect of these institutional structures on refugees' economic lives. This is because Uganda provides three quite different contexts with different institutions and regulatory structures underlying refugees' economic lives. It has urban (Kampala), protracted camp (Nakivale and Kyangwali), and emergency camp (Rwamwanja) contexts. It has therefore offered an auspicious frame of reference for undertaking single-country comparative research.

This has enabled us to make some preliminary and Uganda-specific claims about what distinguishes the economic lives of refugees, and more specifically, what explains variation in economic outcomes for refugees. Indeed, as we highlighted in the first section, variation in income and dependency levels for refugees in Uganda is a product of both structure and agency. It depends on both the institutional context and the particular characteristics of communities and households.

The Ugandan context is by no means representative, and we cannot generalize from it. However, in enabling us to identify differences in institutional characteristics of refugeehood across sites, and the correlation with economic outcomes, our observations provide testable hypotheses that could be explored in subsequent research.

These hypotheses might include the following: H1: The more integrated refugees are into normal *host state governance*, the higher their income levels and the lower their dependency levels. H2: The greater the *geographical scope of infrastructure* available to refugees, the higher their income levels and the lower their dependency levels. H3: The lower the *regulatory barriers* to refugee participation in the formal economy, the higher their income levels and the lower their dependency levels. H4: The higher the *levels of education* available to refugees, the higher their income levels and lower their dependency levels. H5: The more significant and geographically diffuse a refugee's *socio-economic networks*, the higher their income levels and the lower their dependency levels. H6: The greater refugees' *access to start-up capital* for business development, the higher their income levels and the lower their dependency levels.

In order to rigorously test these hypotheses and others, much broader multi-country data would be needed. During the course of our research, we have compiled an unprecedented dataset on the economic lives of refugees in Uganda. What is needed next is to develop what economists call 'panel data'; in other words, data that is both multi-country and time series. Ideally, data would need to be collected from a spectrum of host countries with different regulatory environments, from the generous to the restrictive, in urban and camp contexts, and following the trajectories of refugees over multiple time periods.

In addition to expanded data collection, there is significant scope for methodological and theoretical innovation. As we explained at the outset, too few economists have worked on refugees and forced migration, and we hope that this work will encourage the development of a broader research agenda, building upon some of the work that has been undertaken on the economics of immigration.

However, we are certainly not advocating that the study of the economic life of refugees should be left just to economists. On the contrary, a key feature of our work has been to highlight the importance of interdisciplinary work in this area. Anthropology, sociology, political economy, and geography all have important contributions to make to how we study refugee economies.

Furthermore, our methodology for this research has been greatly enriched by sequencing in-depth qualitative research and quantitative survey methods. Beginning with semi-structured interviews, focus groups, and participant observation allowed a contextual understanding which helped us to engage in survey and in finding causal patterns behind statistical correlations.

During each phase of the research, using participatory methods also ensured we were able to build networks of trust that improved both access and data quality. Without having teams of refugee researchers from across the communities, we would not have been able to develop in-depth qualitative insights nor been able to ensure the credibility of survey responses. Using participatory methods based on training refugees as peer researchers and enumerators also left a legacy with the communities in terms of training. It is an approach that significantly contrasts with most survey methods currently used by both academic and practice-oriented researchers working with refugees.

Implications for Policy and Practice

There is a long history of 'refugees and development', attempting to bridge the relief-to-development gap in order to promote self-reliance for refugees. However, many of these past attempts have been limited by their state-centric approach. Today, there are new opportunities to adopt more market-based approaches. Recognizing and understanding the economic lives of refugees themselves, and the ways in which they interact with markets as consumers, producers, buyers, sellers, borrowers, lenders, employers, employees, and entrepreneurs offers the chance to build on what exists. Supporting refugees' capacities rather than just their vulnerabilities offers an opportunity to rethink assistance in ways that are more sustainable for refugees, host states, and donors.

Such an approach requires recognition that the relevant relationship for refugee protection and assistance is no longer understood as being between 'states and refugees' but between 'states, markets, and refugees'. Rather than regarding durable solutions as just about integration in the state system, it should also involve recognition that there can be no durable solution without integration in the global economy. While states have a crucial role to play to ensure the minimum conditions of protection, it is in creating opportunities for integration in markets that refugees will ultimately achieve autonomy and self-reliance. A number of specific implications for policy and practice follow from our analysis.

First, supporting market-based interventions. Too often at the moment, attempts to support refugees' own income-generating activities are conceived in abstraction from a clear understanding of context, including of the market conditions. At essence, such an approach would attempt to 'build on what already exists'. This is in contrast to many existing livelihood programmes that are too often conceived in abstraction from an understanding of the existing market context. This would represent a significant departure for existing approaches, requiring sound analytical tools for understanding the existing markets within which refugees are often already making a living. Crucially, such interventions can begin as early as the emergency phase.

Second, rethinking the role of the private sector. Within refugee policy debates, the private sector is too often assumed to be synonymous with multinational corporations or large foundations motivated by corporate social responsibility. In reality, the role of the private sector is more nuanced. It exists at the global, national, local, and transnational levels. The private sector has a range of modes of engagement and motives for involvement with refugees, including philanthropy, corporate social responsibility, and core business interests. Refugees and displaced populations can themselves be conceived as part of that private sector.

Third, creating an enabling environment. Refugees and displaced populations are not just passive victims. They have skills, talents, and aspirations. While many are in need of assistance, they have capacities as well as vulnerabilities. Rather than assuming a need for indefinite care and maintenance, interventions should nurture such capacities. Following from many of our key research findings, this is likely to involve improved opportunities for education, skills development, access to microcredit and financial markets, business incubation, better transportation links and infrastructure, and improved Internet access and connectivity, for example.

Fourth, investing in research and data. Governments and international organizations have traditionally invested too little in applied research. Yet, we know surprisingly little about the economic lives of displaced populations. There is a need to develop an ongoing and systematic research agenda on the relationship between forced displacement and development. In particular, comparative case studies are needed (a) in different regulatory environments (restrictive versus open), (b) at different phases of a displacement crisis (e.g. emergency, protracted, and return), and (c) for different categories of displacement (e.g. refugees, internally displaced persons, and people displaced in the context of natural disaster).

Fifth, better political analysis. Markets function in the context of states' policies. Restrictive refugee policies will limit the capacity of refugees to engage with markets in ways that can lead to sustainable opportunities. When refugees are given the right to work and freedom of movement, they are capable of making a contribution to the national economy. Importantly, however, governments' policy choices are the result of national politics. In order to enhance market-based opportunities for displaced populations, it is important to better understand and engage with the political context and incentive structures within which national refugee policies are made.

Regressions on income

Tables A.1 and A.2 regress key variables on the income of refugee households' primary livelihood earners. The first set of regressions are conducted on the entire survey sample from all four sites (one emergency settlement, two protracted settlements, and Kampala).

Table A.1 Regression on income across locations and nationalities

Table A.1 presents results of six regression models of alternative education measures on income (in USD), using data from all surveyed households across three settlements and in Kampala (n = 2213). All variables pertain to households' primary livelihood earners. These models control for geographical location, contrasting households in emergency or long-term (protracted) settlements with those in urban environments. Rwandan, Somali, and South Sudanese households are compared to Congolese households. All survey data from Rwamwanja, Nakivale, Kyangwali, and Kampala are included. Sampling weights are used to adjust for survey design effects and RDS-II weights are used to accommodate data collected using respondent-driven sampling in Kampala.

Variables in the model	1 b (SE)	2 b (SE)	3 b (SE)	4 b (SE)	5 b (SE)	6 b (SE)
Constant	2.798 (0.009)**	3.319 (0.008)**	3.299 (0.008)**	2.206 (0.009)**	3.28 (0.008)**	2.16 (0.009)**
Emergency settlement	−0.836 (0.008)**	−0.794 (0.007)**	−0.734 (0.007)**	−0.611 (0.008)**	−0.685 (0.007)**	−0.517 (0.008)**
Protracted settlement	−0.619 (0.009)**	−0.471 (0.007)**	−0.416 (0.007)**	−0.493 (0.009)**	−0.45 (0.008)**	−0.403 (0.009)**
Somali	0.69 (0.009)**	0.716 (0.008)**	0.746 (0.008)**	0.969 (0.01)**	0.712 (0.009)**	1.054 (0.01)**
Rwandan	0.371 (0.008)**	0.477 (0.007)**	0.494 (0.007)**	0.515 (0.009)**	0.509 (0.008)**	0.562 (0.009)**
South Sudanese	−0.692 (0.049)**	−0.464 (0.04)**	−0.48 (0.04)**	−0.769 (0.054)**	−0.511 (0.042)**	−0.763 (0.054)**
Some primary education	0.07 (0.003)**					
Some secondary education	0.304 (0.003)**					
Some tertiary education	−1.512 (0.005)**					
Years in education		0.031 (0.000)**				
Years in education (squared)			0.003 (0.000)**			
Years in primary education				0.011 (0.000)**		
Years in secondary education					0.096 (0.001)	
Years at university						0.27 (0.003)**
Receive remittances	−0.745 (0.008)**	−0.012 (0.008)	−0.023 (0.008)*	−1.091 (0.009)**	−0.002 (0.008)	−1.074 (0.008)**
Self-employed	0.171 (0.002)**	0.044 (0.002)**	0.048 (0.002)**	0.242 (0.003)**	0.037 (0.002)**	0.242 (0.003)**
Age	0.013 (0.000)**	0.001 (0.000)**	0.001 (0.000)**	0.022 (0.000)**	0.001 (0.000)**	0.022 (0.000)**
Years in Uganda	0.061 (0.001)**	0.036 (0.001)**	0.037 (0.001)**	0.077 (0.001)**	0.044 (0.001)**	0.077 (0.001)**
Female	−0.063 (0.003)**	−0.124 (0.002)**	−0.131 (0.002)**	−0.001 (0.003)*	−0.15 (0.002)*	−0.008 (0.003)*
R-squared	0.467	0.418	0.425	0.349	0.414	0.362

*p < 0.05, **p < 0.001

Table A.2 Regression on income by nationality
Tables A.2.1–A.2.3 present results from the five models in Table A.1 run separately on Congolese, Somali, and Rwandan households. Data collected from Rwamwanja, Kyangwali, and South Sudanese households are excluded. This is because South Sudanese households were only sampled from Kyangwali, and because Nakivale and Kampala are the only sites from which the three remaining nationalities were all sampled. Using data from the same two settlements in each regression model allows for comparison across models run on data from different nationalities. The models below regress alternative education measures on income (log income in US dollars). Sampling weights are used to adjust for survey design effects and RDS-II weights are used to accommodate data collected using respondent-driven sampling in Kampala.
Table A.2.1 Congolese households in Nakivale (protracted settlement) and Kampala (urban)

Variables in the model	1 b (SE)	2 b (SE)	3 b (SE)	4 b (SE)	5 b (SE)
Constant	2.075 (0.034)**	3.46 (0.029)**	3.457 (0.027)**	1.434 (0.031)**	3.3 (0.029)**
Protracted settlement	−0.98 (0.018)**	−0.938 (0.015)**	−0.936 (0.015)**	−0.776 (0.017)**	−0.961 (0.016)**
Any primary education	0.056 (0.023)*				
Any secondary education	0.084 (0.019)**				
Any tertiary education	−0.89 (0.025)**				
Years in education		0.001 (0.001)			
Years in education (squared)			0.000 (0.000)		
Years in primary education				0.029 (0.003)**	
Years in secondary education					0.006 (0.004)**
Receive remittances	−0.574 (0.025)**	0.169 (0.027)**	−0.168 (0.028)**	−0.859 (0.025)**	0.18 (0.028)
Self-employed	0.262 (0.015)**	−0.019 (0.012)	−0.019 (0.012)	0.234 (0.015)**	−0.085 (0.013)**
Age	0.036 (0.001)**	0.006 (0.001)**	0.006 (0.001)**	0.042 (0.001)**	0.01 (0.001)**
Years in Uganda	0.102 (0.003)**	0.08 (0.003)**	0.08 (0.003)**	0.13 (0.003)**	0.085 (0.003)*
Female	−0.161 (0.016)**	−0.377 (0.013)**	−0.377 (0.013)**	0.021 (0.016)*	−0.381 (0.014)**
R-squared	0.535	0.575	0.33	0.502	0.367

*p < 0.05, **p < 0.001

Table A.2.2 Somali households in Nakivale (protracted settlement) and Kampala (urban)

Variables in the model	1 b (SE)	2 b (SE)	3 b (SE)	4 b (SE)	5 b (SE)
Constant	3.257 (0.031)**	4.112 (0.022)**	4.156 (0.02)**	1.69 (0.039)**	4.093 (0.022)*
Protracted settlement	-0.192 (0.024)**	-0.266 (0.017)**	-0.266 (0.017)**	-0.275 (0.034)**	-0.189 (0.019)*
Any primary education	0.45 (0.022)**				
Any secondary education	0.021 (0.021)				
Any tertiary education	-2.899 (0.028)**				
Years in education		0.022 (0.001)**			
Years in education (squared)			0.002 (0)**		
Years in primary education				0.088 (0.004)**	
Years in secondary education					0.053 (0.004)**
Receive remittances	-0.368 (0.016)**	-0.019 (0.012)	-0.014 (0.012)	-0.924 (0.022)**	0.007 (0.013)
Self-employed	0.093 (0.02)**	0.139 (0.014)**	0.14 (0.014)**	-0.064 (0.029)*	0.062 (0.016)**
Age	0.027 (0.001)**	0.004 (0)**	0.004 (0)**	0.064 (0.001)**	0.005 (0.001)**
Years in Uganda	0.021 (0.002)**	0.004 (0.002)*	0.002 (0.002)	0.044 (0.003)**	0.006 (0.002)*
Female	-0.294 (0.02)**	-0.305 (0.014)**	-0.308 (0.014)**	-0.093 (0.027)*	-0.3 (0.016)**
R-squared	0.784	0.40	0.168	0.561	0.156

*p < 0.05, **p < 0.001

Table A.2.3 Rwandan households in Nakivale (protracted settlement) and Kampala (urban)

Variables in the model	1	2	3	4	5
	b (SE)	b (SE)	b (SE)	b (SE)	b (SE)
Constant	2.298 (0.055)**	3.645 (0.036)**	3.795 (0.033)**	1.495 (0.046)**	3.599 (0.035)**
Protracted settlement	−0.515 (0.042)**	−0.477 (0.036)**	−0.547 (0.035)**	−0.42 (0.044)**	−0.567 (0.04)**
Any primary education	−0.044 (0.049)				
Any secondary education	0.371 (0.019)**				
Any tertiary education	−1.122 (0.024)**				
Years in education		0.024 (0.002)**			
Years in education (squared)			0.001 (0)**		
Years in primary education				0.063 (0.006)**	
Years in secondary education					0.077 (0.004)**
Receive remittances	−0.556 (0.023)**	−0.019 (0.023)	−0.01 (0.023)	−0.742 (0.024)**	0.049 (0.024)*
Self-employed	0.701 (0.019)**	0.267 (0.016)**	0.274 (0.017)**	0.679 (0.019)**	0.222 (0.017)**
Age	0.028 (0.001)**	0.003 (0.001)**	0.002 (0.001)**	0.04 (0.001)**	0.003 (0.001)**
Years in Uganda	0.023 (0.002)**	0.004 (0.002)	0.004 (0.002)*	0.021 (0.002)**	0.03 (0.002)**
Female	0.096 (0.016)**	0.045 (0.014)*	0.039 (0.014)*	0.296 (0.016)**	−0.07 (0.014)**
R-squared	0.516	0.23	0.048	0.456	0.078

*pc<0.05, **p < 0.001

APPENDIX B

Regressions on urban–rural selection

Table B.1 shows regression analyses of the association between years of education and location for each nationality and for all nationalities together, controlling for the gender of the primary livelihood earner and the number of children in the household. The results show that years of education are statistically significant and positively associated with living in Kampala rather than in a settlement across the sample as a whole and for Congolese and Rwandan refugees in particular. The results also suggest that the more children there are in a household, the less likely it is that the household is in Kampala and the more likely it is to be in a settlement. This association is statistically significant across nationality groups. Finally, the results suggest that households with female primary livelihood earners are slightly more likely to be in Kampala than in a settlement. The association with gender is statistically significant and largest for Congolese followed by Rwandan households and not statistically significant for Somali households.

Table B.1 Regressions on urban–rural selection

Variables in the equation	Congolese b (SE)	Somali b (SE)	Rwandan b (SE)	All b (SE)
Constant	−3.15 (0.42)**	0.18 (0.3)	−2.85 (0.4)**	−1.68 (0.18)**
Years of education	0.34 (0.03)**	0.01 (0.02)	0.42 (0.04)**	0.22 (0.02)**
Female primary earner	1.34 (0.29)**	0.16 (0.26)	1.04 (0.23)*	1.06 (0.15)**
Number of children	−0.21 (0.07)*	−0.28 (0.06)**	−0.36 (0.09)**	−0.27 (0.4)**

Bibliography

Abbott, K. W. and Snidal, D. (2009). 'The governance triangle: Regulatory standards institutions and the shadow of the state', in W. Mattli and N. Woods (eds), *The Politics of Global Regulation*. Princeton: Princeton University Press, 44–88.

Abramitzky, R., Boustan, L. P., and Eriksson, K. (2012). 'Have the poor always been less likely to migrate? Evidence from inheritance practices during the age of mass migration', *Journal of Development Economics*, 102: 2–14.

Alix-Garcia, J. and Saah, D. (2010). 'The effect of refugee inflows on host communities: Evidence from Tanzania', *The World Bank Economic Review*, 24(1): 148–70.

Al-Sharmani, M. (2004). 'Livelihood and diasporic identity constructions of Somali refugees in Cairo'. Forced Migration and Refugee Studies Program (FMRS) Working Paper 104, New Cairo: American University in Cairo.

Amisi, B. B. (2006). 'An exploration of the livelihood strategies of Durban Congolese refugees'. New Issues in Refugee Research, Working Paper No. 123. Geneva: UNHCR Evaluation and Policy Analysis Unit.

Anderson, J. (2013). 'Policy report on UNHCR's community technology access program: Best practices and lessons learned', *Refuge: Canada's Journal on Refugees*, 29(1): 21–30.

Andrews, B. L. (2003). 'When is a refugee not a refugee? Flexible social categories and host/refugee relations in Guinea'. New Issues in Refugee Research, Working Paper No. 88. Geneva: UNHCR Evaluation and Policy Analysis Unit.

Antoncic, B. and Hisrich, R. (2003). 'Clarifying the intrapreneurship concept', *Journal of Small Business and Enterprise Development*, 10(1): 7–24.

Arrow, K. J. (1962). 'The economic implications of learning by doing', *The Review of Economic Studies*, 29(3): 155–73.

Ashby, J. A. and Sperling, L. (1995). 'Institutionalizing participatory, client-driven research and technology development in agriculture', *Development and Change*, 26(4): 753–70.

Asylum Access (2014). 'Global refugee work rights report: Taking the movement from theory to practice'. Oakland, CA: Asylum Access and the Refugee Work Rights Coalition. Available at <http://asylumaccess.org/wp-content/uploads/2014/09/FINAL_Global-Refugee-Work-Rights-Report-2014_Interactive.pdf>.

Babineaux, R. and Krumboltz, J. (2014). *Fail Fast, Fail Often: How Losing Can Help You Win*. New York: Penguin.

Bakewell, O. (2014). 'Encampment and self-settlement', in E. Fiddian-Qasmiyeh, G. Loescher, K. Long, and N. Sigona (eds), *The Oxford Handbook of Refugee and Forced Migration Studies*. Oxford: Oxford University Press, 127–38.

Bascom, J. (1993). 'The peasant economy of refugee resettlement in eastern Sudan', *Annals of the Association of American Geographers*, 83(2): 320–46.

Bernstein, J. and Okello, M. C. (2007). 'To be or not to be: Urban refugees in Kampala', *Refuge: Canada's Journal on Refugees*, 24(1): 46–56.

Bessant, J. and Tidd, J. (2009). *Managing Innovation: Integrating Technological, Market and Organizational Change*, 4th edn. Chichester: John Wiley & Sons.

Bessant, J. and Tidd, J. (2015). *Innovation and Entrepreneurship*, 3rd edn. Chichester: John Wiley & Sons.

Betts, A. (2003). 'Public goods theory and the provision of refugee protection: The role of the joint-product model in burden-sharing theory', *Journal of Refugee Studies*, 16(3): 274–96.

Betts, A. (2009). *Protection by Persuasion: International Cooperation in the Refugee Regime*. New York: Cornell University Press.

Betts, A. (2016). 'A new solution to old problems: The Solutions Alliance', *Forced Migration Review*, 52: 74–5.

Betts, A. and Bloom, L. (2013). 'The two worlds of humanitarian innovation'. Working Paper No. 94. Oxford: Refugee Studies Centre.

Betts, A. and Bloom, L. (2014). 'Humanitarian innovation: The state of the art'. Occasional Policy Paper, OCHA Policy and Studies Series. United Nations Office for the Coordination of Humanitarian Affairs (OCHA).

Betts, A., Bloom, L., and Weaver, N. (2015). 'Refugee innovation: Humanitarian innovation that starts with affected communities'. Humanitarian Innovation Project. Oxford: Refugee Studies Centre.

Betts, A. and Jones, W. (2016). *Mobilising the Diaspora: How Refugees Challenge Authoritarianism*. Cambridge: Cambridge University Press.

Betts, A., Loescher, G., and Milner, J. (2012). *The United Nations High Commissioner for Refugees (UNHCR): The Politics and Practice of Refugee Protection* (Global Institutions). New York: Routledge.

Betts, T. (1965). 'Draft report of the survey mission concerning a possible project for the integration of refugees in Uganda: Research undertaken November–December 1965', Betts Collection 55. University of Oxford.

Betts, T. (1966, 6 May). *Refugees in Eastern Africa: A Comparative Study*. Betts Collection. University of Oxford.

Borjas, G. J. (2008). *Issues in the Economics of Immigration*. Chicago: University of Chicago Press.

Borjas, G. J. (2014). *Immigration Economics*. Cambridge, MA: Harvard University Press.

Boyden, J., Kaiser, T., and Springett, S. (2002). 'Consultation with and participation by beneficiaries and affected populations in the process of planning, managing, monitoring and evaluating humanitarian action: The case of Sri Lanka'. Prepared for INTRAC. London: ALNAP.

Bradley, M. (2013). *Refugee Repatriation: Justice, Responsibility and Redress*. Cambridge: Cambridge University Press.

Brees, I. (2008). 'Refugee businesses: Strategies of work on the Thai-Burma border', *Journal of Refugee Studies*, 21(3): 380–97.

Brown, D. and Donini, A. (2014). 'Rhetoric or reality? Putting affected people at the centre of humanitarian action'. ALNAP Study. London: ALNAP/ODI.

Brown, D. L. and Woods, N. (2007). *Making Global Self-Regulation Effective in Developing Countries*. Oxford: Oxford University Press.

Buscher, D. (2011). 'New approaches to urban refugee livelihoods'. New York: Women's Refugee Commission.

Buscher, D. (2013). 'New approaches to urban refugee livelihoods', *Refuge: Canada's Journal on Refugees*, 28(2): 17–29.

Calhoun, N. (2010). 'UNHCR and community development: A weak link in the chain of refugee protection?'. New Issues in Refugee Research, Research Paper No. 191. Geneva: UNHCR Policy Development and Evaluation Service.

Callamard, A. (1994). 'Refugees and local hosts: A study of the trading interactions between Mozambican refugees and Malawian villagers in the district of Mwanza', *Journal of Refugee Studies*, 7(1): 39–62.

Campbell, E. H. (2005). 'Urban refugees in Nairobi: Protection, survival, and integration', *Migration Studies Working Paper Series*, 23: 2–19.

Campbell, E. H. (2006). 'Urban refugees in Nairobi: Problems of protection, mechanisms of survival, and possibilities for integration', *Journal of Refugee Studies*, 19(3): 396–413.

Campbell, E. H., Crisp, J., and Kiragu, E. (2011). 'Navigating Nairobi: A review of the implementation of UNHCR's urban refugee policy in Kenya's capital city'. Geneva: UNHCR Policy Development and Evaluation Service.

Carrier, N. (2015). *Little Mogadishu: Eastleigh, Nairobi's Global Somali Hub*. London: Hurst.

Carrier, N. and Lochery, E. (2013). 'Missing states? Somali trade networks and the Eastleigh transformation', *Journal of Eastern African Studies*, 7(2): 334–52.

Castles, S. (2003). 'The international politics of forced migration', *Development*, 46(3): 11–20.

Cernea, M. M. and McDowell, C. (2000). *Risks and Reconstruction: Experiences of Resettlers and Refugees*: Washington, DC: World Bank.

Chalfin, B. (2001). 'Border zone trade and the economic boundaries of the state in north-east Ghana', *Africa*, 71(2): 202–24.

Chambers, R. (1986). 'Hidden losers? The impact of rural refugees and refugee programs on poorer hosts', *International Migration Review*, 20: 245–63.

Chambers, R. (1996). 'Participatory rural appraisal and the reversal of power', *Cambridge Anthropology*, 19(1): 5–23.

Chambers, R. (2007). 'From PRA to PLA and pluralism: Practice and theory'. Working Paper No. 286. Brighton: Institute of Development Studies, University of Sussex.

Chambers, R. (2012). *Provocations for Development*. Rugby: Practical Action.

Chambers, R. and Conway, G. (1992). 'Sustainable rural livelihoods: Practical concepts for the 21st century'. IDS Discussion Paper 296. Brighton: Institute of Development Studies, University of Sussex.

Chimni, B. S. (1998). 'The geopolitics of refugee studies: A view from the South', *Journal of Refugee Studies*, 11(4): 350–74.

Clapp, J. (2009). 'The global food crisis and international agricultural policy: Which way forward?', *Global Governance: A Review of Multilateralism and International Organizations*, 15(2): 299–312.

Clark, C. (2006). 'Livelihood networks and decision-making among Congolese young people in formal and informal refugee contexts in Uganda'. HiCN Working Paper No. 13, Households in Conflict Network, University of Sussex.

Collinson, S. (2011). 'Forced migration in the international political economy', in A. Betts and G. Loescher (eds), *Refugees in International Relations*. Oxford: Oxford University Press, 305–24.

Colson, E. (2004). 'Displacement', in D. Nugent and J. Vincent (eds), *A Companion to the Anthropology of Politics*. Malden and Oxford: Blackwell Publishing, 107–20.

Conway, C. (2004). 'Refugee livelihoods: A case study of the Gambia'. Geneva: UNHCR Evaluation and Policy Analysis Unit.

Cooke, B. and Kothari, U. (eds) (2001). *Participation: The New Tyranny?* London: Zed Books.

Cornwall, A. (2002). 'Making spaces, changing places: Situating participation in development'. Working Paper 170. Brighton: Institute of Development Studies, University of Sussex.

Cornwall, A. and Brock, K. (2005). 'What do buzzwords do for development policy? A critical look at "participation", "empowerment", and "poverty reduction"', *Third World Quarterly*, 26: 1043–60.

Crisp, J. (2003). 'No solution in sight: The problem of protracted refugee situations in Africa'. New Issues in Refugee Research, Working Paper No. 75. Geneva: UNHCR Evaluation and Policy Analysis Unit.

Crisp, J., Morris, T., and Refstie, H. (2012). 'Displacement in urban areas: New challenges, new partnerships', *Disasters*, 36(s1): S23–S42.

Cutler, A. C., Haufler, V., and Porter, T. (1999). *Private Authority and International Affairs*. Albany, NY: SUNY Press.

Czaika, M. (2009). *The Political Economy of Refugee Migration and Foreign Aid*. Basingstoke: Palgrave Macmillan.

De Haan, L. and Zoomers, A. (2005). 'Exploring the frontier of livelihoods research', *Development and Change*, 36(1): 27–47.

De Montclos, M.-A. P. and Kagwanja, P. M. (2000). 'Refugee camps or cities? The socio-economic dynamics of the Dadaab and Kakuma camps in Northern Kenya', *Journal of Refugee Studies*, 13(2), 205–22.

Desert Rose Consulting (2012). 'Consulting report: UNHCR, Kobe Camp, Dolo Ado, 2012'. Addis Ababa: Desert Rose Consulting (unpublished).

De Vriese, M. (2006). 'Refugee livelihoods: A review of the evidence'. Geneva: UNHCR Evaluation and Policy Analysis Unit. Available at <http://www.unhcr.org/4423fe5d2.pdf>.

DFID (1999). *Sustainable Livelihoods Guidance Sheets*. Department for International Development (DFID).

Dick, S. (2002). 'Responding to protracted refugee situations: A case study of Liberian refugees in Ghana'. Geneva: UNHCR Evaluation and Policy Analysis Unit.

Doron, E. (2005). 'Working with Lebanese refugees in a community resilience model', *Community Development Journal*, 40(2): 182–91.

Drucker, P. (1985). *Innovation and Entrepreneurship*. New York: Harper and Row.

Drummond, J. and Crawford, N. (2014). 'Humanitarian crises, emergency preparedness and response: The role of business and the private sector. Kenya case study'. London: Humanitarian Policy Group, Overseas Development Institute. Available from <http://www.odi.org/sites/odi.org.uk/files/odi-assets/publications-opinion-files/8790.pdf>.

Dryden-Peterson, S. (2006). 'Livelihoods in the region: The present is local, the future is global? Reconciling current and future livelihood strategies in the education of Congolese refugees in Uganda', *Refugee Survey Quarterly*, 25(2): 81–92.

Dryden-Peterson, S. and Hovil, L. (2004). 'A remaining hope for durable solutions: Local integration of refugees and their hosts in the case of Uganda', *Refuge: Canada's Journal on Refugees*, 22(1): 26–38.

Duffield, M. R. (2001). *Global Governance and the New Wars: The Merging of Development and Security* (Critique Influence Change 87). London: Zed Books.

Easton-Calabria, E. E. (2015). 'From bottom-up to top-down: The 'pre-history' of refugee livelihoods assistance from 1919 to 1979', *Journal of Refugee Studies* (September): fev004.

Enghoff, M., Hansen, B., Umar, A., Gildestad, B., Owen, M., and Obara, A. (2010). 'In search of protection and livelihoods: Socio-economic and environmental impacts of Dadaab refugee camps on host communities'. Nairobi: Royal Danish Embassy.

Fábos, A. and Kibreab, G. (2007). 'Urban refugees: Introduction', *Refuge: Canada's Periodical on Refugees*, 24(1): 1–19.

Falkner, R. (2005). 'The business of ozone layer protection: Corporate power in regime evolution', in D. L. Levy and P. J. Newell (eds), *The Business of Global Environmental Governance. Global Environmental Accord: Strategies for Sustainability and Institutional Innovation*. Cambridge, MA: MIT Press, 105–34.

Farrington, J., Ramasut, T., and Walker, J. (2002). 'Sustainable livelihoods approaches in urban areas: General lessons, with illustrations from Indian cases'. Working Paper 162. London: Overseas Development Institute.

Fu, X. et al. (2014). 'Innovation in low-income countries: A survey report'. Technology and Management Centre for Development, University of Oxford.

Fuchs, D. A. (2007). *Business Power in Global Governance*. Boulder, CO: Lynne Rienner.

Furubotn, E. and Richter, R. (1998). *Institutions and Economic Theory: The Contribution of New Institutional Economics*. Ann Arbor: University of Michigan Press.

Gale, L. A. (2006). 'Livelihoods in the region: Sustaining relationships across borders: Gendered livelihoods and mobility among Sierra Leonean refugees', *Refugee Survey Quarterly*, 25(2): 69–80.

Gammeltoft-Hansen, T. and Sørensen, N. N. (2013). *The Migration Industry and the Commercialization of International Migration*. London: Routledge.

Garud, R., Tuertscher, P., and Van de Ven, A. H. (2015). 'Business innovation processes', in C. E. Shalley, M. Hitt, and J. Zhou (eds), *The Oxford Handbook of Creativity, Innovation, and Entrepreneurship*. Oxford: Oxford University Press, 339–52.

Geertz, C. (1998). 'Deep hanging out', *New York Review of Books*, 45(16): 69–72.

Giddens, A. (1984). *The Constitution of Society: Outline of the Theory of Structuration*. Cambridge: Polity Press and Los Angeles, CA: University of California Press.

Gleason, S. E. (1978). 'Hustling: The inside economy of a prison', *Federal Probation*, 42(2): 32–40.

Goldsmith, L. (1997). 'History from the inside out: Prison life in nineteenth-century Massachusetts', *Journal of Social History*, 31(1): 109–25.

Golooba-Mutebi, F. (2004). 'Refugee livelihoods: Confronting uncertainty and responding to adversity: Mozambican war refugees in Limpopo Province, South Africa'. New Issues in Refugee Research, Working Paper No. 105. Geneva: UNHCR Evaluation and Policy Analysis Unit.

Gorman, R. F. (1987). *Coping with Africa's Refugee Burden: A Time for Solutions*. Dordrecht: Martinus Nijhoff Publishers.

Gorman, R. F. (1993). *Refugee Aid and Development: Theory and Practice* (Studies in Social Welfare Policies and Programs 17). Westport, CT: Greenwood Press.

Government of Uganda (2006). *Uganda: The Refugee Act 2006*, Act 21, 24 May. Available at <http://www.refworld.org/docid/4b7baba52.html>.

Grabska, K. (2005). 'Living on the margins: The analysis of the livelihood strategies of Sudanese refugees with closed files in Egypt'. Forced Migration and Refugee Studies, Working Paper No. 6. New Cairo: American University in Cairo.

Grabska, K. (2008). 'Brothers or poor cousins? Rights, policies and the well-being of refugees in Egypt', in K. Grabska and L. Mehta (eds), *Forced Displacement: Why Rights Matter*. London: Palgrave Macmillan, 71–92.

Gustavsen, B. (2003). 'Action research and the problem of the single case', *Concepts and Transformation*, 8(1): 93–9.

Haddad, E. (2008). *The Refugee in International Society: Between Sovereigns* (Cambridge Studies in International Relations 106). Cambridge: Cambridge University Press.

Hailey, J. (2001). 'Beyond the formulaic: Process and practice in South Asian NGOs', in B. Cooke and U. Kothari (eds), *Participation: The New Tyranny?* London: Zed Books, 88–101.

Hall, R. B. and Biersteker, T. J. (2002). *The Emergence of Private Authority in Global Governance* (Cambridge Studies in International Relations 85). Cambridge: Cambridge University Press.

Hamid, G. (1992). 'Livelihood patterns of displaced households in Greater Khartoum', *Disasters*, 16(3): 230–9.

Hammar, A. (2014). *Displacement Economies in Africa: Paradoxes of Crisis and Creativity*. London: Zed Books.

Harrell-Bond, B. E. (1982). 'Ugandan refugees in the Sudan, Part 2: The quest for self-sufficiency in planned rural settlements'. UFSI Reports, No. 49. Hanover: Universities Field Staff International Inc.

Harriss, J., Hunter, J., and Lewis, C. (1995). 'Introduction: Development and significance of NIE', in J. Harriss, J. Hunter, and C. Lewis (eds), *The New Institutional Economics and Third World Development*. London and New York: Routledge, 1–16.

Heckathorn, D. D. (1997). 'Respondent-driven sampling: A new approach to the study of hidden populations', *Social Problems*, 44: 174–99.

Hernández-León, R. (2008). *Metropolitan Migrants: The Migration of Urban Mexicans to the United States*. Berkeley, CA: University of California Press.

Holzmann, P., Boudreau, T., Holt, J., Lawrence, M., and O'Donnell, M. (2008). *Household Economy Approach: A Guide for Programme Planners and Policy-Makers*. London: Save the Children.

Horst, C. (2004). 'Money and mobility: Transnational livelihood strategies of the Somali diaspora'. Global Migration Perspectives, No. 9. Global Commission on International Migration (GCIM).

Horst, C. (2006). 'Buufis amongst Somalis in Dadaab: The transnational and historical logics behind resettlement dreams', *Journal of Refugee Studies*, 19(2): 143–57.

Hovil, L. (2007). 'Self-settled refugees in Uganda: An alternative approach to displacement?', *Journal of Refugee Studies*, 20(4): 599–620.

Howland, C. P. (1926). 'Greece and the Greeks', *Foreign Affairs*, 4(3): 454–64.

Hyndman, J. (2000). *Managing Displacement: Refugees and the Politics of Humanitarianism*. Minneapolis: University of Minnesota Press.

InterAid (2009). 'Socio-economic baseline survey for urban refugees in and around Kampala'. Kampala: InterAid.

International Labour Organization (ILO) (1928). 'Refugee problems and their solution', *International Labour Review*: 1768–85.

Jacobsen, K. (2002). 'Can refugees benefit the state? Refugee resources and African statebuilding', *Journal of Modern African Studies*, 40(4): 577–96.

Jacobsen, K. (2005). *The Economic Life of Refugees*. Bloomfield, CT: Kumarian Press.

Jacobsen, K. (2006). 'Refugees and asylum seekers in urban areas: A livelihoods perspective', *Journal of Refugee Studies*, 19(3): 273–86.

Jacobsen, K. (2014). 'Livelihoods and forced migration', in E. Fiddian-Qasmiyeh, G. Loescher, K. Long, and N. Sigona (eds), *The Oxford Handbook of Refugee and Forced Migration Studies*. Oxford: Oxford University Press, 99–111.

Jacobsen, K. and Landau, L. B. (2003). 'The dual imperative in refugee research: Some methodological and ethical considerations in social science research on forced migration', *Disasters*, 27(3), 185–206.

Jacobsen, K., Marshack, A., Ofori-Adjei, A., and Kembabazi, J. (2006). 'Using microenterprise interventions to support the livelihoods of forcibly displaced people: The impact of a microcredit program in IDP camps in Lira, Northern Uganda', *Refugee Survey Quarterly*, 25(2): 23–39.

Jaspars, S. and O'Callaghan, S. (2010). 'Livelihoods and protection in situations of protracted conflict', *Disasters*, 34(s2): S165–S182.

JIPS (2013). 'Livelihood, security, and access to services among urban refugees in Delhi, India'. ESYS144 Final Project. Available at <http://www.jips.org/system/cms/attachments/685/original_Delhi_UrbanRefugees_Livelihood_Services_FINALREPORT.pdf>.

Johnson, S. (2011). *Where Good Ideas Come From: The Seven Patterns of Innovation*. New York: Penguin.

Joskow, P. (2008). 'Introduction to New Institutional Economics: A report card', in E. Brousseau and J. Glachant (eds), *New Institutional Economics: A Guidebook*. Cambridge: Cambridge University Press, 1–20.

Kaag, M., Brons, J., de Bruijn, M., van Dijk, J., de Haan, L., Nooteboom, G., and Zoomers, A. (2003). 'Poverty is bad: Ways forward in livelihood research'. Paper presented at the CERES Pathways of Development Seminar Paper, Utrecht, 6 February.

Kagan, M. (2011). ' "We live in a country of UNHCR": The UN surrogate state and refugee policy in the Middle East'. New Issues in Refugee Research, Research Paper No. 201. Geneva: UNHCR Policy Development and Evaluation Service.

Kaiser, T. (2006). 'Between a camp and a hard place: Rights, livelihood and experiences of the local settlement system for long-term refugees in Uganda', Journal of Modern African Studies, 44(4): 597–621.

Kaiser, T., Hovil, L., and Lomo, Z. (2005). ' "We are stranded here together": Freedom of movement, settlements, and self-settled refugees in Arua and Moyo district'. Refugee Law Project Working Paper No. 14, Kampala.

Kandiyoti, D. (1999). 'Poverty in transition: An ethnographic critique of household surveys in post-Soviet Central Asia', Development and Change, 30(3): 499–524.

Kaplan, J. and Rozeboom, E. (2015). 'Private sector engagement and displacement'. Paper prepared by the Refugee Studies Centre on behalf of the Solutions Alliance Thematic Working Group on Engaging the Private Sector, May.

Kibreab, G. (2003). 'Displacement, host governments' policies, and constraints on the construction of sustainable livelihoods', International Social Science Journal, 55(175): 57–67.

Kibreab, G. (2004). 'Pulling the wool over the eyes of the strangers: Refugee deceit and trickery in institutionalized settings', Journal of Refugee Studies, 17(1): 1–26.

Kibreab, G. (2007). 'Why governments prefer spatially segregated settlement sites for urban refugees', Refuge: Canada's Journal on Refugees, 24(1): 27–35.

Kibreab, G. (2008). 'Civil society and post-conflict peace-building: A case study of the Horn of Africa region', in U. J. Dahre (ed.), Post-Conflict Peace-Building in the Horn of Africa: A Report of the 6th Annual Conference on the Horn of Africa, August 2007. Lund, Sweden: Media-Tryck Sociologen, 21–35.

Kibreab, G., Mahmoud, Y. H., et al. (1990). 'Refugees in Somalia: A burden and an opportunity for the local population and a challenge to the government and the international community'. Uppsala: Department of Economic History, Uppsala University.

Kimmelman, M. (2014). 'Refugee camp for Syrians in Jordan evolves as a do-it-yourself city', New York Times, 4 July. Available at <http://www.nytimes.com/2014/07/05/world/middleeast/zaatari-refugee-camp-in-jordan-evolves-as-a-do-it-yourself-city.html?_r=0#>.

Kloosterman, R., Van der Leun, J., and Rath, J. (1998). 'Across the border: Immigrants' economic opportunities, social capital and informal business activities', Journal of Ethnic and Migration Studies, 24(2): 249–68.

Kok, W. (1989). 'Self-settled refugees and the socio-economic impact of their presence on Kassala, Eastern Sudan', Journal of Refugee Studies, 2(4): 419–40.

Kolchin, M. and Hyclak, T. (1987). 'The case of the traditional intrapreneur', SAM Advanced Management Journal, 52(3): 14–18.

Konings, P. (2005). 'The anglophone Cameroon-Nigeria boundary: Opportunities and conflicts', *African Affairs*, 104(415): 275–301.

Korf, B. (2004). 'War, livelihoods and vulnerability in Sri Lanka', *Development and Change*, 35(2): 275–95.

Krause, U. (2013). *Linking Refugee Protection with Development Assistance: Analyses with a Case Study in Uganda*. Baden-Baden: Nomos.

Kuhlman, T. (1990). *Burden or Boon? A Study of Eritrean Refugees in the Sudan*. Amsterdam: VU University Press.

Kuhlman, T. (1991). 'The economic integration of refugees in developing countries: A research model', *Journal of Refugee Studies*, 4(1): 1–20.

Kunz, E. F. (1973). 'The refugee in flight: Kinetic models and forms of displacement', *International Migration Review*, 7(2): 125–46.

Kunz, E. F. (1981). 'Exile and resettlement: refugee theory', *International Migration Review*, 15(1): 42–51.

Landau, L. B. (2003). 'Beyond the losers: Transforming governmental practice in refugee-affected Tanzania', *Journal of Refugee Studies*, 16(1): 19–43.

Landau, L. B. (2004). 'Challenge without transformation: Refugees, aid and trade in western Tanzania', *Journal of Modern African Studies*, 42(1): 31–59.

Landau, L. B. (2014). 'Urban refugees and IDPs', in E. Fiddian-Qasmiyeh, G. Loescher, K. Long, and N. Sigona (eds), *The Oxford Handbook of Refugee and Forced Migration Studies*. Oxford: Oxford University Press, 139–50.

Landau, L. B. and Duponchel, M. (2011). 'Laws, policies, or social position? Capabilities and the determinants of effective protection in four African cities', *Journal of Refugee Studies*, 24(1): 1–22.

League of Nations (1934). *The League and Human Welfare*. Geneva: League of Nations Union.

Levy, D. L. and Newell, P. J. (2005). *The Business of Global Environmental Governance*. Cambridge, MA: MIT Press.

Lindley, A. (2006). 'Migrant remittances in the context of crisis in Somali society: A case study of Hargeisa'. Humanitarian Policy Group Background Paper. London: Overseas Development Institute.

Lindley, A. (2007a). 'Protracted displacement and remittances: The view from Eastleigh, Nairobi'. New Issues in Refugee Research, Research Paper No. 143. Geneva: UNHCR Policy Development and Evaluation Service.

Lindley, A. (2007b). 'Remittances in fragile settings: A Somali case study'. Working Paper No. 27, Households in Conflict Network, Sussex University.

Lindley, A. (2008a). 'African remittances and progress: Opportunities and challenges', *Análisis del Real Instituto*, 52. Madrid: Real Instituto Elcano.

Lindley, A. (2008b). 'Conflict-induced migration and remittances: Exploring conceptual frameworks'. Working Paper Series No. 47. Oxford: Refugees Studies Centre.

Lindley, A. (2010). *The Early Morning Phone Call: Somali Refugees' Remittances* (Forced Migration 28). New York and Oxford: Berghahn Books.

Loescher, G. (2001). *The UNHCR and World Politics: A Perilous Path*. Oxford: Oxford University Press.

Loescher, G. and Milner, J. (2005). *Protracted Refugee Situations: Domestic and International Security Implications* (Adelphi Series 375). International Institute for Strategic Studies.

Loescher, G., Milner, J., Newman, E., and Troeller, G. (2008). *Protracted Refugee Situations: Political, Human Rights and Security Implications.* Tokyo: United Nations University Press.

Logan, J. R., Alba, R. D., and Stults, B. J. (2003). 'Enclaves and entrepreneurs: Assessing the payoff for immigrants and minorities', *International Migration Review*, 37(23): 44–88.

Macchiavello, M. (2003). *Forced Migrants as an Under-Utilized Asset: Refugee Skills, Livelihoods, and Achievements in Kampala, Uganda.* Geneva: UNHCR.

Magill, M. and Quinzii, M. (2002). *Theory of Incomplete Markets*, Volume 1. Cambridge, MA and London: MIT Press.

Malekinejad, M., Johnston, L., Kendall, C., et al. (2008). 'Using respondent-driven sampling methodology for HIV biological and behavioral surveillance in international settings: A systematic review', *AIDS and Behavior*, 12(S1): 105–30.

Mallett, R. and Slater, R. (2012). 'Growth and livelihoods in fragile and conflict-affected situations'. Social Livelihoods Research Consortium Working Paper 9. London: Overseas Development Institute.

Marfleet, P. (2008). '*Remembering Refugees: Then and Now*. By Tony Kushner', *Journal of Refugee Studies*, 21(1): 133–4.

Massey, D. S., Arango, J., Hugo, G., Kouaouchi, A., Pellegrino, A., and Taylor, J. E. (2008). *Worlds in Motion: Understanding International Migration at the End of the Millennium.* Oxford: Oxford University Press.

May, C. (2006). 'Global corporate power and the UN global compact', in C. May (ed.), *Global Corporate Power.* London: Lynne Reinner, 273–82.

Maystadt, J.-F. and Verwimp, P. (2009). 'Winners and losers among a refugee-hosting population: Consumption, economic activities, and agglomeration'. CORE Discussion Paper, Louvain-la-Neuve, Belgium.

McClure, D. and Gray, I. (2014). 'Scaling: Innovation's missing middle'. Paper presented at the Humanitarian Innovation Conference, University of Oxford, 19 July.

McConnachie, K. (2014). *Governing Refugees: Justice, Order and Legal Pluralism.* London: Routledge.

McCreesh, N., Frost, S., Seeley, J., Katongole, J., Tarsh, M. N., Ndunguse, R., Johnston, L. G. (2012). 'Evaluation of respondent-driven sampling', *Epidemiology*, 23(1): 138–47.

McMichael, C., Nunn, C., Gifford, S. M., and Correa-Velez, I. (2014). 'Studying refugee settlement through longitudinal research: Methodological and ethical insights from the good starts study', *Journal of Refugee Studies*, doi: 10.1093/jrs/feu017.

Mears, E. G. (1929). *Greece Today: The Aftermath of the Refugee Impact.* Stanford, CA: Stanford University Press.

Ménard, C. and Shirley, M. M. (2005). *Handbook of New Institutional Economics.* Dordrecht: Springer.

Metcalf, D. (2012). 'Immigration and the UK labour market', *CentrePiece*, 17(3), Winter: 13–17.

Milner, J. (2009). 'Refugees and the regional dynamics of peacebuilding', *Refugee Survey Quarterly*, 28(1): 13–30.

Monsutti, A. (2005). *War and Migration: Social Networks and Economic Strategies of the Hazaras of Afghanistan*. Oxford: Routledge.

Narbeth, S. and McLean, C. (2003). 'Livelihoods and protection: Displacement and vulnerable communities in Kismaayo, southern Somalia'. Humanitarian Practice Network Paper No. 44. London: Overseas Development Institute (ODI).

Neuner, F., Onyut, P. L., Ertl, V., Odenwald, M., Schauer, E., and Elbert, T. (2008). 'Treatment of posttraumatic stress disorder by trained lay counselors in an African refugee settlement: A randomized controlled trial', *Journal of Consulting and Clinical Psychology*, 76(4): 686–94.

North, D. C. (1990). 'A transaction cost theory of politics', *Journal of Theoretical Politics*, 2(4): 355–67.

North, D. C. (1995). 'The New Institutional Economics and Third World development', in J. Harriss, J. Hunter, and C. M. Lewis (eds), *The New Institutional Economics and Third World Development*. London: Routledge, 17–26.

Olson, M. (1965). *The Logic of Collective Action: Public Goods and the Theory of Groups*. Cambridge, MA: Harvard University Press.

Omata, N. (2013). 'Community resilience or shared destitution? Refugees' internal assistance in a deteriorating economic environment', *Community Development Journal*, 48(2): 264–79.

Omata, N. and Kaplan, J. D. (2013). 'Refugee livelihoods in Kampala, Nakivale and Kyangwali refugee settlements: Patterns of engagement with the private sector'. Working Paper No. 95. Oxford: Refugee Studies Centre.

Palmgren, P. A. (2013). 'Irregular networks: Bangkok refugees in the city and region', *Journal of Refugee Studies*, doi: 10.1093/jrs/fet004.

Pavanello, S., Elhawary, S., and Pantuliano, S. (2010). 'Hidden and exposed: Urban refugees in Nairobi, Kenya'. Humanitarian Policy Group Working Paper. London: Overseas Development Institute.

Phillips, M. (2003). 'The role and impact of humanitarian assets in refugee-hosting countries'. New Issues in Refugee Research, Working Paper No. 84. Geneva: UNHCR Evaluation and Policy Analysis Unit.

Porter, G., Hampshire, K., Kyei, P., Adjaloo, M., Rapoo, G., and Kilpatrick, K. (2008). 'Linkages between livelihood opportunities and refugee–host relations: Learning from the experiences of Liberian camp-based refugees in Ghana', *Journal of Refugee Studies*, 21(2): 230–52.

Price, J. A. (1973). 'Private enterprise in a prison: The free market economy of La Mesa Penitenciaria', *Crime and Delinquency*, 19(2): 218–27.

Radford, R. A. (1945). 'The economic organisation of a POW camp', *Economica*, n.s., 12(48): 189–201.

Ramalingam, B. et al. (2015). 'Strengthening the humanitarian ecosystem'. Humanitarian Innovation Ecosystem Research Project, Final Report, University of Brighton.

R Core Team (2013). 'R: A language and environment for statistical computing'. Vienna: R Foundation for Statistical Computing. Accessible at <http://www.R-project.org/>.

Rodgers, G. (2004). '"Hanging out" with forced migrants: Methodological and ethical challenges', *Forced Migration Review*, 21: 48–50.

Rogge, J. R. and Akol, J. O. (1989). 'Repatriation: Its role in resolving Africa's refugee dilemma', *International Migration Review*, 23(2): 184–200.

Romer, P. M. (1986). 'Increasing returns and long-run growth', *The Journal of Political Economy*, 94(5): 1002–37.

Rosenberg, T. (2011). 'Beyond refugee camps, a better way', *New York Times*, 6 September.

Rothwell, R. (1994). 'Towards the fifth-generation innovation process', *International Marketing Review*, 11(1): 7–31.

Ruf, M., Schauer, M., Neuner, F., Catani, C., Schauer, E., and Elbert, T. (2010). 'Narrative exposure therapy for 7- to 16-year-olds: A randomized controlled trial with traumatized refugee children', *Journal of Traumatic Stress*, 23(4): 437–45.

Ruggie, J. G. (2007). 'Global markets and global governance: The prospects for convergence', in S. Bernstein and L. W. Pauly (eds), *Global Liberalism and Political Order: Toward a New Grand Compromise?* Albany, NY: SUNY Press, 23–50.

Ruiz, I. and Vargas-Silva, C. (2013). 'The economics of forced migration', *Journal of Development Studies*, 49(6): 772–84.

Samuelson, P. A. and Nordhaus, W. D. (2010). *Economía con aplicaciones a Latinoamérica*. Mexico: McGraw-Hill.

Sandler, T. (1997). *Global Challenges: An Approach to Environmental, Political, and Economic Problems*. Cambridge: Cambridge University Press.

Sandvik, K. B. (2011). 'Blurring boundaries: Refugee resettlement in Kampala—between the formal, the informal, and the illegal', *PoLAR: Political and Legal Anthropology Review*, 34(1): 11–32.

Schmidt, A. (2003). 'FMO thematic guide: Camps versus settlements', *Forced Migration Online*. Available from <http://www.forcedmigration.org/research-resources/expert-guides/camps-versus-settlements/fmo021.pdf>.

Schumpeter, J. A. (1934). *The Theory of Economic Development: An Inquiry into Profits, Capital, Credit, Interest and the Business Cycle*, trans. Redvers Opie. Cambridge, MA: Harvard University Press.

Schumpeter, J. A. (1942). *Socialism, Capitalism and Democracy*. New York: Harper and Brothers.

Seddon, D. and Hussein, K. (2002). 'The consequences of conflict: Livelihoods and development in Nepal'. Livelihoods and Chronic Conflict Working Paper 185. London: Overseas Development Institute.

Sen, A. (1999). *Commodities and Capabilities*. Oxford: Oxford University Press.

Sharpe, M. and Namusobya, S. (2012). 'Refugee status determination and the rights of recognized refugees under Uganda's Refugees Act 2006', *International Journal of Refugee Law*, 24(3): 561–78.

Skran, C. M. (1985). *The Refugee Problem in Interwar Europe, 1919–1939*. Oxford: Oxford University Press.

Sohn, C. and Lara-Valencia, F. (2013). 'Borders and cities: Perspectives from North America and Europe', *Journal of Borderlands Studies*, 28(2): 181–90.

Solow, R. M. (1957). 'Technical change and the aggregate production function', *Review of Economics and Statistics*, 39(3): 312–20.

Sood, A. and Seferis, L. (2014). 'Syrians contributing to Kurdish economic growth', *Forced Migration Review*, 47: 14–16.

Stein, B. (1987). 'ICARA II: Burden-sharing and durable solutions', in J. R. Rogge (ed.), *Refugees: A Third World Dilemma*. Totawa, NJ: Rowman & Littlefield.

Stein, B. (1990). 'Refugee integration and older refugee settlements in Africa'. Paper presented at the 1990 meeting of the American Anthropological Association, New Orleans, 28 November.

Stiglitz, J. E. and Walsh, C. E. (2006). *Economics*. New York: W. W. Norton.

Stigter, E. and Monsutti, A. (2005). 'Transnational networks: Recognising a regional reality'. Briefing Paper Series. Kabul: Afghanistan Research and Evaluation Unit.

Suhrke, A. (1998). 'Burden-sharing during refugee emergencies: The logic of collective versus national action', *Journal of Refugee Studies*, 11(4): 396–415.

Svedberg, E. (2014). 'Refugee self-reliance in Nakivale refugee settlement, Uganda', *Independent Study Project (ISP) Collection*, Paper 1778. Available at <http://digitalcollections.sit.edu/isp_collection/1778>.

Taneja, N. and Pohit, S. (2001). 'India's informal trade with Nepal', *Economic and Political Weekly*, 36(25): 2263–9.

Taneja, N., Sarvananthan, M., and Pohit, S. (2003). 'India-Sri Lanka trade: Transacting environments in formal and informal trading', *Economic and Political Weekly*, 19–25 July, 3094–8.

Tarde, G. (1903). *The Laws of Imitatio*. New York: Henry Holt.

Thielemann, E. R. (2003). 'Between interests and norms: Explaining burden-sharing in the European Union', *Journal of Refugee Studies*, 16(3), 253–73.

Trappe, P. (1971). 'Social change and development institutions in a refugee population: Development from below as an alternative: The case of the Nakapiripirit Settlement Scheme in Uganda'. Geneva: United Nations Research Institute for Social Development.

UNHCR (1994). *Review of the CIREFCA Process*. Geneva: UNHCR.

UNHCR (2003). 'Framework for durable solutions for refugees and persons of concern'. Geneva: UNHCR.

UNHCR (2004). 'In pursuit of durable solutions in Zambia'. Geneva: UNHCR.

UNHCR (2005). 'Statement of good practice for targeting development assistance'. Geneva: UNHCR.

UNHCR (2006). *Handbook for Self-Reliance*. Geneva: UNHCR.

UNHCR (2012). 'Livelihood programming in UNHCR: Operational guidelines'. Geneva: UNHCR. Available at <http://www.unhcr.org/4fbdf17c9.pdf>.

UNHCR (2013a). 'Population statistics'. Available at <http://popstats.unhcr.org/>.

UNHCR (2013b). 'Rwamwanja factsheet'. UNHCR Uganda.

UNHCR (2015a). 'Global trends 2014'. Available at <http://www.unhcr.org/558193896.html>.

UNHCR (2015b). 'Community technology access'. Available at <http://www.unhcr.org/pages/4ad2e8286.html>.

UNHCR (2016). 'Global trends: Forced displacement in 2015'. Geneva: UNHCR. Available at <http://www.unhcr.org/statistics/country/576408cd7/unhcr-global-trends-2015.html>.

UNHCR Innovation (2015a). UNHCR Innovation homepage. Available at <http://innovation.unhcr.org/>.

UNHCR Innovation (2015b). 'Refugee housing unit'. Available at <http://innovation.unhcr.org/labs_post/refugee-housing-unit/>.

USCRI (2004). 'World refugee survey: Warehousing issue'. Washington, DC: USCRI.

Verdirame, G. and Harrell-Bond, B. E. (2005). *Rights in Exile: Janus-Faced Humanitarianism*. New York: Berghahn Books.

Voutira, E. and Dona, G. (2007). 'Refugee research methodologies: Consolidation and transformation of a field', *Journal of Refugee Studies*, 20(2): 163–71.

Weber, C. (2013). *International Relations Theory: A Critical Introduction*. London: Routledge.

Weiss, T. G. (2013). *Humanitarian Business*. New York: John Wiley & Sons.

Werker, E. (2002). *Refugees in Kyangwali Settlement: Constraints on Economic Freedom*. Kampala, Uganda: Refugee Law Project.

Werker, E. (2007). 'Refugee camp economies', *Journal of Refugee Studies*, 20(3): 461–80.

Whitaker, B. E. (2002). 'Refugees in Western Tanzania: The distribution of burdens and benefits among local hosts', *Journal of Refugee Studies*, 15(4): 339–58.

White, B. (2015). '17 Years in a refugee camp: On the trail of a dodgy statistic', *Singular Things* [blog], <https://singularthings.wordpress.com/2015/07/04/17-years-in-a-refugee-camp-on-the-trail-of-a-dodgy-statistic/>.

Wilk, R. R. and Cliggett, L. (2007). 'Economics and the problem of human nature', in *Economies and Cultures: Foundations of Economic Anthropology*. Boulder, CO: Westview Press, 31–47.

Williamson, O. E. (1975). *Markets and Hierarchies: Analysis and Antitrust Implications*. New York: Free Press.

Williamson, O. E. (2000). 'The New Institutional Economics: Taking stock, looking ahead', *Journal of Economic Literature*, 38(3): 595–613.

Women's Refugee Commission (2011). 'The living ain't easy: Urban refugees in Kampala'. New York: Women's Refugee Commission. Available at <https://womensrefugeecommission.org/resources/document/701-the-living-aint-easy-urban-refugees-in-kampala>.

World Bank (2013). *Lebanon—Economic and Social Impact Assessment of the Syrian Conflict*. Washington, DC: World Bank. Available from <http://documents.worldbank.org/curated/en/2013/09/18292074/lebanon-economic-social-impact-assessment-syrian-conflict>.

Young, H., Osman, A., Smith, M., Bromwich, B., Moore, K., and Ballosu, S. (2007). 'Sharpening the strategic focus of livelihoods programming in the Darfur region'. Paper presented at the Report of Four Livelihoods Workshops.

Zetter, R. (2014). 'Reframing displacement crises as development opportunities'. Policy Brief. Global Initiative on Solutions, Copenhagen Roundtable, 2–3 April. Available at <www.rsc.ox.ac.uk/files/publications/other/pn-reframing-displacement-crises-2014.pdf>.

Zetter, R. and Ruaudel, H. (2014). 'Development and protection challenges of the Syrian refugee crisis', *Forced Migration Review*, 47: 6–10.

Zetter, R., Ruaudel, H., Deardorff-Miller, S., Lyytinen, E., Thibos, C., and Pedersen, F. S. (2014). 'The Syrian displacement crisis and a Regional Development and Protection Programme: Mapping and meta-analysis of existing studies of costs, impacts and protection', Danish Ministry of Foreign Affairs, February.

Zetter, R., Vargas-Silva, C., Ruiz, I., Fiddian-Qasmiyeh, E., Stav, S.-E., Hoelscher, K., and Horst, C. (2012). 'Guidelines for assessing the impacts and costs of forced displacement'. Washington, DC: World Bank.

Zürcher, E.-J. (2003). 'Greek and Turkish refugees and deportees 1912–1924'. Turkology Update Leiden Project, Working Papers Archive, Department of Turkish Studies, Universiteit Leiden.

Zyck, S. and Armstrong, J. (2014). 'Humanitarian crises, emergency preparedness and response: The role of business and the private sector: Jordan case study'. London: Humanitarian Policy Group/Overseas Development Institute.

Zyck, S. and Kent, R. (2014). 'Humanitarian crises, emergency preparedness and response: The role of business and the private sector: Final report'. London: Overseas Development Institute.

Index

Tables and figures are indicated by a bold t, and f, following the page number. Footnotes are indicated by an italic n followed by note number.

Index

COBURWAS International Youth Organization to Transform Africa (CIYOTA) 173–4
Collinson, S. 189
Colson, E. 50
community-based organizations (CBOs) 95
Community Technology Access (CTA) 174, 182–3
Concerted Plan of Action (CIREFCA) 27
Congolese refugees 10, 49, t66, 67, 86, 87, 206
  and aid dependency 203
  education 205–6, t220
  in emergency camps 140, 141, 142, 144, f146
  and employment 91, t94, 148, 208
  and entrepreneurship 122, 127–8, 135, 136, 149–54, 170–6, 178–9, 181–3, 208–9
  government issues 157–61
  incomes f92, 203, 204, 205, t217, t220
  and land ownership 130, 132
  loan access 89
  and mobility 124–5
  and networking 207
  participatory research with 69, 72, 77, t80
  in protracted camps 111–12, 115, 116
  and street vending 95–7
contract enforcement 127–30
Convention Plus Initiative 7, 14, 32–6, 39
Conway, C. 43
core business engagement 186, 190–1, 199
Cornwall, A. and K. Brock 183–4
corporate social responsibility 190, 194–5
Costa Rica (CIREFCA projects) 27, 28, 31
Crisp, J. 43, 56, 59, 61, 86
Cutler, A. C. et al. 187
Czaika, M. 41

Dadaab refugee camps
  and business engagement 195, 197
  economic effects of 44, 45
  and institutions 48
dairy farms 106–7
Darfur region 43
De Haan, L. and A. Zoomers 42
De Montclos, M.-A. P. and P. M. Kagwanja 43, 53, 60
De Vriese, M. 42, 43, 53, 59, 61
Desert Rose Consulting 62, 150
development issues 2–3, 13–14, 200, 211
  in emergency contexts 139
  and humanitarianism 5–8
  pre-history 15–18
  and private-sector engagement 183, 186, 193
  and refugee innovation 132–3, 171–2, 183, 185, 193
  studies on 41–2
  TDA 33–4

and TSI+ 37–8
UNHCR *Framework* 32
see also CIREFCA; ICARA
DFID 42
Dick, S. 52, 59
discrimination 90, 173
Displacement Economies in Africa (Hammar) 40
Djibouti refugee camp 4–5
documentary films 14n1, 72
Dollo Ado (Ethiopia) 150
  private-sector initiatives 190
  trade in 62
donors *see* funding
Drucker, P. 167
Drummord, J. and N. Crawford 187
Dryden-Peterson, S. 10, 43, 66
Duffield, M. R. 189

Easton-Calabria, E. E. 16, 17
Economic Lives of Refugees, The (Jacobsen) 46
education and training 18, 74, 210
  CIYOTA project 173
  in emergency camps 148–9
  outcomes 205–6, t216–19, t220
Egypt 21
El Quiche returnees 28
El Salvador refugees 28, 29, 30, 31
electricity supply 136, 174
emergency camps 4, 60–2, 139–40
  communication with authorities 157–9
  and employment 143–4, 148
  and entrepreneurship 147–54
  and farming 141, 144–7
  government issues 157–63
  and innovation 169, 177–9, 180, f181
  institutional variation 203
  and mobility 142, 143, 154–5
  and networking 154–6
  and self-reliance 159–61
  and taxation 142, 144, 156–7, 162, 203
  and trading 142
Emergency Market Mapping and Analysis (EMMA) 71
employment
  in emergency contexts 143–4, 148
  and private-sector engagement 195
  in protracted camps 113, 117, 124
  through networking 52, 106–7
  in urban areas 57, 89–103
  wages 44–5, 197
  work permits 52, 89, 202
  see also entrepreneurship
Enghoff, M. et al. 44, 45, 52, 58, 85, 86
entrepreneurship 8, 55–6
  of Congolese refugees 122, 127–8, 135, 136, 149–54, 170–6, 178–9, 181–3, 208–9
  and contract enforcement 127–30